(continued from fro...)

advantage of closer personal c ... shal Stalin than any other We ...

There are vivid portraits c ... who run the Soviet Union, all the way from the members of the all-powerful Politburo to the director of a small collective farm. There are revealing discussions of the efficiency of Soviet industry and agriculture. In the course of his duties General Smith met numbers of Russians of all kinds, and his pages contain fascinating sketches of them, thus building a picture of the life of the ordinary man in a collectivized economy. The American Ambassador had his own housekeeping problems, like the incident of the supply of fresh eggs, which eventually involved ponderous governmental machinery.

Altogether *My Three Years in Moscow* is one of the important books of our time, distinguished in its character and permanent in historical value.

Here is a partial list of the topics discussed:

Stalin—a first-hand portrait of the dictator

Politburo—acute thumbnail sketches of the men who run Russia

Moscow's Foreign Colony

Mechanics of a Police State—what it takes to eliminate the dissenters

Staged Elections—the Russian version of democracy

Industry and Agriculture—how efficient are they?

Religion in Russia—an eyewitness account of the failure to suppress it

The Artist in a Police State—how he is made to serve the party line

Visit to a Collective Farm

Doom of the Individual Farmer—how he is being squeezed out of existence

The Propaganda Machine—thought control, how it works

Cominform and Tito—the inside story of a great diplomatic defeat

Goals of Soviet Policy

War or Peace?

MY THREE YEARS IN MOSCOW

MY THREE YEARS IN MOSCOW

Walter Bedell Smith

J. B. LIPPINCOTT COMPANY

PHILADELPHIA AND NEW YORK

1950

To the men and women
of the American Embassy in Moscow,
1946-1949

CONTENTS

CONTENTS

ILLUSTRATIONS

MY THREE YEARS IN MOSCOW

I

PREFACE TO MOSCOW

I see that some of my predecessors have thought proper to indicate the qualifications and accomplishments which in their judgment would be most useful in an American Minister at this court; and if I attempt to do so, it is from no spirit of officiousness, but merely to give the benefits of my experience and observation, for whatever they may be worth.

. . . I am of opinion that a Minister from the U. States, particularly at this time, ought to be a military man. I mean a man that has seen actual service, and who would be able to maintain his pretensions. This is not suggested for the mere vain show of wearing a uniform, but because the Government of Russia is a military government. . . . There is no question but that a Minister of respectable military attainments and reputation would have much more might than a civilian. The ordinary reasons for such an appointment are, in my judgment, enhanced by the present position and prospects of Russia. Its influence over the rest of Europe is irresistible, particularly with the German states. Its vast military power and military spirit are the secrets of this ascendancy, aided by a system of diplomacy which has perhaps no equal. In short I mean that Russia is such a power that it is important to conciliate by all honorable means, and of these the proper accomplishments of a Minister would certainly be the cheapest to our Government.

—Excerpt from a dispatch of the American
Minister to Russia, Neill S. Brown, dated
St. Petersburg, January 27, 1853

AFTER the end of the war in Europe and eight months of occupation duty in the American zone of Germany, I had returned in January 1946, to the War Department, where I was in the process of taking over the Operations and Planning Division of the General Staff. After the campaigns of North Africa, Sicily, Italy, France and Germany, this was the type of duty to which I had been looking forward. It reunited me with my wife, and we set up housekeeping again in Washington. It gave me the opportunity, after more than four years of almost constant absence, to get reacquainted with my own country.

But I had hardly begun the job in earnest, when the telephone on my desk rang one day and my secretary reported that the caller was Secretary of State James F. Byrnes. The Secretary asked me to come to his office in the Old State-War-Navy Building, directly across Jackson Place on the west side of the White House.

I had no idea of the purpose of the conference with Secretary Byrnes as I proceeded to his office, but he came to the point at once. Without preamble, he said that it was his desire that I should go to Moscow as American Ambassador. He had talked it over with President Truman, who approved. It had been his original idea that I might first be given another diplomatic assignment at one of the European embassies, for a short period of preliminary experience, but the recent Ambassador, W. Averell Harriman, who had been in Moscow since October, 1943, all during the long and tiring days of the war, had been appointed to London, and would be needed there at once. It was not desirable that the Moscow post should long remain vacant.

Secretary Brynes said that he and the President were agreed that at this time the Moscow mission should be headed by someone whom the Russians knew, at least by reputation, and whom they would accept as ready to speak to them frankly and honestly.

It was true, the Secretary pointed out, that American Ambassadors usually were civilians and only infrequently military men, and in the latter case usually retired officers. But it would not be necessary for me to give up my career in the Army—the Administration was willing to ask Congress to pass a special law permitting me to retain my military rank while on assignment for the State Department. A soldier in the Moscow job actually would be an advantage, the Secretary believed, because Generalissimo Stalin had, on a number of occasions, indicated a certain distrust of career diplomats, and had shown some preference for military men.

Secretary Byrnes said further that both he and the President believed that the successful Soviet field commanders, who had been almost deified during the war and who had been accorded almost complete freedom from the political control customarily imposed upon all ranks of the Soviet Army prior to and during the early stages of the war, would continue to have a potent influence upon Soviet policies, and possibly upon foreign relations.

These Soviet military leaders had learned something of the

West as a result of their experiences outside the Soviet Union. They understood, it was to be hoped, the continued necessity for cooperating with the Allies; and my previous association with them might be helpful in breaking through the hard crust that was beginning to form on the surface of the Soviet Union's attitude toward the West. It was possible that an officer who had served in Europe would have a better chance at this stage of international relations of "getting under the Russian skin" and of obtaining frank answers to many of the questions that were beginning to vex us.

The Secretary, realizing that this proposal came as a complete surprise, said that he would not press me for an answer at once. He would give me two or three days to think the matter over, but he hoped that I realized the great importance attached to the Moscow Embassy.

At the moment, I could not think of any intelligent questions. I told the Secretary that I would talk to my chiefs, Secretary of War Patterson and General Eisenhower; that I would think the matter over and give him my answer as soon as possible.

This was not to be Smith' first contact with the Russians

My mind flashed back over previous contacts with the Russians, first in the North African Theater, later in the Mediterranean, and finally during the operations in Europe and the occupation in Germany.

The first direct meeting of the Russians with the Western Allies on day-to-day business in the field had occurred in North Africa, when the Mediterranean Commission was established to advise on matters relating to Italy, the first of the major Axis powers to succumb to the Allied armies. This was in the autumn of 1943, when Russian propaganda organs were highly critical of the Americans and the British for delay in opening a "second front" in Western Europe and in taking some of the pressure of more than two hundred German divisions off the hard-pressed Red Army. Hitler and his propaganda chiefs were doing their best to divide the Allies, playing upon communism's antagonism toward the West and attempting to convince the Soviet Union that the Western Allies were allowing her to exhaust herself through depletion of her manpower in an almost unassisted struggle against the main effort of the Wehrmacht. In Western capitals, Nazi agents and sympathizers spread rumors that the Soviet Union was about to make a separate peace with the Germans, while Moscow heard through similar channels that the Western Allies were talking of a separate peace and later, in league with Germany, would spring upon and rend a weakened Soviet Union.

In the West, there was evident in the public opinion of the time a sincere desire for some concrete evidence that the Western Allies and the Soviet Union, despite the vast differences in their political and economic structures, were actively cooperating to win the war in the shortest possible time. There had been widespread disappointment that Generalissimo Stalin had found himself unable to accept the invitation, in January, 1943, to come to Casablanca for conferences with President Roosevelt and Prime Minister Churchill, and unable or unwilling to accept their alternative proposal to move the meeting from Casablanca some thousands of miles to the East. He had replied that he was too busy running his armies to leave the Soviet Union, and there the matter had to rest for the time being.

However, the Allied invasion of Italy offered an opportunity for a beginning of the kind of cooperation the peoples of the United Nations sincerely desired. The Mediterranean Commission was to consist of political representatives of the Western Allies and the Soviet Union. It was formed to advise the Allied governments on the proper method of dealing with Italy, which was a defeated Axis power, but which now, under a new government headed by the King and Marshal Badoglio, had surrendered to the Allies after the removal of Mussolini and was seeking to work its passage back into the comity of nations as a co-belligerent of the Allies.

The Soviet delegation which came to Algiers for the first meeting of the Mediterranean Commission was headed by A. Y. Vishinsky, then a Vice Commissar for Foreign Affairs and well known as the hard-driving prosecutor of the Moscow "purge" trials of the late nineteen thirties.

It was my privilege, as Chief of Staff, to sit in for General Eisenhower on this first meeting of the Mediterranean Commission. I found Mr. Vishinsky aggressive but likable. His gray hair, piercing blue eyes, alert self-possession and intelli-

gent expression combine to create an excellent first impression.
He has a lively sense of humor and can, when he desires, exercise a great deal of personal charm. I soon found out, however,
as we got down to business, that his outstanding characteristic
is a brusque truculence. With him, as senior military adviser,
was General Vasiliev, now on duty with the United Nations
Military Staff Committee. Vasiliev is quiet, dignified, reserved
and pleasant, and reminds one more of a college professor than
of the experienced soldier who had distinguished himself as
Chief of Staff on the Orel front during some of the most bitter
fighting of the early part of the war in Russia. Another young
Russian general, whose name I have now forgotten, apparently
was more interested in political than in military affairs, and to
one more familiar with the Soviet system than I was at that
time would have readily been recognizable as the MVD (secret
police) officer who habitually accompanies all important Soviet
missions. This officer spoke excellent English and acted as interpreter for the Russian group.

At the first meeting, Mr. Vishinsky made the immediate demand that the Russian military officers be permitted to visit
the Allied front in Italy. We were, of course, aware that American and British officers in the Soviet Union had repeatedly
asked for and repeatedly been refused an opportunity to visit
an active Soviet front against the Germans, but we were aware
also of the contemptuous attitude of the Russians toward the
Allies' "side show" in the Mediterranean and of their feeling
that we might better be putting our effort into a frontal assault
upon Germany. We knew, also, that since this was the first
evidence of direct Soviet collaboration with the Allies in the
field, it might well be a harbinger of greater cooperation. So
without the slightest hesitation I asked General Francis W. de
Guingand, Chief of Staff to General Montgomery, to show the
Russian visitors the front opposite Cassino, where our troops
were then heavily engaged. I asked General de Guingand to
make certain that they saw some real action.

The trip was an unqualified success from our point of view
and it cannot have failed to modify the Soviet impression that
the Italian campaign was only a side show. One of the Soviet
officers, on returning, remarked to me, "I can die for Mother

Russia—in Russia—any time; I don't have to come to Italy to do it."

That was the only time they asked to visit the Italian front, so far as I know, and it was also the only time that I had a direct part in Mediterranean Commission proceedings since I was otherwise engaged. However, I saw the Russians occasionally, for they were quartered near our headquarters in Algiers, and in connection with my duties I became only too familiar with the political difficulties encountered in attempting to define the base and scope of the post-war Italian Government.

There was never any opportunity, in Africa or later, to establish with the Russians the informal, friendly, man-to-man relationships we had with the English and the French. Language undoubtedly was one barrier, but the most important, it seemed to me, was the Soviet habit of regarding with suspicion any of its officials who became too friendly with foreigners of any nationality. One night, however, the Russian officers did invite me to dinner at their house. I was the only foreigner present, and while the talk was informal, they seemed to me to be overemphasizing its privacy and security. Quite ostentatiously, they placed a pillow over the telephone to hamper its possible use as a recording instrument while we talked at the dinner table. The Soviet officers had brought their own servants with them to Algiers, and the dinner was served by a strapping Russian blonde, who was addressed as "Valya."

Assuming that she spoke no English, I remarked to one of the officers, "Good husky girl, isn't she?" Unable to restrain herself, Valya shot back in perfect English, "Okay, you're not so darned thin yourself."

Concerned with fighting the war as I was, I had little direct connection with the political arguments of the Mediterranean Commission that occurred subsequently, and these were handled for the American Government by Mr. Robert Murphy, General Eisenhower's chief political adviser. But at staff conferences I began to get a sense of the basic differences between the Russians and the Western powers over the meaning of the word "democracy" as applied in action. Viewing events in retrospect, it is as easy now, as it was difficult then, to appreciate the nature of Soviet political aims in Italy. We of the West were determined to establish a democratic government with as broad a base as possible, and this made it easy for us to accept Communist participation in the Italian Government, and even to accept, and indeed to facilitate, the return of the Italian Communist leader, Palmiro Togliatti, who had been in Moscow. Even had we been contrarily disposed, it would have been difficult to deny Communist participation in the Italian Government. Disciplined, militant Communist groups, particularly in the industrial areas of Northern Italy, had been the rallying point for Italian opposition to the Germans. The Communists were the hard core of the Partisan movement, and their initial participation in the reconstructed Italian Government was on a cooperative, collaborative basis.

As the battle for Italy went on, and the Russians, for their part, moved across the Dnieper, recaptured Kiev, and continued westward, two important Big Three conferences were held. The first, held in Moscow during October, 1943, was on the Foreign Minister level, and one of its important decisions was the establishment, in London, of the European Advisory Commission, with Soviet, British and American representation. In December, 1943, President Roosevelt, Prime Minister Churchill and Marshal Stalin held at Teheran their long-awaited first meeting. Out of that session, and an earlier one of British and American representatives at Cairo, came the definitive decision that the Western Allies would re-enter the continent of Europe by means of an attack across the Channel into France in late May or early June, 1944. General Eisenhower was named Supreme Commander, and again I accompanied him as Chief of Staff.

I had no direct responsibility in connection with the EAC in London. Our Ambassador, Mr. John G. Winant, represented the United States on this body. However, he maintained the closest and most personal contacts with General Eisenhower and me, and we were both devoted to him. He was hopeful and confident of post-war collaboration by the Soviet Union and ourselves, though sometimes rather bewildered by the attitude of his Soviet colleague, Mr. Gusev. In his innate nobility of character, Mr. Winant attributed Soviet intransigence to lack of familiarity with us, and suspicion of our intentions.

One of the first projects to which EAC addressed itself was the preparation of the unconditional surrender terms for Germany and, surprisingly enough, these were completed some time before we had crossed the Channel to make our first landings on the Norman coast. In fact, a copy of the terms reached my desk at SHAEF about a week before D-Day, and I gave them only the most casual inspection—first, because I was busy with more immediate problems; second, because it seemed like counting chickens before the eggs were hatched; and third, because they had come to me direct from EAC and not through the channels of the Combined Chiefs of Staff. For this reason, I assumed that they were in tentative form only and not a final draft approved by the three governments. My failure to read them more carefully and understand their purport caused us much unnecessary work nearly a year later when we needed such a document. By the time the Germans were beaten and ready to surrender, I had forgotten completely the existence of the EAC document and so had our staff. Faced with the problem of imminent surrender, we at SHAEF worked three days and three nights without let-up, preparing the surrender terms, and, with no reference to the previous Allied agreement, forwarded them to the Russian, British and American governments for approval. This was given quickly, and our terms were used when the Germans surrendered at Rheims. Four or five days later, when I was talking with Ambassador Winant by telephone, he asked why the EAC draft had not been used. I then remembered the EAC paper, and told him I had not thought it approved by all three governments. He assured me that it had been so approved. The Russians, however, never raised any question about the substitution, but, when the Allied Commanders-in-Chief met in Berlin as a Control Council for Germany, after the surrender, they utilized the EAC draft as a basis for the first Control Council order affecting Germany as a whole, since the provisions were somewhat broader than the simple field surrender terms prepared at SHAEF.

During the campaign across France and Germany, we at Supreme Headquarters had little direct contact with the Soviet Union or its representatives. Strategic problems were handled at the Prime Minister-Presidential level, and only in the closing stages when a link-up of the American and Soviet armies seemed imminent, did we find it necessary, for tactical coordination, to send a military mission to Moscow. Air Marshal Tedder, the

Deputy Supreme Commander, headed this mission, and was accompanied by General Bull, Assistant Chief of Staff for Operations, and several other staff officers of Supreme Headquarters.

The Tedder mission was designed to iron out a number of difficult problems. The EAC also had by this time designated future zones of occupation in Germany and we had already penetrated more than two hundred miles into the future Soviet Zone. Because our contacts with the Soviet Union were so limited and communications so difficult, we were not sure exactly how they would react when we actually touched hands. For instance, we asked ourselves, would they stop when we met or would they insist upon continuing immediately to the limits of their occupation zone? How were we to recognize each other's armored vehicles and troops from the air? How would we provide coordination between the Russian and Allied armies if they operated side by side for a time in actual combat with the Germans?

The Tedder mission was received warmly. Our problems were handled simply and expeditiously and our people returned entirely satisfied. Later, when the meeting of the armies finally took place on the River Elbe, there was the greatest enthusiasm on both sides, especially among the junior officers and soldiers from both East and West. But the young American lieutenant who met the Russians first and who reported to General Eisenhower later, had his anxious moments—he suddenly realized that he had no American flag to identify his detachment. So he and his men hastily made one from a white bed sheet painted with red stripes and a blue union. This "flag" they gave to General Eisenhower as a trophy of war.

It was at about this time that I had a disturbing talk with Prime Minister Churchill while dining alone with him at No. 10 Downing Street during a quick trip to London. He was gravely worried about the future and about the difficulties we had experienced in reaching hard and fast agreements with the Russians, looking toward the future of Europe. Discussing the imminent withdrawal of the Western Allies from the Russian Zone of occupied Germany back into the limits of the zone already assigned to them by the EAC, Mr. Churchill said gravely that it would cast a pall over all of Europe when the

Allied troops withdrew from this vast area of Germany which they had conquered by their blood and courage, without having reached a definite settlement with our Russian Allies on many important outstanding questions. He could not overlook the fact that the war would terminate with the Russians holding all of the capitals of Central Europe. However, there was some comfort in the thought, he remarked more cheerfully, that two years ago if someone had told us that the Russian Army was approaching the Rhine we would have been very happy about it.

Before the war finally ended in Germany, we had one final opportunity to demonstrate our complete good faith to the Soviet Union. During the end of April and early part of May, the German front had cracked wide open, both on the east and the west, and Soviet and American troops were advancing almost at will. The Nazis, even after Hitler's suicide, never gave up their effort to split the Allies, and play one off against the other. Their last attempt amounted to the proposal that they should surrender to the British and Americans, but not to the Russians. This the Supreme Commander rejected instantly and conclusively. He sent them a twelve-hour ultimatum: they must surrender or we would close the front and take no more prisoners. During these negotiations, Major General Ivan Susloparov, the Russian Military Attaché in Paris and head of the mission to SHAEF, was kept fully informed. It was he who transmitted the revised surrender terms to Moscow for approval and, at Rheims, signed the surrender document as a witness.

Since the war, impressive evidence has come to light that the Soviet Union actually believed, or at least expected, that we would make such a deal with the Germans, and this causes one to wonder what the Soviet Government would have done if the offer had been made to them instead of to us.

With the war over and Germany under Allied control, I continued as Chief of Staff in Germany, where our principal contacts were with Marshal Zhukov and General Sokolovski, both of whom we admired very much, and who, I felt, would be great men in any country. These two, and their principal subordinates, impressed us not only by their ability, but by their frank and straightforward attitude. In spite of the language barrier—and it is very difficult to feel close to a man whom you

can only address through an interpreter—we believed that we
had reached with them an honest basis of mutual confidence
and understanding.

Marshal Zhukov was obviously sincere in his statement that
world peace depended entirely upon the ability of the Russians
and the Americans to continue and to perpetuate the cooperation and understanding which they had reached during the
course of the war. However, despite the warm feelings which
we entertained toward Marshal Zhukov and General Sokolovsky, and which we felt were reciprocated, there still was an arm's
length between us in our dealings. As in Africa, we had no
informal opportunities to meet as friends and come to know
each other well. Our contacts were on the official level—whether
transacting business or participating in social function.

When we were arranging to entertain Marshal Zhukov and
his staff at Frankfurt, we suddenly came face to face with a
serious problem on the eve of their arrival—we didn't have any
Soviet flags. So seamstresses worked for twenty-four solid hours
preparing flags of proper design to line the airport and city
streets when the Soviet officers arrived. They were met at the
airfield by a guard of honor, consisting of a British Guards battalion, an American Infantry battalion, and a battalion of
American paratroopers. We had rehearsed this formation on
one occasion so that the troops would be sure to know where
they could march without interfering with air traffic. The re-
hearsal had been somewhat protracted, and during one of the
rest periods I walked behind the battalion of British Guards.
As I passed their rear rank, I heard one Tommy say to another,
"It's always this way. 'E says to somebody, 'Come on over for
lunch,' and my God, look wot 'appens!" Soldiers are the same
in any language.

It was on this visit that Marshal Zhukov delivered a stirring
tribute to General Eisenhower's development of unified command, and expressed the "hope that in the future work of the
four Allied Commanders in the Control Council we will be
just as unified." To this, General Eisenhower responded with
a phrase that went round the world, a declaration in the name
of the Allied forces that "we are going to have peace even if we
have to fight for it."

In the first flush of victory, there was a period of very close

Allied collaboration, probably reaching its peak about the time of the Potsdam Conference which was attended by President Truman, Generalissimo Stalin and Mr. Churchill (who was replaced by Prime Minister Clement Attlee after the Conservative Party had been defeated in the election held while the conference was in session). However, it was not long before we began to experience petty annoyances and pinpricks, and ultimately several serious incidents arose that were a prelude to the final great Allied split over the whole German question.

Our first foretaste of difficulty came from Berlin in the form of a letter from the Russian Chief of Staff, giving a list of some two hundred violations of boundary and air corridor regulations by our troops. These were all completely insignificant, but the tone of the Russian letter puzzled me. I replied, quite informally, to the Soviet Chief of Staff that I would if necessary, supply him with a corresponding list of violations by Soviet troops and individuals, but it seemed rather pointless to me for Allies to begin such recriminations, and I expressed the hope that we would be able to avoid correspondence of this nature and that similar questions could be handled on a direct and informal basis.

On this occasion, General Sokolovsky sent back word that he would be willing to proceed informally, but that the reports of air corridor violations had been made by the anti-aircraft and radar units, which were not under Zhukov's command but which operated directly under the General Staff in Moscow. He had, therefore, no option but to forward this complaint and to transmit our reply to Moscow. I am glad to say that during the rest of my stay in Germany, this was the last report of its kind received from Soviet headquarters.

Our most serious problem with the Soviet Government while I was in Germany concerned the implementation of an Allied agreement made at Yalta and reaffirmed at Potsdam, looking toward the return of displaced persons—prisoners of war, slave laborers and others—to their country of origin. Return of Russian nationals to the Soviet Union was the responsibility of a Soviet repatriation mission, headed by General Daridor, who had set up his headquarters in Frankfurt where the headquarters of the American command for Germany had been established in the main offices of I. G. Farben.

Regrettably, the Soviet interpretation and our interpretation of the Yalta agreement differed considerably. We believed that we were talking about facilitating the return to Russia of those Soviet nationals who desired to return, plus, of course, such individuals as might be charged specifically with war crimes. We certainly did not intend to violate the traditional American attitude toward giving sanctuary to political refugees, of whom we found thousands in Germany. Many of these were from the Baltic states, which had been incorporated into the Soviet Union since the war began, and others from those parts of Poland and Rumania which had been recently annexed by the Russians.

I found on one occasion that an American unit, somewhat overzealous in carrying out its responsibilities, actually had begun forcibly to load on a train some of these Russian displaced persons who had refused to return voluntarily to the Soviet Union. Some of these had taken refuge in a church and pleaded with the Americans not to send them back to the Soviet Union. When their pleas seemed unavailing, one or two actually committed suicide.

We immediately issued instructions that we would not forcibly repatriate anybody except actual war criminals, since it was entirely contrary to our principles to force the return to the Soviet Union of any of these people who did not wish to go or who felt they would suffer for their political opinions.

The Russians, for reasons of their own, were determined to repatriate all displaced persons born in areas now part of the Soviet Union to their place of origin, and we had many just reasons for complaint on account of their aggressive procedure which took no account of Allied authority.

They constantly kept changing the make-up of their repatriation mission, and it was quite clear they had brought in more personnel than we had agreed to accept. We had at that time what we thought to be a rather tight rationing system in Frankfurt, with all personnel being fed at a central mess, and I thought this might provide one method of finding out whether the Soviet contingent was overstrength and how the non-accredited members of the repatriation mission were able to obtain food. An investigation disclosed that they were using their admission cards to the officers' mess several times for each meal, and in this way transient Russians traveling in the American zone could stay for an indefinite time without our knowledge. We established a new rationing system to put a stop to that.

I have speculated many times why there is such a violent and active campaign on the part of the Soviet Union to get back into Soviet territory all displaced persons who were born in Russia or in any of the territories now part of Russia, even against the will of the individuals concerned. The facts are that the Soviet officials are thoroughly aware of the possibility of injury to Soviet foreign policy and propaganda inherent in the presence abroad of thousands of persons who can and will testify at first hand on Soviet methods, or who may, through family connections, etc., receive and make public information on conditions and practices in the Soviet Union.

After prolonged experience with the DP question in Germany, I felt that it would be a serious mistake to underestimate the influence of the traditional feudal concepts which still prevail in the Soviet Union. The Soviet idea of the relation of the state and its citizens is very clearly revealed in the prohibition of marriages between Russians and foreigners, in the refusal to permit emigration or to recognize expatriation, and in the isolation of the Soviet public from foreigners.

The DP problem dogged me through my stay in Germany, and I was glad to be clear of it—or so I thought—when I was transferred back to Washington.

These, then, were the previous encounters and experiences with the Russians that I thought about while I considered Secretary Byrnes' offer.

I knew, of course, that I could count on Secretary Patterson and General Eisenhower for good advice, but if I subconsciously expected any encouragement to decline, I was disappointed. Both men have far too high a sense of duty to decline any task themselves, however difficult it may be, or to encourage a subordinate to do so, and both said that I could not refuse.

General Eisenhower's further advice was that I should allow myself a year or a year and a half to try to "break through the crust," as he put it, and, if unsuccessful, to let someone else try. In any event, he thought I should not remain in Moscow for more than two years.

That seemed to settle it. I told Secretary Byrnes I'd take the job.

In preparation for the Moscow assignment, I was subjected to the most intensive educational "cramming" of my entire life. I went on an eighteen-hour-a-day schedule during those last weeks in Washington, for I was not only learning about the responsibilities I was to assume, but I was also in the process of turning over my War Department duties.

My "instructors," with whom I had daily meetings, included the officers of the Eastern European Division of the State Department, then headed by Freeman Matthews, now our Ambassador in Sweden, and Elbridge Durbrow, later Minister-Counselor in Moscow, who had the Russian Desk, and I had the invaluable advice of Charles Bohlen, later Counselor of the State Department and one of the Department's original group of Russian-language experts, who served as interpreter for Presidents Roosevelt and Truman at the Big Three conferences at Teheran, Yalta and Potsdam. In addition, I had the advantage of two conversations with President Truman, one of them long, informal and very informative.

In my last talk with the President, he expressed the kernel of an idea which later was to grow into the North Atlantic Pact. It was obvious that one of the President's major preoccupations was to set things right with the Soviet Union, but without sacrificing further the position and interests of the United States and its Western Allies.

It was clear, too, that the President had familiarized himself in great detail with the situation in Central and Eastern Europe since he became Chief Executive, and that his knowledge of foreign affairs was extensive. During our talk, he took from his desk drawer a map of the Danubian basin, on which he had noted his ideas for a solution of the problems in this vital area where Eastern and Western policies were in violent contradiction and daily clashes.

The President instructed me to call upon Stalin at the earliest possible moment after my arrival in Moscow. He gave me a letter to the Generalissimo asking him to come to the United States as the President's personal guest, and told me to make it very clear to Stalin, and through him to the men who control the Kremlin, that the United States had made agreements in Yalta and Potsdam in good faith, and hoped to be able to carry out those pacts in good faith. But he also wished me to make it very clear to the Kremlin that our continued adherence to these agreements would be made impossible by continued Soviet disregard of their own obligations. He felt even then, I am sure, that if Soviet pressure continued the Western nations inevitably would be forced closer together in mutual self-defense. In such a case, the United States, as the strongest Western nation, would find it necessary to take the lead.

I had several long talks with Averell Harriman and drew heavily upon his knowledge, for he had just spent two and one-half years experiencing the peaks and valleys of Soviet friendship.

I also talked with Mr. Bernard Baruch, whose primary preoccupation was with the vital problem of atomic control, and he wanted me to make every effort to impress upon Soviet statesmen that this was, as Mr. Baruch said in his memorable speech opening the atomic discussions, "a race between the quick and the dead."

My one meeting with Mr. Churchill, during this period of training, came through the accident of my staying temporarily in the same New York hotel immediately after his now famous Fulton, Missouri, "Iron Curtain" speech, for which he was being vigorously picketed and abused by both Communists and fellow-travelers. While I did not subscribe to all the views expressed by Mr. Churchill at Fulton, I wanted very much to see him before I left, because of the affection and respect which I, like my associates at Supreme Headquarters, had come to feel for him during our close association in the war. I telephoned his rooms and asked if I might call informally. He told me to come up at once, since he wished to talk with me for a few minutes before the official reception committee arrived to conduct him to the dinner where he was to make another speech.

I found him in the bathtub, but he called me in; and as he dressed himself I read the speech which he was to make that night.

The former Prime Minister obviously was disturbed by the picketing outside. It was his first experience, in America, of any sentiment other than friendship. But he stood firm in his belief in the correctness of his Fulton analysis, declaring, "Mark my words—in a year or two years, many of the very people who are now denouncing me will say, 'How right Churchill was.' "

Then with deep emotion, he discussed the close relations which had developed between the United States and Britain during the war years.

"Never allow yourself to be persuaded that there is any real rift between us—no matter what the extremists on both sides may say," Mr. Churchill added. "We both have the same ideas of honor, of freedom, of decency and liberty. We must maintain the association forged in war and which is without parallel in history."

Finally the time came when I was crammed with "background" by my tutors until it fairly came out of my ears. Every morning a messenger delivered a hand cart, loaded with books and documents, to my offices in the Ambassadorial suite. The morning study was followed by afternoon conferences, and this went on day by day, until the picture became clearer.

The war had made a vast change in Russia's world position. This change had come about, not primarily from any development within Russia itself, but from the disintegration of the power of neighboring states. As a result of the extensive decline in the principal rival power, Germany, which confronted Russia across her land frontiers at the termination of hostilities, she found herself for the first time in her history without a single powerful rival on the European land mass. Also she was in physical control of vast new areas of this land mass, including Poland, Eastern Germany, Rumania, Bulgaria, Yugoslavia, Hungary, a portion of Austria, and with considerable influence in Czechoslovakia. Most of these were areas to which Russian power never before had been extended. The exact frontiers of Russian interest were purposely kept vague, contingent upon the future. These new areas contained over 100,000,000 people.

This increase in power brought with it a corresponding increase in the responsibilities of the Soviet Union, which would now be morally responsible to the world for the happiness and prosperity of the newly acquired peoples, for developing their resources, for ordering their industrial and cultural relationships, and for securing their military defense.

The word "democracy" had been used extensively at Yalta and at Potsdam. The question was whether democracy meant the same thing to the Soviet Government as it did to the Western governments, and whether Russia would carry out successfully these new responsibilities in accordance with the Allied agreements. The record, to date, so far as these agreements were concerned, was not an encouraging one.

Behind Russian policy for centuries had lain the age-old sense of insecurity of an agricultural people reared on an exposed plain in the neighborhood of fierce, nomadic tribes. Would this sense of insecurity now become a permanent feature of Russian psychology? Would their psychology provide the basis for successful expansion of the new areas to the East and West? And, if initially successful, would it know where to stop? Might it not be inexorably carried forward, by its very nature, in a struggle to reach the whole—to attain complete mastery of the shores of the Atlantic and the Pacific?

Americans, in general, had come to believe during the war that collaboration with Russia, as we visualized it, was entirely possible. They thought this colloboration depended only upon the establishment of popular, personal relations of cordiality in conferences with the Russian leaders. They reasoned that the only solution for our current difficulties was for the United States to find the means to insure renewal of this collaboration. If this was impossible, they feared the other extreme. The more fearful among us would conclude that the war had been fought in vain, that another war was inevitable, and civilization would be faced with catastrophe.

This was not the view of State Department officers, long experienced in dealing with the Soviet Union and familiar with history of Czarist Russia. They felt that the Soviet Union, owing to its peculiar structure and the political philosophy which motivated it, was almost incapable of collaborating with other governments in the manner which Americans have in mind when they speak of collaboration. These officials were of the opinion that the Soviet Union had no intention of permitting anything like the number of personal contacts between the two peoples which would be required to lead to a broad basis of confidence and collaboration.

Their experience had been, through a dozen years of diplomatic relations between the two countries, that the United States had consistently taken the initiative in trying to establish relationships of confidence and cordiality, but that these efforts had been met from the Soviet side almost invariably with suspicion and rebuff—and that this would not and could not be otherwise in the foreseeable future.

These men had reached the conclusion that while the type of intimate open collaboration for which the general American public yearned was impossible, it was not actually essential for the future of world peace. They felt that the Soviet Government, as a body thoroughly versed in the realities of power, understood this well, and that very probably, in the absence of real collaboration, it would be possible to establish a reasonable stability among the great powers for decades to come by preserving a reasonable balance of strength between them, and a realistic understanding of mutual vital interests.

I was inclined to take a more optimistic view, encouraged by my conversations with senior Russian officers. It seemed to me that even if the extreme cordiality and confidence for which we hoped could not be attained, at least a measure of it was possible, and that this would be sufficient to insure long-term collaboration. I felt that the first essential was an effort to restore confidence and mutual understanding.

The answer, of course, lay in the future, and the only way to find out was to go, see, and try. It was in this mood that I was ready to leave Washington for Moscow.

II

THE MISSION STARTS

. . . Russia cannot boast of a single invention in mechanics, that has been practical or copied out of the country. All they have is borrowed, except their miserable climate, and even upon that they are paying an enormous rate of usury, in the defences and privations of winter. They fight their battles on borrowed capital, and make loans to build their railways. Their best vessels are built in England and the United States. And all their arts and pursuits, though cultivated and pressed, with commendable diligence and a good degree of success, are the products of foreign genius, duplicates of inventions and discoveries of a people wiser than themselves. No nation has more need of foreigners, and none is so jealous of them. These remarks have no special reference to Americans. On the contrary the Americans rank as high here as any other people, and though republicans they are known and acknowledged not to be propagandists.

—Excerpt from a dispatch of the American
Minister to Russia, Neill S. Brown, dated
St. Petersburg, November 6, 1851

THE physical preparations for departure proved to be almost as arduous as the professional briefing. You can't just get on an airplane and go to Moscow as you might go to Paris, or London, or Brussels or Buenos Aires; you have to prepare carefully for any extended sojourn in the Soviet capital. The Moscow Embassy's "Post Report," a guide for future diplomatic appointees, made it discouragingly clear, even before we had left Washington, that we were not heading for any paradise of plenty.

After thirty years in uniform, with only an occasional opportunity to wear civilian clothes, I anticipated, of course, an extensive and expensive New York shopping tour for myself and for my wife, who would, of necessity, require a much more elaborate wardrobe as mistress of an embassy than she had ever possessed in the modest capacity of a Regular Army wife.

Such a clothes-buying expedition would have been required regardless of the Embassy to which we were assigned, but neither of us had expected to have to buy out a sizable part of the local five and ten cent store until we came across this paragraph in the "Post Report":

"Two general ideas should govern what is brought to the Soviet Union: (1) nothing is obtainable there, and (2) it is cold, both indoors and out, a good deal of the year."

There followed, in the coldest blue type I have ever read, a detailed list of the articles needed in Moscow but unobtainable there and frequently overlooked by travelers. The list, in full, follows:

Extras—watch, watch straps, fountain pen, mechanical pencil, lighter fluid and flints, razor and blades.

Electrical Equipment—radio, sun lamp, hair dryer, lamps, flatirons with extra elements, percolator, toaster, vacuum cleaner.

Miscellaneous—stationery, ink, books, playing cards, poker chips, score pads, calling cards, Christmas cards, Christmas tree decorations, table covers, table decorations, pictures, ash trays, bookends, candles, clocks, linen, silver, cocktail shaker, victrola, records, needles, flower bulbs and seeds, complete sewing kit, clothes hangers, laundry soap, non-inflammable dry-cleaning fluid, starch, mothballs, shoeshine kit, extra shoe laces, miscellaneous small tools, picture wire and fasteners, thumbtacks, wrapping paper, string, corkscrew, can opener, fly swatter and fly paper, flashlight, matches, thermos bottle, Sterno, hot water bottle, ice pack, any special medicines, dental floss, first-aid kit, Kleenex, cosmetics, manicure materials, scissors, bobby pins, hairpins, dark glasses, picnic kit, skis and skates, tennis rackets and balls, miscellaneous small gifts for servants, birthdays, etc.

I had selected as my personal staff: former Major Ruth Briggs of the Women's Army Corps, who had been my staff secretary in North Africa and at SHAEF and who now, fortunately for me, was in the State Department; Sergeant Greiner, who had been my driver in Washington; and former Sergeant Mirion Blazejczak, who, born in America, had lived in Poland since he was twelve and who had been liberated from the Buchenwald concentration camp with the fall of Germany. He was to be invaluable because he spoke Russian, and could help Mrs. Smith in running the Embassy household. All of them were pressed into duty with the shopping list, because they had to buy for themselves as well as for us.

Because my civilian wardrobe was practically non-existent, I had to start from scratch. Time was short, but my friend, Bernard Gimbel of New York, cooperated handsomely and everything was ready on time.

My own needs included three business suits, the diplomatic "uniforms" of tails and morning coat and, of course, heavy overcoats and other heavy clothing suitable for wear in an extremely cold climate.

And, as the word got around that we were flying to Moscow in a C-54, everybody who had friends in Moscow wanted us to carry packages there, with the result that we were loaded with everything from fur coats down to altar candles for the small Roman Catholic church which is open in Moscow under the terms of the Litvinov-Roosevelt agreement providing for diplomatic recognition of the Soviet Union by the United States.

Finally everything was ready, and on March 24, 1946, we took off from the Washington Airport, after saying goodbye to a small group of State Department officials, Army personnel, and a few newspaper correspondents whom I had known and become fond of in Europe, and who did us the kindness to come and say farewell.

The flight to Berlin was uneventful, broken only by short stops at Orly Field near Paris, where I saw and talked with our Ambassador to France, Jefferson Caffery, and at Frankfurt, where I renewed for a few moments old-time associations with Army officers I had left behind when I relinquished my post in Germany.

At Berlin, we were met at the airfield by our old and dear friends, General and Mrs. Lucius Clay and Ambassador Robert Murphy, and we spent the night and following day as guests of the Clays in their house in the American zone. The Clays' house was to be a haven of refuge to us for the next three years.

The principal Russians in Berlin, Marshal Sokolovsky and his political adviser, Ambassador Seminov, paid formal calls and I was glad to see Sokolovsky again. He seemed as friendly as before, but a little more reserved than he had been during our talks when I was his opposite number as a Chief of Staff. Mr. Seminov, an intelligent, clean-cut, quiet, and obviously capable political officer, who speaks excellent English, interpreted Marshal Sokolovsky's statements on the necessity for understanding and cooperation.

I had brought gifts from General Eisenhower for Marshal Sokolovsky's wife, and I asked him to what address in Moscow they might be sent. At first he avoided the question, but when I pressed him, he asked me to send them to his aide at his headquarters in Berlin. I told him that they were packed with my baggage and that it was impossible to find them until we had arrived in Moscow. He reiterated, however, that they should be sent to the aide in Berlin. This surprised me, but, as I found out later, Soviet officials dislike or are timid about giving the addresses of their families to any foreigner en route to Moscow, presumably because they fear that overtures to their families may arouse suspicion in high places in the Secret Police and perhaps even in the Kremlin itself.

In a negative sort of way, perhaps the most striking experience of my Berlin stop was an opportunity to review the Berlin garrison at Tempelhof Airport. I had seen such a review once before in Berlin, with General Eisenhower, and we had watched the march past of one of our famous airborne divisions, battle-tested, veteran officers and men who had complete equipment of the most modern sort in perfect condition for immediate action, and who were capable of giving a magnificent account of themselves under any circumstances. That this is a conservative statement needs only to be checked against the records of the Battle of the Bulge, where the single airborne division defending Bastogne during the Ardennes counteroffensive held its position against a total of ten attacking German divisions.

General Clays' men (and women, for a WAC detachment was included) were everything to make an American proud, except in strength of numbers. Here they were only a faint shadow of the mighty Army I had left in Europe. Here, I thought, as I looked at the Russian officers in the reviewing stand behind us, was the most impressive evidence in the world of the American desire for peace. Here, in the hottest spot in Europe, if not in the world, was the unmistakable evidence that the United States had demobilized in record time and had liquidated the most efficient and most powerful armed forces ever assembled. This was, of course, the result of the "bring the boys home" campaign, which, launched just before a Congressional election year, had reached such intensity, inside as well as outside the

Army, that no governmental official could withstand it. And the result was, it seemed to me, that we had reduced our defense force to a greater extent than was justified by world conditions.

There was, however, one contingent which was both comforting and encouraging. Our Air Force elements, gathered from various places in Germany outside Berlin, passed in review in still impressive, although attenuated, strength, and the B-17's flying low in tight formation were a story in themselves which no potential aggressor who saw the ruins of Berlin around us could disregard.

We left for Moscow from Berlin in the early hours of March 28, 1946. By now our C-54 was fully loaded, since we had picked up at Paris, Frankfurt and in the former German capital scattered members of the Moscow Embassy who had been in Western Europe on government business or on leave, and who welcomed the chance for a speedy, direct-flight return to their posts in Moscow.

The flight time from Berlin to Moscow is about five and one-half hours by the most direct route, which took us about midway between Koenigsberg (now renamed Kaliningrad), the former capital of East Prussia but now a part of the Soviet Union, and the Masurian Lakes. Below us was a vast and formidable terrain, the site of Eastern European battlefields of the immediate and distant past.

It was here that two of the decisive battles of the first World War were fought, ending in defeat and annihilation for the Russians, and it was here, too, that the Russians won some of their great victories of the most recent war; victories which sent the Wehrmacht fleeing in disorder behind the Oder line, the last defensive position before Berlin itself was overrun. In the first World War, the Russian forces, led by Rennenkampf and Samsonov, had been routed at Gumbinnen and destroyed at Tannenberg after the two armies had separated and were prevented from giving mutual assistance by the impassable area of the Masurian Lakes, behind which Hindenburg had deployed his waiting Eighth Army. This campaign illustrated a weakness which had been frequent in Russian armies throughout history and which was eliminated only by Bolshevik discipline and iron control—that is, a tendency to jealousy and hatred between Russian senior officers. Hindenburg accurately took the measure of his opponents, noting that Samsonov and Rennenkampf had long been bitter enemies as the result of a disagreement arising during the Russo-Japanese War. He believed that either would prefer to see the other defeated than to win a battle himself, and that either would wait too long to reinforce the other in the case of a German attack. His estimate was correct, and the Russian debacle resulted.

From the time we left East Prussia, the landscape, unfolding below like a map, seemed almost lacking in roads and other means of communication. There were few cities, or even villages of any appreciable size. The terrain was impressive for its enormous wooded areas, dark forests of pines and firs alternating with the lighter color of birches.

General Eisenhower had told me that when he flew across the same area on his trip to Moscow with Marshal Zhukov, the Soviet soldier had pointed out the few signs of human habitation and had explained the fact by saying that the Germans had destroyed everything, even small crossroads towns and clusters of farmhouses. I believe this to be true—but the sparsity of the roads and the only occasional sight of a railroad line are also evidence of the limited population in this area before the war.

This was, of course, the historic route for invading armies, not only in the twentieth century but for hundreds of years. It was over these plains that the Mongolian hordes moved steadily westward until a courier brought word that the great Khan had died, and they sped back to their capital to fight the battle for succession. Four times since the eighteenth century, Russian armies had stood at the Elbe. They took Potsdam from Frederick the Great, and played a major part in the capture of Paris from Napoleon.

As we flew over this part of the vast plain, completely lacking in major geographical obstacles and exposed to invasion from every direction, it was easy, in the light of history, to understand why the government of the Soviet Union was so preoccupied with providing security against invasion, and why it was so intent upon constructing a security belt around its borders through a chain of buffer states.

If this were, in fact, the only objective, it would be understandable. But already there were alarming signs that the Pan-Slav imperialism, so disturbingly defined by enthusiastic Russian writers, seemed even at this time to be reasserting itself in spite of Lenin's frequently repeated renunciation of any plans to conquer other nations, because, as he said, "We Russians have never been able to make anything but serfs of conquered people."

The ground below was covered with snow and the lakes still were frozen. This I took as confirmation of what I had been told about the Russian winter; that its length was even more trying than its actual severity.

For hundreds of miles, on the approaches to Moscow, the land was flat, and without visible signs of human habitation until we had reached the immediate vicinity of the capital.

It was almost noon when the plane circled the Moscow Central Airport. The weather was clear, except for a few low-hanging clouds and an occasional snow flurry, and we had a good view of our future home before we landed. Our first impression was of a vast, sprawling city of low buildings and wide streets. There seemed to be few trees in the city itself, although the environs of Moscow are heavily forested.

As we came in low for a landing, we saw that the airfield itself was covered with snow and the landing strip was difficult to distinguish. Looking down, I saw a small collection of motor vehicles and a huddled little group of people, obviously the welcoming personnel of the Moscow mission. As the plane rolled to a stop, my first impression of my future colleagues and assistants was a sort of general and cheerful shabbiness. Most of them were wearing slightly moth-eaten fur-lined coats, and the women were so thoroughly bundled up it was hard to tell what they looked like. The men were crowned with a nondescript collection of headgear, which obviously had been selected for warmth rather than appearance.

We were welcomed warmly, first by George Kennan, Minister-Counselor of the Embassy, who had been acting as Chargé d'Affaires ad interim from the time of Mr. Harriman's departure (and who is now Counselor of the State Department), and then by all of the staff who were not absolutely required to be on duty.

The Soviet Chief of Protocol, looking extremely smart in his gray Foreign Office uniform, with its military-cut greatcoat, gold embroidered shoulder boards, and high gray astrakhan hat, delivered the usual formal greeting in French, and a number of my future diplomatic colleagues came forward with kind expressions of good will.

We shook hands all around before we got into a car and started for the Embassy, which is in the center of the city. None of us will ever forget this first drive through the streets of Moscow.

My first impression was one of general grayness. Moscow is at its worst in the early spring, because the successive layers of snow and soot have gradually melted together and the entire city seems drab. Its people showed acutely the aftermath of years of war and a prolonged state of military mobilization. The majority, both men and women, were wearing the quilted cotton coat and head-shrouding shawl which reminded me immediately of a street scene in Peking in winter. Men, women and children—even tiny babies—wore the Russian felt boot, which is the only really warm footgear that one can use during a Moscow winter.

The most colorful spots in the otherwise drab landscape were the babies. They were wrapped in bright-colored comforters, usually red, so that they resembled clothing rolls with hardly an inch of baby showing.

It was just time for the luncheon recess at primary schools and kindergartens, and on almost every street was a procession of solemn little gnomes, dressed like their elders in quilted jackets, fur- or fleece-lined hats with ear-flaps, heavy mittens and small felt boots. Looking like a procession of Lilliputians, they walked along, two by two, hand in hand, preceded and followed by instructors.

Many of the buildings seemed in an advanced state of disrepair, although I saw no evidence of serious bombings such as London and Berlin had experienced. Part of this is due to the fact that until recently most Russian brick production had been of non-weatherproof brick and, as a result, most of the buildings were faced with stucco, which cracks and flakes during winter weather. Many of the houses were built of logs, lathed over and stucco-faced.

The entire city looked mildewed, and that went, as well, for

Spaso House, which was to be my future home, and which was
a far cry from the elegance of the London and Paris embassies
which I had visited.

Tired, cold and hungry after our long trip from Berlin, our
small party had lunch, distributed itself about the bedrooms of
Spaso House, and spent the rest of the afternoon trying to get
temporarily settled and a few necessities unpacked.

Next morning, I made my first trip to the Chancery of the
Embassy, a seven-story former apartment building which Americans usually called "Mokhovaya," taking its name from its
location on Mokhovaya Ulitsa, the enormously broad avenue
and square adjoining Red Square itself, just north of the red
brick Kremlin wall. Here I met the staff again and had my
first real opportunity to look at and get acquainted with the
people who were to share my work of the Moscow mission, and
who had looked so much alike, because of their clothing, at the
airport when I arrived the day before.

I could not actually become a functioning Ambassador in
Moscow until I had formally presented my credentials to the
head of the state, and, it turned out, this could not be arranged for approximately a week. While most of the world
undoubtedly considers Generalissimo Stalin the head of the
Soviet state, the title technically is held by Nikolai Shvernik, a
former trade union leader who is President of the Supreme
Soviet, which is, in theory, the supreme governing body of the
Soviet Union. Stalin is, of course, the man who wields the real
power, but his title is President of the Council of Ministers, or,
in Western terms, Prime Minister.

During the period while I waited to present my credentials, I
paid a series of informal calls on V. M. Molotov, the Foreign
Minister, and his principal deputies, and upon my colleagues
in the diplomatic corps.

Mr. Molotov received me, two days after my arrival, at his
office in the Foreign Office building (he has another office in
the Kremlin itself). The Ministry, which all Muscovites, Russian and foreign alike, call the "Narcomindyel" (an abbreviation of its Russian title, the People's Commissariat for Foreign
Affairs), is a dingy, unimpressive, grayish red stone building,

standing just across the street from Moscow's famous political prison, the Lubianka.

There are no guards outside, but you encounter them just as you enter the revolving door. Although the outside of the building was covered with soot from Moscow's furnaces, the interior was spotlessly clean, with the wood floors and light paneling well waxed and highly polished. A uniformed attendant, obviously an ex-soldier of long service, possibly even a holdover from the Czarist regime, who was notable for his smiling peasant face and courteous, almost courtly, manner, took my hat, as a girl secretary from Mr. Molotov's office met me at the elevator to take me to the Foreign Minister's suite, where I was greeted again by an MVD officer and a civilian receptionist.

Mr. Molotov's suite, which consisted of this outer reception room, a large conference room and a smaller private office, is a formal, and rather uncomfortable, place to visit. The furniture is what we would call mid-Victorian, or its Russian counterpart. The walls are paneled two-thirds of the way to the ceiling with golden oak and the floors are of hardwood parquet. The atmosphere was one of quiet and orderly efficiency.

Promptly at the moment set for our appointment (I was to learn later that Russian officials are extremely punctual in keeping appointments), I was ushered into the conference room, where Mr. Molotov and his interpreter, Mr. Pavlov, were waiting.

This first conversation was of the usual brief, formal but pleasant nature appropriate to the first meeting of a new Ambassador and the Foreign Secretary. Molotov asked about my trip, inquired about my family, and referred to my service during the war, with which he said he was familiar. He spoke of his own visits to the United States in 1942 and again in 1945, when the United Nations Charter was written at San Francisco, and asked about my first impressions of Moscow.

We both expressed our hope for pleasant and effective association, and our belief in the necessity of closer contact and better understanding between our two countries.

As I prepared to leave, Mr. Molotov assured me that the Foreign Office would be of assistance to me whenever it could, and he promised that I could have access to him at any time, and this was one promise which was kept meticulously. Never was I refused a prompt audience when I requested it.

Sitting there talking with him, I noted particularly Molotov's fine eyes, bright, brown and intelligent. He did not appear completely at ease, then or in subsequent conversations. Later I found that he lacks both the sense of humor and the capacity for quick irritation and sarcasm so characteristic of Vishinsky.

During the following days I paid similar calls on the Vice Ministers of Foreign Affairs, Messrs. Vishinsky, V. G. Dekanozov, I. E. Lozovsky, and Maxim M. Litvinov. The best known of these, of course, was Mr. Litvinov, the Foreign Minister of the Soviet Union from 1928 until just before the Nazi-Soviet pact of 1939 and generally believed to be on his way out of the Foreign Office—a forecast which subsequent events proved correct.

Vishinsky, at this time, was almost as well known as Litvinov, and has since, of course, become much better known to the world in general. His has been a varied and remarkable career. A brilliant lawyer from a good family, his revolutionary activities brought him into the Russian Social-Democratic Party at an early age, and he initially was a member of the Menshevik faction. That group, while accepting Marxian tenets, rejected the idea of forcible and illegal seizure of power by a minority political group, subscribing instead to a program for political success through public education and propaganda. Later, he accepted the victory of the Bolshevik faction. He first came to wide public knowledge as Public Prosecutor in the great purge trials of the late nineteen thirties, where his presentations were often a classic example of savage invective. Even in the case of Bukharin, one of the intellectual giants of the Revolution, who was the only one who had the better of the agile-minded Vishinsky from the witness stand, he still managed to obtain one of those remarkable "confessions" which have so puzzled and confused the outside world. Mr. Vishinsky has a disarming sense of humor and his quick lawyer's mind enjoys an argument, which he sometimes intentionally provokes purely for the interest it creates. As I had known him before, our meeting was less formal and our brief talk less stilted than in the case of Mr. Molotov, although it followed the same general lines. But this meeting was of particular interest to me, not only because of our past association on the Mediterranean Commission, but because Vishinsky was charged in the Foreign Office with supervising the branch which dealt with American affairs.

The other two Vice Ministers, Lozovsky and Dekanozov, did not remain long in the Foreign Office after my arrival. Lozovsky, a short, alert, intelligent man, with gray hair and beard, was responsible for Far Eastern affairs. Like Mr. Litvinov, he is a Jew, and with his departure from the Foreign Office, shortly after that of Litvinov, the last high-ranking Jewish official was eliminated from direct connection with foreign affairs. Lozovsky had the reputation in the diplomatic corps, and especially in the American Embassy, of being one of the most difficult officials in the Foreign Ministry to deal with, but during our brief association I found him pleasant and actually more co-operative than his associates. Indeed, he was the only Foreign Office official other than Mr. Molotov who ever gave me a quick decision or positive answer during the initial discussion of any question.

Mr. Dekanozov was primarily responsible for British Empire affairs in the Foreign Office, and I had few dealings with him, except on the occasions when, in the absence of Messrs. Molotov and Vishinsky, he served briefly as Acting Foreign Minister. He is short, blond and pale, with light blue eyes, and a personality I regarded as rather negative.

April 4 at 11 A.M. was the hour set by the Foreign Office for presentation of my credentials to Mr. Shvernik in his Kremlin office. Although the Soviet Union is proud of the description, "Dictatorship of the Proletariat," the presentation of credentials is as formal a ceremony here as it is in the most fastidious Royal Court. It was the first time I had worn morning coat, striped trousers and a silk hat.

Waiting for us in Mr. Shvernik's reception room was the familiar figure of Mr. Vishinsky, with several uniformed officials of the Foreign Office and the Chief of Protocol, Mr. Molotchkov, with his assistants and interpreter. We chatted briefly and informally for a few minutes, and then Mr. Shvernik entered the room.

As I was presented to him, I handed him the usual formal letter of credence. These credentials are similar in wording when addressed to any chief of state, as they follow an old diplomatic formula. Mine read:

Harry S. Truman
President of the United States of America

To His Excellency
    The President of the Presidium of the Supreme Soviet
    of the Union of Soviet Socialist Republics.

Great and Good Friend:

I have made choice of Walter Bedell Smith, a distinguished citizen of the United States, to reside near the Government of Your Excellency in the quality of Ambassador Extraordinary and Plenipotentiary of the United States of America. He is well informed of the relative interests of the two countries and of the sincere desire of this Government to cultivate to the fullest extent the friendship which has so long existed between them. My knowledge of his high character and ability gives me entire confidence that he will constantly endeavor to advance the interests and prosperity of both Governments and so render himself acceptable to Your Excellency.

I therefore request Your Excellency to receive him favorably and to give full credence to what he shall say on the part of the United States and to the assurances which I have charged him to convey to you of the best wishes of this Government for the prosperity of the Union of Soviet Socialist Republics.

May God have Your Excellency in His wise Keeping.

Your Good Friend,
Harry S. Truman

Washington, March 22, 1946.

When this had been accepted, I introduced my staff, after which Mr. Shvernik and I, according to custom, retired to an adjoining private office for a conversation which lasted about fifteen minutes. In appearance, Shvernik very much resembled an American businessman, although his road to success had been via the avenue of Soviet trade union leadership and, of course, party politics. Of slightly less than medium height and, like most Soviet officials, a little overweight, he has black hair and mustache, a clear ruddy complexion, and the fine bright eyes which characterize so many Russians.

His opening remarks were pleasant and friendly. He inquired about the health of President Truman, expressed good wishes for success on my mission, and reiterated his agreement with the President concerning the necessity for increasing friendly relations between our two countries.

Possibly because of my military background, Mr. Shvernik next referred to an article he had recently seen quoted from the American press concerning the problems of the United States in connection with the rehabilitation of discharged veterans. He said that he was, in some respects, concerned with a corresponding problem in Russia. He asked a number of questions about our veterans' program, and especially about the G.I. Bill of Rights. He expressed interest, too, in our program for veterans' education and asked whether it had been successful.

He wanted to know what our experience had been in relation to the mental attitude of veterans returning to civilian life.

Shvernik remarked that in the Soviet Union it had been found that soldiers who had just returned were reluctant to resubmit themselves to the discipline of farms and factories. Most veterans, he said, wanted a rather prolonged period of rest and comparative freedom from restraint.

To these questions, I replied in as much detail as time and good taste permitted.

President Shvernik and I then returned to the outer assembly room, where the entire group posed for press photographs, and, though I had always thought as a result of my experiences in America and abroad that press photographers, who frequently give orders to the President of the United States, were the same irreverent, demanding types the world over, I found that the Kremlin photographers were considerably more restrained and not demanding at all. They appeared to be overawed by the Kremlin atmosphere, taking only the minimum number of shots without the inevitable request for "just one more" and without attempting to rearrange the group.

This ended the conference, and the American group drove back to Spaso for a glass of sherry all around to celebrate the fact that I had become legally the Ambassador. But I could stay with the group only a few minutes, because I had to retire to my own room with Mr. Kennan and one or two of the senior officers to review my instructions and prepare for the first conference with Generalissimo Stalin, which had been set for 9 P.M. that night.

III

STALIN

You are well enough acquainted with the character of this Government and court to appreciate the difficulties of obtaining correct information of what is meditated on any subject. It is only by weighing circumstances that opinions can be arrived at; and formed in this way they are always liable to be fallacious. These difficulties are increased by the fact that the policy of Russia seems not to be based, at present, any more than it was at former periods, on settled principles or to be guided by any fixed landmarks. Expediency is the great test. And what may be expedient today under a given state of facts, may be inexpedient tomorrow under the same state of facts.

—Excerpt from a dispatch of the American
Minister to Russia, Neill S. Brown, dated
St. Petersburg, February 29, 1852

THE Russians, only a few weeks before my first interview with Stalin, had failed to keep a treaty commitment to remove their troops from Iran, and that small neighbor to the south had brought its complaint before the United Nations Security Council at its first session in New York City. The fate of the whole United Nations effort seemingly hung in the balance, for a period, on this question. A. A. Gromyko, the Soviet representative, had stalked angrily from the Council Chamber when the other world powers, led by the United States and Secretary of State James F. Byrnes, insisted upon discussing the Iranian case without delay. The Soviet Government paid no heed to the United Nations resolutions, but, under the pressure of world public opinion, unilaterally established a new date, May 5, for the withdrawal of Soviet forces from Iran. The world wondered whether the Russians would keep their word this time.

There were difficulties and tensions involving the Russians in China, in Korea, and over the repatriation of Japanese prisoners of war. In Europe, since the beginning of the war in 1939, the Soviet Union had taken over Latvia, Lithuania, Estonia, and parts of Poland, Rumania, Czechoslovakia and Finland. Governments responsive to the Kremlin were firmly in control

46

in Poland, Bulgaria and Yugoslavia, and virtually in control in Rumania. Communist members of coalition governments in Czechoslovakia and Hungary were becoming more aggressive, and it was clear that new political crises could be expected in both countries. In France and Italy, Communist parties already had substantial minority representation in the parliaments; they controlled the labor movements of both countries; and they were obviously biding their time to make their bids for control of the entire government. Finland and Sweden and, to a certain extent, Norway had recurrent attacks of apprehension. The Soviet Union had violated one agreement after another in the dynamic expansion which was extending the influence of the Kremlin across great areas of Europe and Asia.

It was against this background that the conference with Stalin took place. My presentation had been carefully considered, in advance, in consultation with the President, with Secretary Byrnes and with the best informed State Department authorities on the Soviet Union. The President also had written a cordial personal letter to Stalin, which I carried, inviting him to visit the United States as the guest of the American people; and he also had told me to ask some very direct questions of the Soviet leader. I had told Foreign Minister Molotov of this instruction from the President at our first meeting.

I had believed myself more or less immune to excitement, after the stress and strains of more than four years of war, but I must confess that I experienced a mounting feeling of tension as the hour for the interview with Stalin approached. I thought the meeting might be a stormy one, and for that reason I chose to go alone, not taking any of my senior Embassy officers or even an interpreter with me. Mr. George Kennan, then our Minister-Counselor in Moscow, who had been in the Soviet Union for extended periods since our first diplomatic mission was established in 1933, and other Embassy officers, dined with me at Spaso House that night, but we did more talking than eating as we tried to anticipate the course of the coming conversation, the importance of which we felt strongly. I read and re-read a page and a half of closely typed notes, headed "Possible Points To Be Stressed in Conversation with Stalin," which had been prepared in the State Department before I left Washington.

The night was clear and cold and the sky filled with stars when I left Spaso House just after 8:30 P.M. The Embassy car, flying the American flag, moved rapidly over the soot-covered snow and slush down the Arbat, which is, I daresay, the most heavily policed street in the world because it is the route taken by Stalin and other members of the Politburo from their Kremlin offices to their houses in the country. It is said, probably with good reason, that the occupants of the shops and dwelling places on either side of this street are investigated and frequently re-investigated by the secret police with the most scrupulous care, and that every guest and visitor is checked and constantly watched. There is at least one policeman at intervals of one hundred yards, and two to four at each intersection.

With the approach of an official car having so-called "Kremlin privileges," all traffic lights are turned green and the vehicle is given the right-of-way. As we came to the sally port at the west wall, the automobile was halted by MVD officers, whose duty it is to assure themselves of the identity of the passengers and to take a quick look at the inside of the car. A pilot automobile, stationed outside the gate awaiting the visitor, convoyed the Embassy car through the main gate, while an alarm bell, set off by an electric eye, rang continuously until we had passed inside the Kremlin enclosure. At the gate itself, we were not halted to be checked again, but were passed with a salute by guards and officers of the MVD on duty.

The drive from the gate over the broad interior boulevard to the building which houses the offices of Generalissimo Stalin and other important Politburo members took us past the Kremlin Museum, the Hall of Soviets within which former ballrooms have been converted into assembly chambers of the legislative body of the Soviet Union, the ancient and magnificent Greek Orthodox churches, and the bell tower, at the foot of which is the great broken bell familiar as an illustration in every school child's geography. As we approached the lighted entrance to the building, I saw an usher in the Kremlin uniform of dark gray with inconspicuous red braiding on the collar and cuffs. Standing with him was a tall officer with the gold shoulder boards of a colonel, very soldierly in his olive drab tunic with red braiding, dark blue breeches with red stripes, and high soft black leather boots. Like all military personnel on duty at the

Kremlin, he wore a belted pistol in a black leather holster. As the usher opened the door of the car, the colonel greeted me with a friendly smile and a salute, said a few words in Russian, and motioned to me to follow.

An elevator took us to the third floor, and we walked down a long, narrow, high-ceilinged corridor, where a uniformed and armed MVD guard was stationed at each turn. The entrance to Generalissimo Stalin's suite of offices is through a high double door, covered with dark green padded and quilted leather, which opens into a succession of reception rooms, in the second of which were several MVD officers standing near a desk at which was seated a short, elderly, very bald, uniformed official whose shoulder boards bore the insignia of a General. I learned later that this was Stalin's Cabinet secretary.

We paused here only long enough to be announced, and I was ushered immediately into a paneled conference room at the farther end of which stood Stalin, Molotov and Pavlov, the likable young Soviet Foreign Office official who had served as interpreter for the Big Three at Teheran, Yalta and Potsdam.

As I moved toward him, Stalin greeted me formally. I shook hands with Molotov and Pavlov, after which Stalin motioned us to the table. He sat facing me at one end of the table, with his back to the wall, on which hung portraits of the great Russian Marshals Suvorov and Kutuzov. Molotov sat at Stalin's right, but took no part in our subsequent conversation, except on one or two occasions when he whispered a brief reminder to the Generalissimo. Mr. Pavlov sat at the other end of the table between Stalin and myself and served as interpreter for both of us, taking down in shorthand the sentences of each speaker in turn and then translating as he read the notes. His English, of course, is excellent.

Stalin began the conversation with the usual semi-formal greeting, a query about my trip from the United States and a question about President Truman, expressing the hope that he was in good health. He referred to our association in war, remarking that I was well known to the Russian Army and people, who had hoped to greet me earlier at the time of General Eisenhower's visit to Moscow.

I immediately handed President Truman's letter to Pavlov, who read it in Russian. Stalin listened impassively, and nodded when Pavlov had finished but, to my surprise, offered no comment whatever. It was not, in fact, until nearly two hours later, when our conversation had come to an end, that he reverted to the President's invitation and remarked:

"I would like very much to visit the United States, but age has taken its toll. My doctors tell me that I must not travel long distances and I am kept on a strict diet. I will write to the President and tell him why I cannot now accept his invitation. A man must conserve his strength. President Roosevelt had a great sense of duty, but he did not save his strength. If he had, he would probably be alive today."

The first question I put to the Soviet leader was "What does the Soviet Union want, and how far is Russia going to go?" I explained that when I left the United States this had been the most important question in the minds of the American people. The United States, I said, could appreciate and understand the desire of the Soviet Union for security. At home, we knew and deeply sympathized with the suffering that the Soviet people had endured at the hands of the German aggressor, and we appreciated fully the magnificent effort of the Red Army in the defeat of Germany. We understood the desire of the Soviet Union for security and for a share of the world's raw materials, and, consequently, our people did not strongly criticize what seemed to be some of the Soviet objectives.

It was the methods which were being used by the Soviet Union in an effort to attain these objectives which were causing grave apprehension in the United States, I went on. These, to be honest, were giving the impression in America that the Soviet Government did not mean what it said in its statements since the end of the war regarding its peaceful, non-aggressive intentions and its policy of non-interference in any way with the rights, liberties and political freedoms of neighboring states. The American people were willing and anxious to meet the Soviet Union halfway, because they were convinced that if our two nations understood and cooperated with each other the peace of the world was assured. Indeed, we felt that we had already gone more than halfway.

I paused frequently so that Pavlov could translate my remarks and Stalin could reply, if he wished, but he made it clear that he wanted me to finish my statement. His face was expressionless as I talked. He did not look at me directly, but kept his head turned to one side, taking an occasional puff from a long Russian cigarette.

I continued, touching on a number of situations, then politically important, including those in Iran, Turkey and the United Nations. We could not, I said, take seriously the possibility of aggressive action against the Soviet Union by any nation or group of nations in the world today. We were in the process of demobilizing our armed forces at great speed, which should be sufficient proof of our own non-aggressive intentions, and we would, in fact, like to disarm to a greater extent if the current atmosphere of suspicion and apprehension could be removed.

Until now, Stalin had kept his head turned slightly to one side, but at this point he began to glance at me from time to time and, as he often does when he is interested, to "doodle" with a red pencil. His drawings, repeated many times, looked to me like lopsided hearts done in red, with a small question mark in the middle.

We wanted, I said, greater evidence of Soviet cooperation in supporting the principles of the United Nations Charter. The President had asked me to say that both he and Secretary Byrnes had always believed that when Stalin made a commitment, he meant to keep it. The American people hoped that events would confirm that belief. But it would be misinterpreting the character of the United States to assume that because we were basically peaceful and deeply interested in world security, we were either divided, weak or unwilling to face our responsibilities. If the people of the United States were ever to become convinced that we were faced with a wave of progressive aggression on the part of any powerful nation or group of nations, we would react exactly as we had always done in the past.

When I concluded, there was a short pause, after which Stalin asked, "Have you finished?" I said that I had. He at once began to reply, speaking quietly and pleasantly, and at length. The sequence and length of his remarks made me feel that either he has a remarkable memory and great power of concentration, or that the points which would be raised by the United States had been anticipated. His statement included a number of counter-charges against the United States, including the allegation that it had definitely aligned itself with Great Britain against the U.S.S.R.

He discussed in detail the Iranian oil question, including a history of Soviet-Iranian relations from the time of the Treaty of Versailles. He commented rather bitterly on the fact that the United States had pressed for debate on Iran's complaint before the United Nations, and had opposed Gromyko's request for postponement. He stressed the need of the Soviet Union for a greater share in the exploitation of the world's oil resources, and said that Great Britain and later the United States had placed obstacles in the way of Russia when she sought oil concessions.

"You don't understand our situation as regards oil and Iran," he said. "The Baku oil fields are our major source of supply. They are close to the Iranian border and they are very vulnerable. Beria [the head of the MVD] and others tell me that saboteurs—even a man with a box of matches—might cause us serious damage. We are not going to risk our oil supply."

He reaffirmed Soviet support of the United Nations Charter, charging that the American press and statesmen had given an entirely incorrect idea of Russia's actions in the United Nations. Turning to the charge of Soviet domination of neighboring governments, he said that the U.S.S.R had no intention of taking over the Balkan nations. Indeed, he added, even if it had, this would be no easy matter, because the Balkan nations were determined to maintain their national integrity.

He expressed strong resentment over the Iron Curtain speech made at Fulton, Missouri, by former Prime Minister Winston Churchill. This speech, Stalin said, was an unfriendly act; it was an unwarranted attack upon the U.S.S.R. Such a speech, if directed against the United States, never would have been permitted in Russia.

Later in the conversation I asked Stalin why he thought that any power or group of powers seemed a threat to the U.S.S.R.

"Churchill," Stalin replied. "He tried to instigate war against Russia, and persuaded the United States to join him in an armed occupation against part of our territory in 1919. Lately he has been at it again.

"But Russia, as the events of the past few years have proved, is not stupid. We can recognize our friends from our potential enemies."

"Is it possible that you really believe that the United States and Great Britain are united in an alliance to thwart Russia?" I asked.

"*Da* [yes]," Stalin replied.

"I must affirm in the strongest possible terms," I said, "that this is not the case. In the first place, I know Mr. Churchill well, having in a sense served under him as an Allied staff officer. He is far-seeing in international affairs, but I could never visualize him as an instigator of war. I hold no brief for his Fulton speech, but I must say that it reflects an apprehension which seems to be common to both the United States and Britain.

"In the second place," I continued, "the Soviet Government will understand that while we have many ties with Britain, including a common language and many common interests, our primary concern is world security and justice. This concern and responsibility extend to small nations as well as large, and while recent events have required the United States to vote with Britain in the United Nations Assembly and in the Security Council, this was because we felt that justice required us to do so.

"All that you have said so far is interesting and encouraging," I concluded, "but it does not answer the question I asked at the very beginning and which I said was uppermost in the minds of all the American people: 'How far is Russia going to go?' "

Looking directly at me, Stalin replied, "We're not going much further."

"You say 'not much further,'" I observed, "but does that 'much' have any reference to Turkey?"

"I have assured President Truman and have stated publicly that the Soviet Union has no intention of attacking Turkey, nor does this intention exist," Stalin said. "But Turkey is weak, and the Soviet Union is very conscious of the danger of foreign control of the Straits, which Turkey is not strong enough to protect. The Turkish Government is unfriendly to us. That is why the Soviet Union has demanded a base in the Dardanelles. It is a matter of our own security."

"It seems to my government that this is exactly the kind of

problem that should be handled by the United Nations," I
replied. "We have set up the United Nations to provide just
this security. If the Soviet Union is sincere in its assurances
of support for the United Nations, that agency will be able to
provide such security. Soviet security can be assured without
aggression toward Turkey."

"It is possible that the Soviet Union could agree that, as an
alternative, the Security Council of the United Nations might
be able to undertake this responsibility," Stalin replied.

By this time the conference had lasted more than two hours,
and I felt that I had made the position of my government quite
clear. I indicated that I had said all I wished to say, by sum-
marizing briefly my main points and by restating our desires for
a closer relationship and mutual understanding with the Soviet
Government, which we considered essential for world peace
and toward which I was directed by the President to work.

"Prosper your efforts," Stalin said. "I will help you. I am
at your disposal at any time."

He then reaffirmed his desire for peace and adherence to the
United Nations, and his belief that, though we had differences
in our political ideologies, the position of our two countries
was not incompatible.

"We should not be alarmed or apprehensive because of differences of opinion and arguments which occur in families
and even between brothers, because, with patience and good
will, these differences could be reconciled," Stalin said as the
interview ended.

Is it possible that we can come to an understanding with
Stalin? Is he an absolute dictator, as bad or worse than Hitler
or Mussolini, bent upon conquering the world and responsible
for the anti-American policy of the Soviet Union, which has
cost us so much in time, energy and money, and inflicted upon
the post-war world the terrible enervating fear of another war?
Or is he, on the contrary, the leader of a pro-Western *minority*
bloc within the Soviet Politburo, who would like to come to
a reasonable arrangement with us and who would carry it out
in good faith to insure the future peace of the world, but who
is unable to do so because he is outvoted by his colleagues of
the ruling oligarchy within the Kremlin?

These questions, which I have been asked hundreds of times since I returned to the United States, reflect conflicting currents within American public opinion. Until recently, this opinion has swung between extremes of optimism and pessimism under the influence of reports of something that Stalin has said or done. It has ranged from the despairing view of a handful of extremists who see Stalin as an absolute and hostile dictator and who believe a preventive war now is the only solution, to the wishful thinking of others who visualize him as an altruistic leader who, given some "encouragement," could persuade his colleagues to abandon their basic ideological strategy for Communist domination of the world and make possible a firm and lasting peace based on international cooperation. And from the others, who are interested only in the question of whether we can do business with Stalin in the foreseeable future, there is the reflection of a basic middle-of-the-road let's-get-along-for-the-moment-and-let-the-future-take-care-of-itself attitude.

I subscribe fully to the dictum of Paul Winterton, the distinguished former Moscow correspondent of the London *News Chronicle,* that "there are no experts on the Soviet Union; there are only varying degrees of ignorance." For three years, my office in the American Embassy was just across broad Mokhovaya Ulitsa from the red-bricked, crenelated Kremlin walls, the seat of all Soviet power, yet I entered those walls on business less than a score of times, and to talk at length to Stalin only four times. But four lengthy talks and one or two brief social meetings with Stalin were more than any other Western diplomat enjoyed during the period I was in Russia, and those opportunities to meet the leader of the Soviet peoples face to face, climaxing careful study of what he has said and what he has done during the past years, make it possible to differentiate the Stalin of *fact* from the Stalin of legend.

From that experience, I have drawn certain conclusions about Stalin in the sixty-ninth year of his life and his twenty-fifth year in power:

He is not, for instance, an absolute dictator, on the one hand, nor a prisoner of the Politburo, on the other; his position, I would say, is more that of chairman of the board with the decisive vote. There doubtless are divisions on policy and

cliques within the Politburo, but none of them is anti-Stalin-
ist. All of his foes have been liquidated, exiled or "re-educated."

The aggressive and expansionist foreign policy of the Soviet
Union in the post-war period has been Stalin's policy. It could
not, under the present Soviet system, have been put into effect
and continued without Stalin's sanction and approval. He must
be viewed as its champion, and not as a reluctant supporter.

When Stalin tells foreign statesmen or journalists that capitalism and communism can co-exist peaceably in the future, he
contradicts his own words, or is speaking in a limited sense.
In his writings and speeches to the leaders of the Communist
Party, he has repeatedly reaffirmed Lenin's basic theory that a
future struggle is inevitable between the Soviet Union and the
capitalist world which encircles it.

As to his health, Stalin shows signs of his advanced years,
which certainly should be expected, considering the enormous
burden of work and responsibility that he has carried for many
more years than has any other living national leader. There
have been rumors of heart attacks, and he has said to me and
other foreigners that the regimen imposed by his doctors requires careful dieting and prevents long trips by sea or air.
But he is a Georgian, a race in which centenarians are not un-
common, and he has already begun to conserve his strength. I
see no reason, therefore, why he should not be able for a number of years to retain the reins of power.

What manner of man is this Stalin, who rules the 200,000,000
persons of the Soviet Union, controls the destinies of another
100,000,000 or more in Soviet Russia's Communist-dominated
neighbors, and whose every major policy statement brings hope
or fear to the hearts of hundreds of millions of others around
the rest of the world?

It is doubtful whether any man, during his own lifetime,
has been the subject of as many and as widely differing ap-
praisals as has Stalin. One American writer, who saw him often,
is repelled by his physical appearance and emphasizes his pock-
marked face and his bad teeth. A former American Ambassador to the Soviet Union writes of his kind and gentle brown
eyes and says "a child would like to sit on his knee." Winston

Churchill described him, after their initial meeting as wartime Allies, as a man of inexhaustible courage and energy, and said that Stalin left him "with the impression of a cold and deep wisdom and a complete absence of illusion of any sort." A non-Russian Communist acquaintance of mine is in such awe and fear of Stalin that even in private conversation he avoids mentioning the name, referring almost in a whisper to "the man with the mustache."

Certainly Stalin was hated and feared by many of his colleagues in the formative years of the Soviet Union, and these people now are in exile or dead. Lenin, himself, who undoubtedly had great enthusiasm for Stalin's talents during most of his career, is alleged by some biographers, hostile to Stalin, to have made a final political testament in which he urged Stalin's replacement as General Secretary of the party because of his rudeness and his lust for power.

The probability is that most of those who have interviewed Stalin and written about him have done so from a fixed point of view politically, and objectivity, however desirable, toward a man who will fill more pages of world history than Napoleon, is almost impossible.

The fact is that very few people in the world, even very few Russians, know Stalin. He is the most powerful and least accessible of the world's rulers, cut off from his own people as well as from foreigners by the forbidding Kremlin walls, the multitude of police agents assigned to protect him, and the deep secrecy maintained concerning his personal life. Americans in Moscow are not even sure where Stalin lives when outside the Kremlin. They believe his country residence to be in an area northwest of the city, where other government officials are known to live and where there are evidences of extensive police protection, but they cannot point to his house. Even Russians do not know whether he has married again since the death of his second wife in 1932.

To most of them, Stalin is a name and a symbol, the man they never see. At the great demonstrations in Red Square, where he reviews proceedings from the top of Lenin's tomb, he is visible to the marchers in the square, but the ordinary crowd is too far away even to get a glimpse of him. So far as we know, he never takes a walk on a Moscow street, and he rarely, if at all, visits a factory, mine or collective farm. During the war, he is said to have made a few trips "to the front," but there is no evidence that he was seen on these trips by any except a very few high-ranking officers, and certainly none that soldiers in the line recognized him or knew of his presence.

We have never heard of him stopping at a Soviet hotel overnight. There is no record that he has ever traveled extensively inside the Soviet Union and been seen by the people. The most informal of his public appearances have been at the annual sports festival at the huge Dynamo Stadium on the outskirts of Moscow. His speeches are always made to limited audiences, such as the Supreme Soviet (the Russian Congress) or a Communist Party meeting, never to throngs of tens of thousands such as turned out to hear a Roosevelt, a Churchill or even a Hitler and Mussolini, when they spoke at outdoor meetings to carry their arguments on major policy questions direct to the people.

But Stalin is omnipresent in every Soviet village or hamlet across one-sixth of the world's surface. He is literally deified. It is impossible for a Westerner to imagine or understand the fulsome public flattery with which he is deluged. To millions of Soviet people he is that combination of demigod and loving parent which the Russian national psychology seems to require. His picture hangs in every Soviet office, schoolroom, party agency, and Communist home. His statue is in every park, in most railway stations and airports, and, indeed, in nearly every public building, including not only major governmental offices, but also hotels and stations of the Moscow subway. On state occasions, such as the anniversary of the Revolution, celebrated on November 7, huge pictures of Stalin and leading members of the Politburo adorn every city and village.

It is from such inanimate evidence that the Soviet people "know" about their leader. The pictures had for many years remained unchanged, and the Russians were genuinely shocked in the closing days of the war when new pictures were issued in which Stalin was portrayed with graying hair. These pictures, first posted for sale in the windows of Moscow book shops, attracted large crowds which studied them closely. Nearly everyone commented, with surprise, upon the evidence that Stalin, too, was growing old. Because of their lack of contact with him, the people of Moscow, like those of the Soviet Union generally, had come to think of him as ageless.

News of his day-to-day activities is never published. No list of his official callers, such as the White House releases to the American press, is ever made known, except that occasionally there is a communiqué that he has received a foreign ambassador or statesman or been host to a group of visitors at a Kremlin banquet. Plans for Stalin's future activities, whether they involve travel inside Russia or not, are kept as closely secret in peace as in war. When he goes on vacations to the Black Sea, where he has been spending more and more time in recent years, there is no announcement of this fact, and foreigners find out about it only when some diplomat requests a conference with Stalin and is advised that it is impossible because the Generalissimo is not in the city. The Russian people never know.

To us, this seems a strange and remote life. Even Stalin's working hours at the Kremlin office are the reverse of ours. They run from late afternoon to early morning, which is why the rare interviews granted to foreign diplomats are usually scheduled between 9 P.M. and midnight. Other senior Soviet officials, quite naturally, have molded their own working day to conform to his. The result is that Americans, who by custom maintain the Western-style 9 A.M. to 5 P.M. office schedule, find it almost impossible to accomplish any work involving contact with ranking Russian officials during the hours before lunch and, indeed, until mid-afternoon.

Met face to face, Stalin is not by any means the unattractive personality which some writers have depicted. Indeed, he has genuine charm when he chooses to exercise it. While not tall, he is square and erect, giving the impression of great strength. Since the beginning of the war, he has abandoned his old party uniform of khaki trousers and a plain tunic that buttoned up to the neck, on which he wore no insignia, and he now appears in public and receives foreign visitors in the uniform of a Marshal of the Soviet Union, with usually only a single decoration —the treasured gold star of a Hero of the Soviet Union.

I scarcely noticed the pockmarks which some American writers have emphasized. The most attractive feature of Stalin's

face is his fine dark eyes, which light up when he is interested.
They did not impress me either as "gentle," as one observer
thought, or "cold as steel," as others have remarked, but they
are alert, expressive and intelligent. His manner is calm, slow
and self-assured, and when he wishes to warm up during a conversation he seems at times actually benign. There is no question but that he can be brutally abrupt, and I have been told
that he has sometimes referred to himself, half-apologetically,
as "a rude old man."

I have often referred back mentally to that first interview.
Stalin had told me that Russia was not going "much further";
that though we had different political and economic systems our
forms of government and ways of life were not "incompatible";
and that we could, with patience and good will, resolve any differences which arose. It is statements like these, taken at their
face value, which have so often aroused the hopes of the world
during the past four years, and which time and events have so
often proved misleading that I now marvel at the way world
public opinion can still swing from the depths of gloom to the
heights of optimism and back again on the strength of Stalin's
latest statement to a foreign visitor or his reply to an interroga-
tory by a foreign correspondent. There is, I think, a widely
held and possibly a dangerous misconception that while other
Soviet leaders, such as Molotov and Vishinsky, may be difficult
and hostile, Stalin is basically reasonable, and that if one can
only manage to gain direct access to him, state the problem and
get it across to him, everything will be all right.

A cartoon published a few years ago illustrated this point
very well. The usual four by four cartoon square was divided
into sixteen smaller squares. In the first of these the world, depicted as a small cringing dog, was wriggling with pleasure as
it received a pat on the back from a benign, pipe-smoking Stalin.
The second square showed the dog yowling in pain as it took
a hard kick from Molotov. The third square was a repetition of
the first, and the fourth of the second, and so on through the
sixteen frames. Apparently we only learn the hard way. We
forget that the principles and objectives of Bolshevism have
been stated again and again, first by Lenin and then by Stalin,
who has repeatedly reaffirmed that he is Lenin's most faithful

disciple. As recently as January 21, 1946, on the anniversary of Lenin's death, the Communist Party's principal theoretician, Alexandrov, said in the presence of Stalin and other Politburo members that "our Soviet land can take pride in its leaders who, in the field of foreign policy of our state, work according to the tactics of Lenin."

What, then, did Lenin teach? He made two important statements on the peaceful co-existence between the Soviet Union and capitalist states which are constantly repeated in Communist circles and which have been widely quoted elsewhere. At the party congress in 1919, he said: "We are living, not merely in a state, but in the system of states, and the existence of the Soviet Republic side by side with imperialist states for a long time is unthinkable. One or the other must triumph in the end. Before that end supervenes, a series of frightful collisions between the Soviet Republic and the bourgeois states will be inevitable."

Then in 1920, in a speech to the Moscow party members, Lenin repeated this theory in the following words: "As long as capitalism and socialism exist, we cannot live in peace. In the end, one or the other will triumph, a funeral dirge will be sung either over the Soviet Republic or over world capitalism." He went on to say, "We are at present between two foes. If we are unable to defeat them both, we must know how to dispose of our forces in such a way that they fall out among themselves, because, as is always the case, when thieves fall out honest men come into their own; but as soon as we are strong enough to defeat capitalism as a whole, we shall immediately take it by the scruff of the neck."

At another party congress, that of 1918, Lenin had said: "In order not to get lost in the periods of retirement, retreat, or temporary defeat, or when the enemy throws us back, the important and only theoretically correct thing is not to cast out the old basic program."

In the years since Lenin's death, we have yet to see this old basic program cast out. It has been modified and added to, yes, but never rejected or forgotten.

When Stalin made his first post-war election speech on February 9, 1946, he reaffirmed Lenin's theory of capitalist hostility. This speech, remember, was addressed to the Soviet people and not to foreigners, and, whereas so many of his other remarks have been contradicted from his own lips or by events, nothing has occurred to contradict the essential theory of this speech, which reaffirmed the basic hostility of the two systems. Stalin said, in part:

> It would be incorrect to think that the war arose accidentally or as the result of the fault of some of the statesmen. Although these faults did exist, the war arose in reality as the inevitable result of the development of the world economic and political forces on the basis of monopoly capitalism.
>
> Our Marxists declare that the capitalist system of world economy conceals elements of crisis and war, that the development of world capitalism does not follow a steady and even course forward, but proceeds through crises and catastrophes. The uneven development of the capitalist countries leads in time to sharp disturbances in their relations, and the group of countries which consider themselves inadequately provided with raw materials and export markets tries usually to change this situation and to change the position in their favor by means of armed force. As a result of these factors, the capitalist world is sent into two hostile camps and war follows.

When comparisons are made between what Stalin has said to foreigners and what he has said to his own people in the basic literature of the Communist Party, in which their program is clearly spelled out, it is impossible to avoid the conclusion that the Generalissimo is capable of contradicting himself and even, on occasion, of deliberately deceiving his auditor.

It is therefore important to an understanding of the Soviet Union today to remember certain points about Stalin. In the first place, he is a Georgian, not a Russian. It is strange how often in history great peoples have accepted the leadership of obscure and untypical persons from their borderlands, and in this respect, at least, Stalin is comparable to Napoleon and Hitler. He probably does not now think of himself as a Georgian, and certainly he has become one of the greatest of *Russian* national figures, but he still has all the qualities, good and bad, that are his birthright. Courageous but cautious; suspicious, revengeful and quick to anger, but coldly ruthless and pitilessly realistic; decisive and swift in the execution of his plans when the objective is clear, but patient, deceptive and Fabian in his tactics when the situation is obscure, he is, as one of my most experienced officers put it, "like a true Georgian hero—a great and good friend or an implacable dangerous enemy. It is difficult for him to be anything in between."

In the second place, he is insulated from the outside world and isolated from his own people. Lenin, for years, walked about freely, mingled with the peasants and workers, and saw life as others see it. Stalin, since his accession to power, has never done this. He moves back and forth between the Kremlin and his country *dacha* by the same carefully guarded route, and such careful precautions are taken for his safety that he cannot possibly know his people today except through the eyes of others. Since this is so, how much more ignorant must he be of the Western world! His formative years and young manhood were spent in the atmosphere of revolutionary conspiracy. Much of his life has been lived underground or in exile. Nothing of his experience could have mitigated the Oriental trend of his thinking. It would be impossible for him to understand Western thought or to appreciate Anglo-Saxon tolerance of opposition and temperate approach to the solution of major national and international problems, even if these were accurately interpreted to him by representatives abroad whom he trusted implicitly. However, it is most unlikely that these representatives report either accurately or objectively. The views of the Soviet official are manufactured for him by the party in such detail that they must color all his observations. Thus, Stalin must be, by character, experience and environment, almost completely dependent on a few close friends and advisers within the walls of the Kremlin.

It is not only in authoritarian states that the continuous struggle for access to the Chief of State, and for control of his sources of information, is a major factor in political life. In the Soviet Union, where secrecy and suspicion are rife, this must be particularly intense. Because of Stalin's ignorance of the West, his suspicious Georgian character and his isolation, the power of his few political intimates must be very great. It is in the character of these advisers, and in their relationship with Stalin, that we must seek the answers to many of the perplexing manifestations of Soviet foreign policy and of the Soviet attitude toward the United States and Western Europe.

IV

MEN OF THE KREMLIN

The leadership passed completely and entirely into the hands of one party, into the hands of our Party, which does not share, and must not share the guidance of the state with any other party. This is what we mean by the dictatorship of the proletariat.

—Stalin: *October Revolution* (1934)
"Three Basic Slogans," p. 141

THE members of the Politburo are the only political personalities in the Soviet Union who are known on a nation-wide basis. Since the Russian people seldom see their leaders, they become acquainted with them through their portraits, displayed on public buildings on national holidays; and membership in the Politburo is a prerequisite to inclusion in this picture gallery. Lesser political figures, including Cabinet Ministers, are known regionally or to a part of the population, but not to the people as a whole.

Most Americans, I think, visualize the Politburo as a sort of super-Cabinet—at the pinnacle of an authoritarian governmental structure—which shares dictatorial power with Stalin, but is subordinate to him. In a broad and general sense, this is true, because the members of the Politburo are the men who run the Soviet Union, but a number of distinctions must be recognized.

In the first place, the Politburo is an arm of the Communist Party, and not of the Soviet Government itself. This difference, of course, is more apparent than real in a political system where only the one party is permitted, but it is a distinction and an important one. Since the time they seized power, the Bolsheviks have been concerned that their rule should be exercised through governmental instead of through party machinery. As the *Agitator's Handbook* said in 1947, "The All-Union Communist Party of Bolsheviks is the *organizing and directing force* in the

64

Soviet Government, the heart, brain and spirit of the people, the leader and teacher of the workers."

Secondly, the supremacy of the Politburo rests upon the form of organization dictated by Stalin after he established absolute control over both the party and the government. In theory, and party statutes, the organization is only a sub-committee of and subordinate to the All-Union Central Committee of the Communist Party, which is supposed to be the supreme tribunal of the party between congresses. The Central Committee originally consisted of a small number of the party elite who met frequently and arrived quickly at decisions. But as the party came into power, with increasing membership and increasing responsibilities, the size of the Central Committee increased until it became unwieldy. It was found expedient to create a smaller, inner group for the discussion and determination of political policy, subject, of course, to the approval of the Central Committee. Other groups set up at the same time were an Organization Bureau and the Secretariat. Stalin became a very important member of all three organizations while Lenin still was alive and in power, but it was his job as head of the Secretariat which enabled him to place men of his own choice in key positions. He thus created for himself a strong organization of his own selected men when the struggle for power with Trotsky began, and when this battle was won, he was able to force the Central Committee to accept the supremacy of his Politburo and to elect to it men of his choice. And, by 1929, Stalin emphasized the end of the cleavage within the party and his own mastery by announcing that decisions of the Politburo were being taken unanimously. Through a system of "interlocking directorates," the Politburo controls both the party and the government.

Who, then, are the men who share power with Stalin and who by their constant association with him wield such great influence upon his decisions because he is so isolated both from the Russian people and first-hand knowledge of events in the world outside? Since the death of Andrei Zhdanov in 1948 and the unexplained removal of Nikolai Voznesensky in the spring of 1949, the Politburo consists of these eleven men in addition to Stalin who run the gov't

VYACHESLAV MIKHAILOVICH MOLOTOV, 59, native of Russia, First Deputy Chairman of the Council of Ministers, member of the Politburo since 1926, member of the Supreme Soviet, and former Minister of Foreign Affairs.

GEORGI MAXIMILIANOVICH MALENKOV, 48, native of Georgia, Deputy Chairman of the Council of Ministers, member of the Politburo since 1946, General Secretary of the Communist Party, member of the Orgburo, and member of the Supreme Soviet.

LAVRENTI PAVLOVICH BERIA, 50, Georgian, Deputy Chairman of the Council of Ministers, member of the Politburo since 1946, member of the Supreme Soviet, Marshal of the Soviet Union, former Minister of State Security and Internal Affairs, and reputed head of the special intelligence service on atomic energy.

NIKOLAI ALEXANDROVICH BULGANIN, 54, native of Russia, Deputy Chairman of the Council of Ministers, and former Minister of Armed Forces, alternate member of the Politburo since 1946, and full member since 1948, member of the Supreme Soviet, member of the Orgburo, and General of the Army.

LAZAR MOISEEVICH KAGANOVICH, 56, Ukrainian-born Jew, Deputy Chairman of the Council of Ministers, member of the U.S.S.R. Supreme Soviet, and member of the Politburo since 1930.

ANDREI ANDREEVICH ANDREYEV, 54, native of Russia, Deputy Chairman of the Council of Ministers, Chairman of the Council for Collective Farm Affairs, member of the Politburo since 1932, member of the Orgburo 1926-1946, Chairman of the Commission on Party Control, and member of the Supreme Soviet.

NIKITA SERGEEVICH KHRUSHCHEV, 59, Ukrainian-born, Chairman of the Council of Ministers of the Ukrainian S.S.R., member of the Politburo since 1939, and member of the Supreme Soviet.

ALEXI NIKOLAYEVICH KOSYGIN, Deputy Chairman of the Council of Ministers, alternate member of the Politburo since 1946, and full member since 1948, member of the Supreme Soviet, and Minister of Finance.

ANASTAS IVANOVICH MIKOYAN, 54, Armenian-Georgian, Deputy Chairman of the Council of Ministers, Politburo member since 1935, member of the Supreme Soviet, and former Minister of Foreign Trade.

NIKOLA MIKHAILOVICH SHVERNIK, 61, native of Russia, Chairman of the Presidium of the Supreme Soviet (titular Chief of State), alternate member of the Politburo since 1944, former Secretary General of the All-Union Council of Trade Unions from 1930 to 1944.

KLEMENTI EFREMOVICH VOROSHILOV, 68, native of Russia, Deputy Chairman of the Council of Ministers, member of the Politburo since 1926, member of the Supreme Soviet, former Commissar of Defense from 1925 to 1939, and former Chairman of the Allied Control Commission for Hungary from 1945 to 1947.

These men are, in every sense of the word, dedicated men. As a group, they represent the most effective form of authoritarian dictatorship; that is, dictatorship by committee. They are, without exception, intelligent, able, disciplined and indefatigable. I doubt if any statesmen in the world work half as hard as do those of the Soviet Union. They are Stalin's men, loyal to him and owing their advancement to him and to his appreciation of their merits and abilities.

I believe also that they are completely ruthless and even cynical in their determination to retain power for themselves and for a Communist Party in which the doctrine of "Stalinism" has replaced pure Marxism. Those apologists for the Soviet system who argue that what we believe to be iron tyranny could not have produced the heights of courage and endurance which the Soviet people exhibited during the years of the war ignore the fact that Russian serfs exhibited equal courage and endurance on previous similar occasions without the hopes which the party held out during the most recent one; but it is certainly true that none of the weak and venal Czarist governments in Russia's history could have withstood even a fraction of the strain and adversity which the disciplined Communist Party government endured and overcame, to triumph in the end and to emerge even stronger.

The most significant thing about this small group at the supreme pinnacle of Soviet power is that for almost ten years, and until very recently, there had been practically no change among them. Prior to 1938, there was a period when changes in high governmental positions occurred with a rapidity equalled only during the historical periods of revolutionary chaos. Thereafter, the most important figures in Soviet political life seemed so permanently fixed as to justify the cynical remark of one foreign observer that no one could have survived the purge years who was not endowed with the gift of immortality. There were not even any important deaths, until the recent death of Zhdanov. That of Mikhail Ivanovich Kalinin, the venerable Chief of State so respected and loved by the peasants, which took place shortly after my arrival in Moscow, occurred after Kalinin had retired from active political life because of age and ill health. Very recently, one alternate member, Voznesensky, was dropped without the slightest explanation, but his departure did not negate the generally held idea that the Politburo was a dead-end street from which the only exit was via the undertaker. During this decade, also, there have been no really important changes in the composition of the Central Committee of the Communist Party, or even in the leading provincial party positions.

This would be a remarkable thing in any country that had been through two major changes of foreign policy and a military struggle that threatened the very existence of the state. And it is a phenomenon of the first order in a political system like that of the Soviet Union, which has never failed to produce a few political sacrificial victims whose confessions explain every major reverse in the fortunes of the country.

And so the same small group has remained in power for a long time. Its average age now is over fifty-seven. There is no sign yet of the introduction of new and younger men into this select circle, but this may come at the next party congress, the first since 1939, which apparently will be called in the near future.

Except for Molotov and Mikoyan, these men have little knowledge of the outside world or of foreign statesmen. The vast pattern of international life, political and economic, can provide few associations and hold little significance for them except in what they conceive to be its bearing on the problems of Soviet security and internal development. Independence of

judgment is not a characteristic of Communists, who must follow a rigid party line, and to keep a head level enough to avoid
becoming self-intoxicated by the propaganda and auto-sugges-
tion with which the Soviet Union has been flooding the world
for years would tax the best efforts of a very cosmopolitan mind
—and these men are anything but cosmopolitan. Yet the images
and impressions that are created in their minds by what they
hear of life beyond the borders of the Soviet Union, the conclusions they draw from these, and the recommendations they
make based on these conclusions are of vital importance to the
world. What these conclusions will be, and how they will influence the policy of the Soviet Union toward the West, we can
only guess from what we know of the background and personalities of those among them who seem to have the greatest influence with Stalin.

There was, quite naturally, extreme curiosity throughout the
world last spring when both Molotov and Mikoyan, the men
with the greatest knowledge of the outside world, were relieved
of their posts as Minister of Foreign Affairs and Minister of Foreign Trade, respectively. The communiqué announcing the
change was terse and brief, and merely said they would continue as Deputy Vice Premiers. There was wild speculation
everywhere about whether this meant a new split in the Soviet
authority, whether Molotov and Mikoyan were being demoted
or promoted. Since a shift in Cabinet personnel usually accompanies shifts in the tactical line followed by Moscow, there were
many who wondered if A. Y. Vishinsky had been put into the
Foreign Office to soften up the "tough" line followed by Molotov, which had not been successful and which had, in fact,
caused the West to unite in the North Atlantic Pact and beat
the Berlin blockade.

No one outside the upper Soviet hierarchy can give even an
approximate picture of what is happening inside the higher
strata of the Bolshevik Party. One can only piece together scattered facts. It seems now, however, that the shift which relieved
Molotov and Mikoyan of separate Cabinet assignments was little
more than a reversion to Soviet practice before the war, when
ministries were headed by technicians rather than by statesmen-
politicians of the first rank. That policy kept Politburo mem-

bers free of administrative responsibility and gave them more
time for attention to over-all governmental problems.

But while the Molotov-Mikoyan shift may not have been
an important change in the ranking of the Soviet hierarchy, it is
certain, as the ouster of Voznesensky demonstrates, that the relative positions of influence of members of the Politburo within
the organization itself have been and are changing.

When I think of the straws which we watched in an effort
to determine the direction of the Soviet political wind, and to
arrive at reasonably intelligent answers to questions which
would be freely and openly discussed in every newspaper in
every non-Communist country in the world, I am always reminded of a paragraph written by the French observer, De
Custine, who visited Moscow in 1839:

> If better diplomats are to be found among the Russians than
> among the most highly civilized peoples, it is because our
> papers warn them of everything that happens or is contem-
> plated in our countries, and because, rather than prudently
> disguising our weaknesses, we expose them passionately each
> morning, whereas their Byzantine policy, on the other hand,
> working in the shadow, carefully conceals all that is thought,
> done and feared in their country. We walk in broad daylight;
> they advance under cover. The game is one-sided; the igno-
> rance in which they leave us blinds us; our sincerity enlightens
> them; we have the weakness of chattering; they have the force
> of secrecy. There above all, is the cause of their cleverness. . . .

That was written 110 years ago, but De Custine might have
been speaking for any diplomat in Moscow today when he complained of the paucity of information to be found in the Soviet
press. We were forced, by necessity, to lean on many weak
reeds. In Moscow we always used to study with interest the
published lists of Politburo members who were candidates for
government office, in the thought that these lists, since they were
not arranged alphabetically or in the order of party seniority,
might be a fairly accurate barometer of the order of their actual
standing after Stalin.

These lists for the elections of January, 1946; January, 1947,
and November, 1947, gave the names of the Politburo members
in the following order:

January, 1946	January, 1947	November, 1947
1. Stalin	1. Stalin	1. Stalin
2. Molotov	2. Molotov	2. Molotov
3. Beria	3. Beria	3. Zhdanov
4. Malenkov	4. Zhdanov	4. Voroshilov
5. Mikoyan	5. Voroshilov	5. Beria
6. Voroshilov	6. Mikoyan	6. Kaganovich
7. Andreyev	7. Andreyev	7. Andreyev
8. Zhdanov	8. Kaganovich	8. Mikoyan
9. Kaganovich	9. Khrushchev	9. Malenkov
10. Khrushchev	10. Malenkov	10. Khrushchev
11. Shvernik	11. Voznesensky	11. Voznesensky
12. Voznesensky	12. Shvernik	12. Shvernik
	13. Kosygin	13. Bulganin
	14. Bulganin	14. Kosygin

It will be noted that Stalin and Molotov held firm in the Number 1 and Number 2 spots. Beria, who had been third in January, 1946, and a year later, had dropped to fifth by November, 1947. Zhdanov, now dead, but looked upon for a long time as the leading heir-apparent, had been eighth in January, 1946, fourth in January, 1947, and third eleven months later. Malenkov, who was fourth in 1946, dropped to tenth in the January, 1947, listing, but had climbed back up to ninth in November of that year.

Color was added to the idea that these lists might to some extent indicate party prominence by the announcements of nominations to the Moscow City Soviet during the last election. Both *Pravda* and *Izvestia* featured the story of Stalin's nomination on Page 1; and, on Page 2, separate stories covered the nominations of Molotov and Zhdanov. The other Soviet leaders were lumped together in a long article giving their names. Molotov was described, in these articles, as Stalin's "closest colleague and the executor of the Leninist-Stalinist foreign policy." Zhdanov was called "the greatest worker of the Bolshevik Party and the Soviet Government," and "a great theoretician of the Bolshevik Party—a fiery fighter against subservience to foreigners." Voroshilov was commended for his part in the creation of the Soviet Army. Beria was not mentioned for any particular contemporary function, probably because the nature of his present task is shrouded in secrecy (he is believed to be in charge of atomic development, among other things), but he was cited for wartime service in increasing munitions production. Malenkov was lauded for increasing agricultural production last summer, and for his war work.

The most popular and continuous guessing game in Moscow and, indeed, in every Foreign Office around the world and in newspaper and magazine offices as well, is, "After Stalin, Who?"

For the answer, of course, we must look to the Politburo, and especially to those men who, because of their background and personalities, and by the prominence accorded them in Communist Party activities and in the Soviet press, seem to be closest to Stalin.

Of these Molotov is best known both inside and outside the Soviet Union. The *Soviet Encyclopedia* of 1943 describes him as the closest companion-in-arms of Stalin, but *Pravda,* on January 9, 1947, said exactly the same thing about Voroshilov. Certainly Molotov has, for more than thirty years, been one of Stalin's closest associates, and he is indebted to Stalin for his career. In his book, *Stalin & Co.,* Walter Duranty relates a story still current and accepted in Moscow. Stalin had suggested to Lenin that Molotov, as an old and trusted member of the party and one of the founders of *Pravda,* should be a member of the Central Committee of the party. Lenin squinted his Tartar eyes and asked, "Why that one?" Stalin enumerated Molotov's services, and Lenin said: "Well, if you like. But you know what I think of him—he's the best filing clerk in Russia." If Lenin intended this remark in a disparaging sense, Molotov's services to the Soviet Union have demonstrated its inaccuracy.

Molotov joined the Bolshevik faction of the Russian Social Democratic Party in 1906. After the Revolution he carried out with ability a succession of increasingly important party assignments, until in 1926 he received the accolade of membership in the Politburo. In December, 1930, he became Chairman of the Council of People's Commissars, now the Council of Ministers, and occupied the office corresponding to Premier until Stalin himself took it over in 1941. He replaced Maxim M. Litvinov as Foreign Minister on May 3, 1939, and by foreigners he is always thought of in this capacity. But during the war he also was in charge of Soviet tank production and was a member of the all-powerful State Committee of Defense.

To me, Molotov's personality is unattractive. While he is always correct and courteous, he is repellingly colorless, and it seems impossible for him to be really at ease in the presence of foreigners. Even when attempting to be humorous, he appears stiff. Only once have I heard him laugh without constraint. This was at a dinner at Spaso House during the Moscow Conference of Foreign Ministers. At the opposite end of the long table Mr. Bevin and Mr. Molotov were sitting at either side of Mrs. Smith, Molotov drinking scotch and water with Bevin. As my wife told me afterward, the two had been exchanging stories, via the interpreter. Mr. Bevin countered one of Mr. Molotov's with a very funny, but very irreverent joke about Lenin, which sent Molotov into a gale of laughter. Young Troyanovsky, the interpreter, was so shocked that he remarked stiffly in English to the British Foreign Minister: "In the Soviet Union we do not joke about Lenin."

In his dealings with representatives of other countries, Molotov has been systematically aggressive, stubborn and unyielding. In conferences he seems at times deliberately to bait and irritate his opponents. Yet the blandness with which he can execute a political somersault is remarkable, even for a Communist. His party statements about the United States have been particularly sarcastic and bitter. His stubbornness in negotiations justifies his party name (*Molot* means "hammer"—his real name is Skriabin).

Before the war he was believed by most foreign observers to favor Germany as against France and Britain, and when he replaced Litvinov as Minister of Foreign Affairs in 1939, a change in Soviet policy was confidently expected, since it has been usual Soviet practice to change men when policy changes. Accordingly the failure of the poorly handled last minute Anglo-French military mission to Moscow could have been no surprise to the relatively few informed observers of the Soviet scene.

Molotov is credited with having engineered the German-Soviet non-aggression pact which followed a few weeks later, and which he described as having made narrower the zone of possible military conflicts in Europe. In November of the following year Molotov made his first trip abroad, a visit to Germany. Advertised as a return call on Ribbentrop, this visit was certainly for the purpose of trying, if possible, to smooth out the growing difficulties between the Soviet Union and Germany, and, of course, to find out everything possible about Germany's intentions. There is a good deal of question about what took place at this visit. Goering told me, after his capture, that Molotov had demanded the withdrawal of German troops from Finland and Rumania, and bases for Soviet troops on the Bosporus. As Goering described it, "When I heard Molotov's demands, I almost fell out of my chair." Hitler presumably was convinced by this time that an attack on the Soviet Union should not long be delayed. In any event, the visit increased rather than diminished the tension between the two countries, although the Soviet Union continued to supply Germany with food, oil and strategic raw materials, in accordance with the existing commercial treaty, and even offered more. Many of the German bombing planes that flew over London were serviced with Soviet-produced oil, and the first German sea raider that entered the Pacific via the northern passage, with disastrous effect on British and Australian shipping, was convoyed by Soviet ice breakers.

Molotov first visited the United States in 1942, and he has been here twice since. Madame Molotov visited us much earlier. She was here in 1936 and lunched at the White House. She has a brother, Sam Karp, who is an American citizen, in business in Connecticut.

Like nearly all important Soviet officials, Molotov, so far as foreigners know, is without redeeming minor vices. He has none of the human qualities of humor or sudden anger that make Vishinsky rather attractive among a class of officials who are rigidly correct and reserved in their relation to foreigners. He is usually coldly self-possessed.

On occasions, when irritated or in difficulty during a debate, he stammers noticeably. Only once have I seen him really flustered. When the Kasenkina affair occurred, Molotov's secretary called me shortly before midnight and asked me to come to the Foreign Office. I must have arrived sooner than expected, for Molotov's outer office, usually a model of orderly quiet, was in considerable confusion. However, I was admitted to his conference room after a wait of only about five minutes. I could see that the paper from which he read his official protest was a hastily marked up first draft, with many corrections. His stammer was very pronounced and he was obviously angry and disturbed, understandably so, since, as head of the Foreign Office, the consulate from which Madame Kasenkina escaped came under his official responsibility. We had a very sharp exchange for a few minutes, as I denied his allegation of United States Government complicity in what he called "the activities of White Guards and bandits" who had "lured away and captured" Madame Kasenkina. Before the conference ended, however, he had recovered his poise and was again the self-possessed and correct Foreign Minister.

Most foreign observers have identified Molotov directly with the hardening of Soviet policy toward the West. My own impression is that there really was a decided difference of opinion in the Politburo concerning relations with the West. I believe that there is a moderate group which wishes closer understanding, for the reason that the Soviet Union needs a period of peace of at least ten to fifteen years to reconstruct its economy and consolidate the enormous gains made during the war. I do not mean by this that these "moderates" would renounce the basic Soviet objective of Communist world domination through world revolution, but simply that they believe more time is required to prepare for the clashes which this policy envisages. Opposed to this, a stronger militant group supports the Molotov policy of constant pressure, aggressive action and intransigence. Beria and, until his death, Zhdanov were thought to be of this faction, while Malenkov was estimated by foreigners in Moscow to be more moderate in his views, although the amount of information about him is so limited, and his foreign contacts have been so slight, that it would be difficult to prove this theory. Whatever the reason, it is evident that events which preceded Zhdanov's death last year reflected some discord in the ranks of the Politburo.

Zhdanov had not been entirely well for several years. I sat next to him at a Kremlin dinner, in the fall of 1947, and noticing that he ate and drank nothing, commented on his lack of appetite. He replied briefly that he was on a "regime." He looked well at this time, and his illness, whatever it was, did not keep him from the long hours of hard work to which he had been accustomed for years. There are many indications that the final heart attack which preceded his death from "paralysis of the heart" was the culmination of a covert struggle which had been going on ceaselessly for several years between Zhdanov and Malenkov and their respective factions within the Soviet power apparatus.

Andrei Zhdanov was Stalin's first deputy for Cominform and Communist Party affairs, and the best known party theoretician. He was considered one of the most anti-Western and anti-foreign members of the upper Soviet hierarchy. If it was this xenophobia which led him to advocate or support the Soviet policy that failed in Yugoslavia, Finland and Berlin, he paid dearly for his responsibility, although, since Soviet policy is officially adopted by the Politburo as a whole and individual members cannot be publicly accused of making a mistake, his loss of influence was ostensibly the result of a much less cogent matter. His enemies attacked and humiliated him by discrediting Yuri Zhdanov, generally believed to be his son, and others of his supporters who took the wrong side in the much publicized "genetics" argument. When it became an article of party faith, announced by the Soviet seed expert, T. D. Lysenko, with the prior approval of the party Central Committee, that acquired characteristics could be inherited, and that adherence to Mendel's law was party heresy, the younger Zhdanov and others of the Zhdanov faction were discredited and disgraced; Zhdanov, as the leader, under Stalin, of party ideology, was discredited also, and as his star declined and set, that of Malenkov rose.

Georgi M. Malenkov is still in his forties and, in my opinion, is the outstanding personality of the younger generation of Bolsheviks. He has been a member of the Communist Party since 1920. He became an alternate member of the Politburo in 1941, at the same time as Beria, and in 1946, also with Beria, he was made a full member. He was once Stalin's private secretary, and it was Stalin himself who trained Malenkov to handle the administrative machinery of the Communist Party, intrusting him little by little with important party functions. In 1939, when only thirty-seven, Malenkov was elected a member of the Central Committee of the Communist Party and in 1946 he became one of the Secretaries of the Central Committee of the party, the other Secretaries of which are now Stalin, Suslov, Popov and Ponomarenko. In spite of the enormous responsibilities he carried during the war as reorganizer of the aircraft industry and later as president of the committee for restoration of liberated areas, he has never given up direction of the Orgburo or of the administration of personnel of the Central Committee. These two party agencies give him control of the appointments of all major party officials and the opportunity to place talented supporters in key positions. Thus he followed the same road to power previously taken by Stalin.

Malenkov is fat and flabby-looking, with a round, expressionless face. Mentally, he is anything but flabby, as his impressive accomplishments during the war, in a series of positions of great responsibility, give ample evidence. As Stalin's principal "party man," he always appears in the now very much outmoded party "uniform," with drab-colored coat, buttoned up to the throat, with a turned-down collar. His infrequent public statements have been forceful, sensible and realistic.

Malenkov has had his ups and downs. He seems to have been removed from the Secretariat of the Central Committee in 1947 after having been appointed thereto, and he reappeared in that capacity in mid-July of 1948. This reappearance, which marked the beginning of the end for Zhdanov, placed him again in the inner circle of Stalin's advisers, together wth Beria and Molotov.

These three, Molotov, Malenkov and Beria, now represent the most important functions of Soviet Government—Molotov, as First Vice Premier and Stalin's principal lieutenant for many years, has vast experience in the field of foreign relations; Malenkov has the party machinery; and Beria, who rose with Malenkov in the party, has the apparatus of state security and the secret police—the cement which holds together the whole great pyramid of the Soviet political structure.

Lavrenti P. Beria, like Stalin, is a Georgian. Like Malenkov, he is still relatively young—he became fifty in 1949. He joined the Communist Party in 1917, did important underground work in Baku and Azerbaijan during the civil war, and headed the Soviet security organization in the Caucasus from 1921 to 1929 and from 1929 was Georgian Commissar for Internal Affairs. Thereafter he became party secretary of the Caucasus area, a post which he held for seven years. As principal party official in this area of mixed nationalities, he performed noteworthy service, and he holds the Orders of the Red Banner of both the Georgian and Azerbaijanian Soviet Republics and the coveted Order of Lenin. In 1934, he was elected a member of the Central Committee of the Communist Party, and in the summer of 1938, when the great purge was at its height, with the party shaken to its foundations, terror rampant and leadership in industry and the Army in a state of moral collapse, he was made vice-chief of the NKVD, second in command to Yezhov (whom he replaced five months later), with the mission of restoring the situation.

The job ahead of the secret police had been a fatal one. A series of Beria's predecessors went from that position of power to meet the fate which each, in his turn, had inflicted on so many others. Beria, however, was as different in personality from such men as Yezhov, Yagoda, and Dzherzhinsky as he was in appearance. He looks like a teacher or a scientist, with high forehead, steady eyes and a firm mouth. His expression is calm and reserved. Although he has the rank of Marshal of the Soviet Union, I have rarely seen him in uniform, and few pictures of him in uniform are published.

After the war, during which he again performed distinguished service in connection with increasing the production of arms and munitions, he was awarded the decoration of Hero of Socialist Labor. In 1947, he became one of the Vice Premiers and resigned from his duties as Minister for Internal Affairs in January, 1946. Presumably, his principal duties in the Politburo are supervision of the Ministries of Internal and State Security, the MGB and MVD, with their widespread activities and large military strength of highly disciplined and politically reliable troops, in and out of uniform. This probability is reinforced by the fact that both these ministries, primarily concerned with the enforcement of internal security, are headed by minor personalities who have been closely associated in a subordinate capacity with Beria for years.

Beria has also been one of Stalin's closest associates for many years, and his personal loyalty to his chief is unquestioned. In return, Stalin has demonstrated his complete confidence in Beria on so many occasions that Beria's prestige in the inner party circle cannot be doubted. He is rumored to have been made responsible for all atomic research and development.

The stability of the Soviet regime depends to a large extent on a powerful and efficient police system, and Beria has demonstrated his ability to cope with any problem involving the security of the state.

These three men—Molotov, Malenkov and Beria—represent, respectively, foreign policy and general direction of the governmental machine, party policy and organization, and internal security. Malenkov, the party man, may also become responsible for general supervision of Soviet economy, a field in which he has had experience. Or, since the death of his rival, Zhdanov, he may have inherited the all-important function of directing, under Stalin, the party's ideological policy.

Two other members of the Politburo, whose influence seems now to be somewhat less than the big three, are also closely associated with Stalin and likewise have major responsibilities. These are Bulganin and Kaganovich.

Bulganin is the Politburo member now most directly identified with matters of national defense. He is about fifty-four, and a veteran of the civil war. Originally a factory worker, he developed into an able administrator and executive and a brilliant speaker. His experience is wide. He has, for instance, been President of the Soviet State Bank, Mayor of Moscow, and Lieutenant General in active operations on the Orel front. Later he was Minister of the Armed Forces. The older Voroshilov, sixty-eight, who was Commissar for Military and Naval Affairs (afterward called Commissar for Defense) for fifteen years, is now generally considered a military elder statesman.

I have met Bulganin only casually at large social functions, where he was distantly courteous. His appearance is attractive, for he is well groomed, faultlessly turned out in his new uniform of a Marshal of the Soviet Union, and rather handsome. Incidentally, he wears a goatee—the only one in the Politburo. The few foreigners who have dealt with him have thought him reasonable, intelligent and able.

When Stalin resigned the portfolio of Minister of Defense to Bulganin, the latter's prestige rose greatly and it was further enhanced by his promotion to Marshal. I have read arguments that his selection for the post of Minister of Armed Forces was an indication that the Soviet Union was less aggressive in a military sense than some foreigners believe, for the reason that he is an executive and administrator rather than a professional soldier. I do not think this argument is valid. Stalin unquestionably thinks of himself as the first strategist of the Soviet Union, and he is, as his title of Generalissimo indicates, the supreme commander of the Soviet Armed Forces.

Kaganovich, the "Iron Commissar" and Stalin's troubleshooter, is still young enough to have an important future. He is usually referred to as the only Jew in the Politburo, but this may not be correct, for Beria, the Georgian, is also rumored to be Jewish although no confirmation of this fact has been revealed. Kaganovich is the best administrator in the Soviet Union. He has been shifted from place to place wherever great executive ability is needed and has always turned in an outstanding performance. He is another remarkable example of the ability of the Bolsheviks to select talent, because Kaganovich started life as a shoemaker in the Ukraine and was still a shoemaker when he joined the Communist Party in 1911. Seven years later he was playing a major role in the organization of the Red Army. He supervised the building of the Moscow subway, which, while still not extensive, is the most beautiful subway structure in the world, and of the great Dnieperstroy power installation. I have never spoken to Kaganovich, and he does not make many public or social appearances, but Russians have described him to me as colorful, forceful and energetic.

These rulers of the Soviet Union are united in purpose and they are loyal to Stalin. Such internal differences as have developed among them are personal and have not militated against this party unity and loyalty, nor will they while Stalin lives and retains the general control of Soviet policy. His enormous authority and prestige, and the stern party discipline, will insure that all his associates work together harmoniously under the guidance of the inner circle of advisers whose names I have mentioned.

It is to this inner circle that Stalin must look when he remembers the crisis through which the party passed after Lenin's death and the struggle for power from which he himself emerged victorious at such great cost to the Soviet Union, and when he plans, as undoubtedly he has, to prevent the repetition of this crisis. Stalin is well aware that since rumors of the deterioration of his health became rife, the outside world has speculated wildly on what would happen when he was no longer able to rule, and it is inconceivable that he has not taken measures to prevent another political crisis and another struggle for power.

The question is, Will these measures be successful? Like Lenin, Stalin stands so far above all of his contemporaries that it is impossible to compare any of them with him. But this was not always so. When Lenin occupied the pinnacle of power, he was equally pre-eminent among his contemporaries, of whom Stalin was one and Trotsky was another. Stalin's ultimate succession to Lenin's position of power was the result of a struggle which lasted for years, cost innumerable lives, and placed an almost unbearable strain on the structure of the Soviet state. This transition from the power of Lenin to the power of Stalin is the only one which has taken place in the Soviet Union. Will the violent events of that period repeat themselves, or will the next transition take place quietly and without explosive repercussions?

Stalin's struggle for power was within the party, and he won it by the simple and direct tactic of exterminating the opposition.

Americans would do well to ponder that fact—"he won it by the simple and direct tactic of exterminating the opposition." For us, with our habit of accepting the November election result every four years on the Presidency without the slightest hesitation despite the heated charges and counter-charges of campaign oratory, it is difficult to grasp the full import of those words.

How did Stalin do it? He began early, from his post as General Secretary of the party, to pick out his friends and enemies who would help or hurt his efforts to take over Lenin's mantle. His friends were strengthened in authority and position; and his enemies were isolated. Finally he was ready for the showdown struggle with Trotsky which was to send his more brilliant colleague into exile first in remote Alma Ata, then in Norway, and finally in Mexico where he was later brutally assassinated. Into exile or prison went all of Trotsky's associates but still the political crisis deepened. History was rewritten and Trotsky's role in the Revolution and in the early post-war years was minimized while Stalin's was enhanced. But still the Georgian found the going hard, and it was necessary to charge that Trotsky and some of the giants of the Revolution had been traitors to Russia by conspiring with foreign agents. This culminated in the bloody purges of the late nineteen-thirties when hundreds faced firing squads and literally tens of thousands were sent to forced labor camps. When it was over, there were none left who dared to challenge Stalin's authority.

When Stalin disappears from the political scene, there may be an opportunity for one or more ambitious leaders within the party to attempt, by the same methods, to extend their own authority. A dictatorship is usually so organized about the personality of the dictator that when he dies a political vacuum occurs, and the release of violent, unpredictable forces is likely to take place.

The feeling is so strong in many quarters outside the Soviet Union that the pattern of the Stalin-Trotsky struggle must inevitably repeat itself after Stalin dies that it has strongly influenced some national foreign policies. It must be remembered, however, that toward the end of the war, most observers of the Soviet scene believed that it would be impossible for the party to re-establish complete control over the Army, whose victorious leaders had become veritable demigods to the Soviet people. Important changes appeared inevitable. Great concessions had been made by the party to the people during the war years, and the war-weary people seemed to be in no mood to relinquish them. Nothing like this happened. The party maintained its dominant position, apparently without the slightest difficulty. Great military leaders like Zhukov, whose ideas about cooperation with the West presumably conflicted with the "Molotov" policy, disappeared from the Moscow scene to posts of relative obscurity so quietly that it was hardly noticed. A new series of five-year plans and a drastic currency reform were inaugurated, and the party recaptured all the concessions it had been forced to make during the strained years of war. The leadership and structure of the regime underwent no significant changes. A few important people disappeared, a few new personalities arose, but the strong party nucleus which directs the destinies of the Soviet people remained basically the same. However, all this took place under Stalin's strong leadership, and whether the redistribution of power in the event of his death or disability can be accomplished with equal facility is a question which only time can answer.

Long-range predictions regarding an organization about which so little is known as the Politburo are certainly dangerous, but one thing is certain. As long as Stalin lives he will continue to assert supreme authority; therefore, he is not likely to vest a major measure of power in any one person. The responsibilities he centralized in his own hands during the war, he now appears to be dividing among those close associates whose personal loyalty to himself has been most thoroughly tested. The ones who now seem to be sharing the major portion of this delegated power are Molotov, Malenkov and Beria.

It is inconceivable to me that any single one of these men can take Stalin's place. During the war years his stature became so great that it dwarfed all of his associates. His mantle is now too large for any one of them to wear. My own belief is that when Stalin dies his power will be divided among these three. Or possibly, there may be associated with them the other two who appear to be next to them in prestige—Kaganovich and Bulganin. As they are now carrying out his general directions, so they would, after his death, carry on the functions of his dictatorship.

The question whether, when that time comes, personal antagonisms and ambitions, suppressed in Stalin's presence, may assert themselves and disturb the cooperative relationship, is impossible to answer. Although it is true that the Soviet regime, like other dictatorships, is linked with the personality of its leader, the fact remains that because it is basically dictatorship by committee, this is less significant in the Soviet Union than it has been elsewhere.

However, I think it is quite likely that one or more of the directorate which succeeds Stalin, or even some new leader whose name is still unknown, eventually will be tempted to make a bid for supreme power.

But I believe also that no struggle is likely to occur that is any way commensurate with the battle of giants which took place after Lenin's death. This, it will be remembered, was at a time when the Soviet Union was far less strong, and the Communist Party much less firmly entrenched than now, after the successful trial of a great war; but the system, though seriously shaken then, was not disastrously damaged. In its present day of strength, a palace revolution might hardly cause a ripple on the surface of Soviet political life, and the Soviet people are inured to political purges. Other nations have, in the past, been governed by a minority class, and though one palace revolution after another has gradually weakened their political structures, these have nevertheless endured for generations, and even for centuries. I am convinced that we must, for many years to come, accept the Politburo as a force to be reckoned with.

V

FOREIGNERS IN MOSCOW

The position of a Minister here is far from being pleasant. The opinion prevails that no communication, at least of a public nature, is safe in the Post-Office, but is opened and inspected as a matter of course. Hence those Legations that can afford it, maintain regular couriers and never send anything by mail. The opinion also prevails that Ministers are constantly subjected to a system of espionage, and that even their servants are made to disclose what passed in their households, their conversations, associations, etc. Of all this I have no positive evidence, but I believe there is some foundation for such charges. To be made to apprehend such a state of things is exceedingly annoying. If therefore I do not write as often as may be desired, this is my apology. And if I do not furnish matter of more interest, it must be attributed in part, at least, to the great difficulty of obtaining correct information. No courtesy or liberality whatever is shown in this respect by the Government. But I do not believe I have any grievances on this subject but what are common to other Legations. Secrecy, and mystery, characterise everything. Nothing is made public that is worth knowing. You will find no two individuals agreeing in the strength of the army and navy, in the amount of the public debt, or the annual revenue. In my opinion it is not intended by the Government that these things should be known.

—Excerpt from a dispatch of the American
Minister to Russia, Neill S. Brown, dated
St. Petersburg, January 28, 1852

THE popular notion that Ambassadors lead lives of luxury and ease while they conserve their energies for dealing with only such top level tasks as require the abilities of a statesman is certainly not based on Ambassadorial service in Moscow.

I found that high diplomacy is an art that is required only occasionally; that the system limited my business calls on Russian officials to about three or four a month; and that these usually concerned not momentous issues of peace settlements, but more practical matters, such as whether the Soviet Government would recognize our assertion of American citizenship for persons residing within the borders of the Soviet Union.

Much of my time was taken up with administrative matters, and the problems of existence were complicated.

The personnel of the Moscow mission consisted of twenty-five to thirty State Department officers and attachés, and thirty-

85

five to forty clerks, about half of the latter being wives of staff members. There were approximately fifteen Army, Navy and Air Force officers in the attachés' offices, together with some twenty-five enlisted men, the majority of whom were employed in operating the Embassy's communications system. Much of the clerical work in the Consular and Administrative sections was performed by Soviet employees, who averaged about one hundred when one included, in addition to the clerks, chauffeurs, firemen, janitors, and similar employees.

I found that I had inherited an excellent staff but a woefully inadequate and very run-down plant.

The senior diplomatic officer of the mission was the Minister, George Kennan, who had been in charge in the interim between Averell Harriman's departure and my arrival, and who was to be my mentor and principal adviser during my first months in Moscow. A career officer of wide experience and an outstanding Russian specialist, he was the first member of Ambassador Bullitt's staff to arrive in Moscow after we reestablished relations with the Soviet Union in 1933. He spoke Russian perfectly, and was actually more cultured in Russian than are most Russians. Knowing at first hand and largely through personal experience all the details of Soviet-American relations, and learned in Soviet political history and ideology, he was the best possible tutor a newly arrived chief of mission could have had. Both he and his attractive wife were to become valued friends.

The only member of the staff whom I had known previously was Frederick Reinhardt. He had served with me at SHAEF during the war as assistant to our Political Adviser, Robert Murphy, and I was extremely fortunate to get him again in Moscow. A Russian specialist with experience and a career officer of superior ability, he possessed great personal charm. He lived with us at Spaso House, as did my secretary, Ruth Briggs, now Vice-Consul and Administrative Officer at our Belgrade Embassy. Ruth, a former WAC major, had been one of my staff secretaries during the war and was one of the first five WAC officers to be sent overseas. Like many other professional soldiers, I had viewed with a jaundiced eye the project for using women officers in an active theater, excepting always the Army nurses. Consequently, when during a quick trip to the United States I was directed by General Eisenhower to establish qualifications for women officers as staff secretaries, I set the standard extremely high. Nevertheless, Colonel Hobby, head of the Women's Army Corps, was able to produce candidates who met all the requirements, and five, one of whom was the then Lieutenant Briggs, were shipped off to North Africa, only to be neatly torpedoed off Oran by a German submarine. Since I had promised Mrs. Roosevelt to keep a special eye on this first consignment, I flew to Oran the day after their rescue, and five more forlorn little objects it would have been impossible to imagine. Their ship had been sunk at two o'clock in the morning, with the loss of all their clothing and personal effects, and they had been in open boats for about twelve hours. Ruth had headed the clerical staff contingent, which we furnished for both the Casablanca and Teheran conferences, and there her efficiency had attracted the attention of Secretary Byrnes, who offered her a post in the State Department after the war, and who very kindly allowed me to take her with me to Moscow. A typical New Englander with great ability, she kept my office running smoothly and maintained me in a state of official comfort during my entire period of service in Moscow.

The others of my personal staff were my soldier-chauffeur, Sergeant Greiner, and a personal employee, a former sergeant in the Polish Artillery, Mirion Blazejczek, who came to me during the war, after he was liberated from four and one half years in Buchenwald.

Instead of driving my car, Greiner helped run the Embassy commissary, and Blazejczek acted as steward and storekeeper for Spaso House, where he saved me much money and much trouble, by virtue of his knowledge of the Russian language and of Russian characteristics.

Captain Ronald Allen, USNR, also lived with us. A fluent linguist, who had worked in Russia for a number of years, he was loved by all of us, and if my efforts to make him look military in uniform were a complete failure, I could, as Reinhardt remarked, comfort myself with the thought that high-ranking naval officers, including Admiral Stanley, had also tried and failed. I did manage, just before our first formal reception, to prevent Ronnie from attaching his aiguillette to the front of his white dress uniform with a large black safety pin, and in the triumph of this accomplishment completely overlooked the fact that he was not wearing a Navy aiguillette at all, but half of one borrowed from an Army officer. When Allen left, his place in the household, and in the affections of the family, was taken by Richard Davis, one of the younger and most able of the new group of career officers specializing in Soviet affairs. Davis was in Moscow when we arrived. He finished his tour, returned for two years' service in the United States, and re-joined me in Moscow some time before my own departure.

The Chancery officer next in seniority to Kennan was John Davies, for years a Far Eastern specialist. Born in China, and with long service there, he was extremely valuable in interpreting trends and events in that area, and I found him a very loyal and very capable officer of sound judgment. His beautiful and talented wife, herself the daughter of an Ambassador and a former Assistant Secretary of State, worked in the Chancery, as did almost all the Embassy wives.

Indeed, it would have been impossible for the Moscow mission to function had the wives not worked and relieved us of the necessity for importing more clerks, for the amount of housing made available to the Embassy by the Soviet Government was completely inadequate to meet even our minimum needs.

These, and the remainder whom I have not named, but who stood equally high in our affections, were a loyal and devoted little group. Officers, staff officers and clerks alike, they always did a little more than anyone had a right to expect from them. As they left for the United States, or to other foreign assignments, they were succeeded by others as carefully selected, as capable and as devoted.

It was in the Soviet Union, of all places, where men and women supposedly had equal rights and all class distinctions allegedly had been wiped out by the Revolution, that an effort first was made to introduce a caste system into the Smith household.

The question arose on an issue—eggs for breakfast—which, to us at least, seemed highly important.

In Indiana, where I come from, breakfast is not a matter to be taken lightly. It usually consists of a couple of eggs with a healthy slice of ham or several strips of bacon, and it is just about the most important meal of the day. Mrs. Smith thinks so too.

Food rationing was in effect when we arrived in Moscow. Because I was Ambassador, and not because I was any hungrier than the rest of the family, my ration was fixed by the Soviet authorities at fifteen eggs a month, or at the rate of one-half egg a day. Mrs. Smith didn't have quite so much rank, so she drew ten eggs a month, or one-third of an egg a day. The other members of my household drew varying numbers, ranging down to five eggs a month.

That hardly seemed enough, but it was the amount fixed by the Soviet Government for our purchases at the special fixed-price store maintained for foreigners. Of course, it would have been possible to go into the open market, where prices were determined by the inflationary law of very small supply and very high demand. With the value of the ruble arbitrarily fixed at twelve to the dollar (later reduced to eight to the dollar) for the diplomat, eggs cost thirty to forty cents each, depending upon the season of the year, with a sharp variance, too, of age and quality. The price alone was enough to discourage us, without calculating the other imponderables of freshness and edibility.

It so happened that in our first weeks of cleaning up the garden of Spaso House, we had come across an old, unused chicken house and a small wired enclosure. This suggested the logical solution of buying some hens and producing our own eggs.

That was simple to say, but not so simple to accomplish. In a Communist land where the means of production belong to the people but are controlled by the government, you can't just get in your car, drive out in the country to a farm, and buy some chickens. Such transactions must be made through governmental channels, and the ways of bureaucracy are devious and slow.

The first step was to call in one of the Soviet nationals, employed by the Embassy as "expediters," and charge him with the preliminary arrangements. His first call was upon an agency known as Burobin, the abbreviation of a name which, translated literally, means "The Administration for Services to the

Diplomatic Corps." Burobin is responsible, theoretically at least, for every requirement of a foreigner in Moscow, and must be consulted. One can't telephone directly to a plumber if the bathroom fixtures do not work, or to a carpenter if the roof needs repairing. You must proceed through Burobin; and Burobin is a very large, unwieldy and suspicious organization.

To Burobin, our representative declared with great formality, in order to impress them with the urgency of the matter, that the American Ambassador, personally hungry for eggs but even more anxious to keep peace in the family by removing an inequitable distribution of available supplies, wanted to buy some chickens and keep them in pens upon the property of the American Embassy to produce more eggs for Spaso's table.

Burobin expressed sympathy and understanding but, naturally, it couldn't do anything by itself. It was only a middleman. Burobin's next step was to pass the request along to one of the branches of the Ministry of Agriculture, specifically the one charged with poultry raising.

Days passed, as the egg shortage continued and the Smiths kept wondering what it would be like to have a typical American breakfast again. Our representative kept needling Burobin, and Burobin kept reminding the Ministry of Agriculture. Finally, the word came that our request had been approved and that on a designated day we were to come to the Ministry of Agriculture where we would meet an official who would conduct us to a chicken farm outside Moscow. Since arrangements had become so formal, and since the prestige and influence of the American Ambassador had been called into play, I decided to go along.

Promptly at 2 P.M. we arrived at the Ministry of Agriculture, trailed by the small black automobile carrying my MVD bodyguards. The Soviet official was waiting to join me in my car, and there was an additional car with another group of bodyguards. The Russian official got into my car, which made it somewhat crowded, so I sent two members of my personal staff —Sergeants Raymond Greiner and Mirion Blazejczak, and the family cocker spaniel—back to ride with the MVD agents, who seemed somewhat surprised by being asked to transport foreigners, but took them in with true Russian hospitality.

We had a pleasant drive of about twenty-five miles out the

Yaroslavskoe Chausée, passing on the way a silver fox farm which appeared to be very well run, and finally arrived at an experimental poultry farm, the Russian name for which would literally be translated "Factory for Raising Up of Birds."

Here we were greeted by the director and several members of his staff, and given a complete tour of the establishment, including the incubator house, the brooder house and the laying bins. The poultry population, consisting primarily of White Leghorns, barred Plymouth Rocks and Rhode Island Reds; and one or two European varieties which I did not recognize, were obviously aristocrats of their respective breeds. There also was a section devoted to the raising of ducks and turkeys, and I mentioned to the director that a friend of mine in the United States raised a special variety of white turkey. When he expressed interest, I said that I would arrange for him to receive a setting of eggs, and this I later was able to do, although it necessitated carrying them in my lap most of the way from New York to Moscow.

When the inspection was over, the director escorted us to his house, it then being time for the heavy Russian meal of the day —a late afternoon *uzhin,* or dinner. This consisted of chicken prepared several ways, sliced fried turkey breast, fried and hard-boiled eggs (how the Smith mouths watered over these scarce items), and vegetables with the usual sour cream dressing. This was strictly a hearty country meal, with all the food placed on the table, but there was champagne, presumably contributed by our escorting official. We prefaced our meal with toasts in vodka and brief speeches of mutual friendship and admiration.

During the meal, we had a glass or two of champagne, but it was, by the standards Russians employ in entertaining foreigners, a fairly simple meal—not to be compared with a multi-course state banquet.

Afterward, the director escorted us back to the pens and announced that the time now had come for me to select the chickens I wished to buy.

I countered by asking what variety had the best sustained record for egg production.

He paused for a moment, as though considering the question, and said that White Leghorns had the best production record so far. There were two strains of White Leghorns, one British and the other American. Of the two, he continued, the record of the British strain was the better; adding quickly, and obviously to avoid offending my national pride, that this doubtless was due to the fact that the British variety had been in the Soviet Union longer. Taken by itself, that last statement would have seemed a rather charming example of Russian chauvinism, but I understood what he meant—that the British hens were laying better because they had been longer in Russia and therefore were better acclimated to local conditions than were the hens hatched from eggs sent from America.

Laughing, I replied that I would never for an instant allow my national pride to interfere with getting the largest number of eggs for Spaso's inhabitants, and I would, therefore, like to buy twenty-four hens of the British White Leghorn strain.

The chickens were delivered to Spaso later that afternoon, and the entire household gathered to cheer their arrival. The example caught on in the diplomatic corps and was copied by others, notably the British Ambassador, Sir Maurice Peterson, who held his flock in such high regard that he wintered them inside the attic of the British Embassy. Mine, poor things, were kept in a small, otherwise unsuitable room in the middle of the garage, warmed by a single electric heater in the depths of Moscow's cold, cold winters. But they came through with flying colors, and I never felt that Sir Maurice's pampered flock outproduced mine, which maintained a fairly consistent record of eighteen to twenty eggs a day for nearly two years, after which they were replaced by new stock.

Other, and much more important, food problems faced the Embassy—I was directly responsible for the thirty-eight residents and servants fed at Spaso, and, in general, for the welfare of the more than 150 other American and Soviet employees—and these did not yield so easily to solution.

There were grave shortages of every important item in the Western diet, and, because of the arbitrary and exaggerated value given to the ruble even at the diplomatic rate of exchange, prices were exorbitant. While the diplomatic *gastronome* (food store) was operating, we did receive a fair supply of rationed goods at reasonably low prices. (At least the costs seemed reasonable when compared with the charges made in the state-operated "commercial" stores, which were kept open in a governmental effort to sop up surplus ruble purchasing power in the hands of the Russian people, or in the "open" markets where peasants and farmers were allowed to bring for sale supplies produced in excess of their quota of fixed deliveries to the state.) But with the end of rationing in December, 1947, the diplomatic store was closed and all foreigners as well as Russians, had to buy their food in the state stores or on the "open" market.

American women who had been through the peak of postwar inflation in America never get over the shock of their first dealings in the Moscow stores. Mrs. Smith continues to recall ruefully the day she spent a total of $25 for ten eggs and approximately ten pounds of soup meat at the Ukrainian market in Moscow. Other prices, as of June, 1948, at the state stores, which were the cheapest, together with the comments of our experienced shoppers, are quoted: black bread, 37½c a kilo (2.2 pounds) (not palatable under present circumstances); white bread, 62½c to $1.12 a kilo (few Americans use it—most bake their own); butter, $8.50 to $9.25 a kilo (edible if your cook or shopper buys it); margarine, $3.75 a kilo (edible if your cook or shopper buys it); eggs, $3.12 to $4.37 for ten eggs (quality varies even more than prices); bacon, $7.25 to $7.75 a kilo (extremely short supply); poultry, $4.62 to $6.25 a kilo (edible but lightweight); beef, $4.62 to $6.25 a kilo; lamb, $4.75 to $5.12 a kilo (short supply); liver, $4.37 a kilo (extremely short supply); sausage, $5 a kilo; ham, $8.25 to $8.75 a kilo (short supply); fish, $2.50 to $5 a kilo (only seasonably fresh); sugar, $2.87 a kilo (short supply); conserves, $3 to $3.75 a jar; plain biscuits, $5 a kilo; cabbage, $1 a kilo; carrots, 62c to $1 a kilo; beets, 25c to 50c a kilo; onions, $2.25 to $3.12 a kilo; cucumbers, 30c to 50c a kilo; stewed fruit, $2 a jar; apples, $2.25 a kilo; prunes, $4.12 a kilo; fresh milk, 50c a liter; rice, $4.25 a kilo; barley, 87c to $1 a kilo; macaroni, $1.87 a kilo; and potatoes, 25c to 50c a kilo.

Food items at such prices were, of course, beyond the means of employees on government salaries, even taking into account a cost of living allowance granted by the United States Government to its employees to equalize the value of the dollar more fairly in terms of purchasing power in relation to the high value placed by the Soviet Government upon the ruble.

Therefore, we operated a small commissary on a cooperative basis. Every member of the Embassy made a contribution to the commissary's working capital, in proportion to his or her salary, and we ordered staples and canned goods from America, which were sold to our people at cost plus operating expenses, which included very high charges for transportation and insurance, and considerable loss by pilferage. But even with this large addition to the original United States price, we were able by this means to provide less expensive food for the Americans in Moscow for a long time.

I supplemented these shipments by bringing in a load of food every time the Embassy plane came in from Berlin, where it was based, as I had the privilege of purchasing at the Berlin Army commissary until the blockade cut off this source of supply. An average load consisted of about 150 pounds of beef, 100 pounds of poultry, and other varieties of frozen meat, eggs, citrus fruits, and other staples of the American diet, many of which were unobtainable in Moscow.

But then the Soviet Government cracked down and imposed heavy restrictions on the amount of goods which could be imported duty free. All our arguments that this was a heavy penalty upon the handful of foreigners in the Soviet Union, whose imports could not conceivably have any effect at all upon the Soviet economy, had no effect, and it was necessary to reduce the commissary orders to a few absolute essentials. This forced our personnel to buy food at high prices on the local market in order to obtain a balanced diet.

Americans with their corner drugstores, supermarkets and five and ten cent stores will find it difficult to imagine the conditions of life for foreigners in Moscow in an economy marked by the complete absence of the other ordinary daily necessities which we take for granted.

Housing was our other principal problem.

I could not have been more depressed by the sight of the American establishment during my first days in Moscow. The Ambassador's residence is the famous Spaso House, which takes its name from its location on Spasopeskovskaya Square, which in turn was named from the near-by little church of Our Savior of the Sands, now ruined, but obviously once a gem of old Russian ecclesiastical architecture.

Built by a wealthy Russian merchant and completed just before the Revolution, Spaso has housed the American Ambassador since our relations with the Soviet Union were established in 1933. It showed the neglect and overcrowding inevitable during the busy war years when repairs and maintenance had been impossible.

Spaso House is a two-story masonry and stucco structure, with a good deal of waste space. I have often thought that the pre-revolutionary Russian millionaire who built it was primarily interested in a large reception hall, extending from the ground floor to the roof, and that he put most of his money in the magnificent gold and crystal chandelier which hung at the top of the reception room and must have weighed a ton. With the small sum remaining, he then added on the living quarters as a sort of afterthought.

On the ground floor, in addition to the central reception hall and a ballroom added during Ambassador Bullitt's residence, were smaller reception rooms, a large state dining room, a smaller dining room, a billiard room, and the pantries. There are two principal bedroom suites and a number of smaller bedrooms on the second floor. In the basement are the kitchens, a modern laundry, servants' dining room and living quarters, with a small amount of storage space. Behind the house, the former stables have been converted into a two-car garage, with additional rooms for servants above the garage, and a large basement where in the fall we stored our winter supply of potatoes and cabbages.

Pre-revolutionary Russian construction obviously was not well engineered, since large cracks were visible in Spaso's outside walls when I first arrived and remained when I left, despite strenuous efforts to have them repaired. The interior was depressing. During the war, an enormous increase in the size of our Moscow diplomatic and military mission had forced Mr. Harriman to convert his residence into a combination barracks-hotel-office building, and he retreated into his own bedroom, where he lived and did most of his work.

The central heating system had proved inadequate, and

almost every room was equipped with an oil-burning stove sitting in a large sandbox, with the stovepipe suspended by rusty wires and passing out through the windows.

The handsome plaster cornices and frescoes were mildewed and flaky. Wall coverings, some of once expensive silk or satin, were dirty, split and hanging down in long shreds. Floor coverings were dismally stained or completely absent.

The pride of the Embassy was that magnificent chandelier, which was plated with gold to a thickness of almost one-sixteenth of an inch and laden with a mass of beautifully cut enormous crystals, some of them a foot long and weighing perhaps twenty-five pounds each. But this constituted a hazard to life and limb, for the wires attaching the crystals to the chandelier were about to rust through when I arrived. It cost $800 to have this wire replaced in order to make it safe to walk through the main reception room.

The business office of the Embassy is the Chancery, usually known in Moscow as Mokhovaya, taking this name from its location on Mokhovaya Ulitsa, to the north of and facing Red Square, St. Basil's Cathedral and Lenin's tomb. This building, which is seven stories high and very shallow in depth, was originally constructed by the Soviet Government to house writers and artists, but was rented to the American Government in 1933. It is in two connected sections, each with an elevator which operates about half the time. In addition to the Embassy offices, there are seventeen small apartments in this building. They are occupied by officers of the Embassy and their families, and by women clerks.

The cultural and information activities of the Embassy are housed in a building on Vesnina Ulitsa, which originally had been rented by the American Red Cross, from whom the Embassy obtained the lease. One or two of our families and several of the unmarried girls usually lived in this building. There were also ten small rooms in the basement, housing ten Russian families not connected with the Embassy who shared one kitchen and one bathroom.

The male clerical personnel of the State Department and our Army and Navy enlisted men were quartered in a barracks-like structure called American House, about one mile from the Chancery. This rather dreary two-story building contained a

Ambassador Smith about to enter his car in front of Spaso House, the residence of American Ambassadors in Moscow.

Great chandelier and central reception hall at Spaso House with Mrs. Smith giving instructions to the butler.

number of large and medium-sized rooms, each occupied by one or two men. In addition, there were some recreational facilities, including a poolroom and assembly room, where motion pictures could be shown. A central mess was operated in a large dining room.

The overflow, always considerable, was housed in the National Hotel adjoining the Embassy and the Savoy and Metropole Hotels near by, in dreary, poorly furnished, ill-heated rooms, and constantly under pressure to move so the rooms could be given to others.

My first thought, after surveying this collection of inadequate and run-down buildings, was that this might be a good time to renew the proposal for construction of a new Embassy, Chancery and apartment house, all within the same compound, with the Russians providing the building material and labor and the American Government paying the Soviet Government with some of the vast stores of surplus war materials remaining in Europe, which were being sold at a fraction of the original cost.

I knew, of course, that the Russians had indicated a desire to buy a large quantity of this material, and had submitted a list of the things they wanted, principally trucks, heavy road-building equipment and similar items. The things the Russians wanted most were not available, but I went to see Mr. Molotov shortly after I arrived to press the case for a new Embassy to be financed by surplus property of other kinds. I had not expected, nor did I receive any immediate reaction, favorable or otherwise, from the Soviet Foreign Minister, but I did make arrangements with the American authorities in Paris who had charge of liquidating these surplus properties to earmark about $10,000,000 to $12,000,000 worth and to give me a list from which the Russians might choose.

When this list was ready, I called upon Mr. Molotov again. He was pleasant but non-committal, and finally said that matters of this nature came within the province of A. I. Mikoyan, then the Minister of Foreign Trade. An appointment was arranged at once, and Mr. Mikoyan received me in his office. Several members of his Foreign Trade staff, including a senior Army officer, also participated in this conference.

When I had stated my case, Mr. Mikoyan replied that he

knew nothing of the proposed plan to build an American Embassy, but he agreed to examine our lists of surplus property. I tried to do a good job of salesmanship, pointing out with enthusiasm hundreds of items which I felt certain would be of value to the Soviet Union. Included on my lists was very modern hospital equipment—all of which I knew was in short supply in Russia—and large quantities of drugs, including penicillin, blood plasma and other items which simply could not be obtained in Moscow pharmacies. There were modern office equipment and machines of the best types, as well as many other equally interesting things. I had hardly expected to receive a positive answer at this first interview with Mr. Mikoyan; but the fact is that I never heard from him again, which I felt was unfortunate for both of us, since the Americans desperately needed a new Embassy and the Russians certainly could have used to advantage all the things we offered.

But our greatest complaint against the Soviet Government's treatment of us stemmed not from our physical discomfort, but from the restrictions placed upon our freedom as individual human beings.

The Russians require the Moscow foreign colony to live what amounts to a ghetto existence, as isolated as the Kremlin and the men in it from the stream of life in the Soviet capital.

Of course, it is not to be imagined that the foreign colony literally lived within something like the thirty-acre red-walled Kremlin area. Far from it. We were, in fact, scattered all over the city.

But high walls or not, the Soviet Government saw to it that the strictest kind of segregation was enforced between the foreigners, who numbered perhaps five hundred, and Soviet citizens, with a very few exceptions. We were completely cut off from the great bulk of the Russian people by constant police surveillance, by propaganda and by the fear of punishment. It still is easy for any Russian to recall the hysterical purge period of the late nineteen thirties, when Muscovites were moved permanently to Arctic Siberia and its slave labor camps to be "re-educated" for no greater crime than friendship with and association with foreigners.

One of the newspaper men in Moscow had a cynical but

accurate lament about the situation. Perhaps it would be better, he said, if there literally were a wall stopping us in our efforts to get through to know and understand the Russian people. If that were the case, we would hit our heads against this wall, and we would have something to show for it—perhaps a bump or a thin trickle of blood on the forehead. But the present system is worse—you slam your head again and again against a barrier which is a mental vacuum. And when you fall back you still have not even a bruise to show for it.

The result was that the foreign colony lived together constantly. We worked together and we played together. We read the same translations of the same newspaper articles and we exchanged impressions and information. We entertained each other at afternoon parties, dinner parties, dances, movies, badminton games, etc. We saw the same ballets, operas and dramas.

On the Ambassadorial level, our professional contacts with top Russian officials was limited to not more than two or three a month, on the average. Socially, we saw them even less frequently. Meetings with other Russians, except our servants, usually were on a most formal basis, involving some state function at which the Soviet Government was entertaining, or on the infrequent occasions when the Soviet Government would allow carefully chosen Russians to attend a party given in a foreign embassy.

We made every possible effort, consistent with reasonable dignity, to improve our social relations with the Russians. The funds available to a Moscow chief of mission for official entertaining are limited, but with careful economy I was able to give a large party on the Fourth of July and several formal dinners during the winter. Our first Fourth of July invitation list included all important Soviet officials of the Ministry of Foreign Affairs and of the other Ministries with which we had contact, as well as senior officers of the military services, writers, artists and other intellectuals and members of the professions. Of the three hundred or more invited, about twenty-five came. I was very disappointed until I discovered that this was a better than average response to an invitation from a representative of a Western nation. Rarely was there an acknowledgment of an invitation, and we hardly ever knew until the last minute whether we would have Soviet guests or not. All of our invitations were extended by way of the Foreign Office, and on several occasions I found out afterward that the intended recipient had never received the invitation intended for him. One Soviet Army officer, of more than usual independence of action, said to me, "I never received your invitation. Here is my phone number. If you want me to come, telephone me." This, of course, was before the passage of the "State Secrets Act," which finally dropped the Iron Curtain around us in Moscow.

When Field Marshal Montgomery visited Moscow, as the guest of the Soviet Union, I gave a dinner for him, to which I invited Marshal Voroshilov and Marshal Konev. The latter accepted and came. However, the Foreign Office asked that I extend an invitation to a senior officer other than Voroshilov, who was ill, and this I did. The two Marshals were pleasant and friendly, but they ate little and left early.

We could always count on an acceptance from one or two of the younger officials of the Office of Protocol of the Foreign Ministry, as it is part of their job to go to parties. Those who came to us I believe really enjoyed themselves. However, toward the end of my tour, as the cold war became more intense, only these, plus the brief appearance of one of the Vice Ministers, could be counted on, even at the celebration of our national holiday.

On the other hand, we were always invited to Mr. Molotov's official entertainments, always went, and were always received with irreproachable courtesy. When I first went to Moscow, these Soviet official entertainments were very lavish, with quantities of expensive food and drink. Later they became more austere.

There is one unique feature about official Soviet entertaining. Separate rooms are arranged, to which the guests are conducted in order of rank. Ambassadors and Soviet officials of corresponding rank are grouped together. In an adjoining room are ministers, senior diplomatic secretaries and generals. The juniors are in still other rooms, and the quantity and quality of the refreshments seem to be graduated proportionately.

On our national holidays at Spaso House, all Americans came together, regardless of rank or job, but we compromised with Soviet custom to the extent of having a separate table at which we could seat our ranking Soviet guest. Further than this I would not go.

My Counselor of Embassy, Foy Kohler, during one month gave a cocktail party each week, to each of which he invited twenty Russians and a number of other guests. On a few occasions, one or two Russians came, but usually his invitations were ignored. All the other Western representatives had similar experiences. It was only to social functions given by the satellite missions that Soviet representatives appeared in numbers. The rest of us had to depend on each other.

We were aware, of course, that this lack of outside influences produced a sterility of new thought and a dreadful uniformity of old ideas, but we were, in a very real sense, victims of the system which could not be changed by our efforts; a system, by the way, not new to the Russia of the Soviets, but as old as the Russian nation's historic suspicion of foreigners.

In fact, we often made fun of ourselves over our dilemma. One of the favorite pranks at a large diplomatic party was for an attaché, upon entering the room, to confide to a colleague the most fantastic rumor that he could imagine, so outrageous as to be beyond the limits of possibility. Within ten minutes, the story would have made the entire circuit of the room and would be told back to the inventor usually with some embellishment and all the trappings of complete authenticity. An effort would then be made, of course, to advise those present that the story wasn't true to begin with, but it was not always possible to catch every junior official who had heard it, with the result, no doubt, that some of those whoppers have been solemnly recorded in various Foreign Office Chanceries.

As far as the British and American Ambassadors were concerned, the Soviet Government saw to it that the Moscow citizenry was neither too friendly nor too inquisitive. They provided us with guards who followed us in automobiles wherever we went, entering stores with us, going fishing or skiing with us, and waiting patiently outside our own or foreign residences when we made calls.

One reason for this, as I have said, was for our own protection. The Russians have the Oriental concept of hospitality toward foreigners and are determined that no harm shall come to them while in their country. The Soviet Government is acutely aware that two attempts, one of them successful, have been made upon the lives of foreign envoys in Moscow, and of the embarrassing and annoying aftermaths. They have no intention of permitting incidents of this kind to occur again. I did not believe personally that such precautions were necessary while I was in Moscow, whose citizenry's regimented discipline was so well known that fifty thousand captured Germans were paraded through the streets at the peak of the war without even arousing hoots or catcalls.

But the guards were there, twenty-four hours a day, on orders of the Kremlin, and whether the purpose was to protect me or to limit my contacts with Russians, they achieved both objectives equally well.

Perhaps my most amusing experience with them was an occasion when, on the spur of the moment, I drove in my car to the Moscow Sea, without advance warning to my guards, and persuaded the director of a small cooperative fishery to take me fishing in the one and only small rowboat visible on the premises.

I assumed that the guards would stay behind with their car until my return, but I could not have been more mistaken. In a few minutes, we heard an enormous splashing, and I looked behind to see another small boat, obviously leaking badly, following us with my faithful escort. One was rowing the boat while the other two bailed steadily. They kept just far enough away to allow me casting distance, sitting over their ankles in water. I was about to take pity on them and go to shore, when another rowboat, occupied by two Russian women, approached. The guards hailed the newly arrived boat, and after a brief wordy exchange both boats rowed to the shore, where they dispossessed the two women, expropriated their less leaky boat, and resumed their post. Even so, when I returned to the dock they were sitting ankle deep in cold water; but I never saw more rugged souls and they didn't seem to mind at all.

After their experiences with my predecessor, Mr. Harriman, the MVD had come to believe that all American Ambassadors must be excellent skiers, and my guard in winter always included some of the best skiers in the Soviet Union. It must have been a shock for them after watching Mr. Averell Harriman's graceful swift movements on skis to see me fall on the smallest hill; but they always moved in quickly, set me on my feet again, brushed me off, and stayed just far enough to the rear so they could pick me up the next time.

It is only the British and American Ambassadors who are honored with this open escort, although other diplomatic personnel are watched more or less closely, depending on the state of relations between their respective countries and the Soviet Union. This surveillance makes any real contact with the Soviet people impossible, since the Russians do not wish unnecessarily to attract the attention of the secret police. However, during 1946 and part of 1947, a number of Russians came to our official entertainments at Spaso House, and to our Sunday night movies which were attended by most of the foreign colony. Our Soviet guests were usually from the intellectual or artistic groups—writers, artists and a few people from the theater and the ballet—who were considered public personalities and who seemed to be allowed considerable latitude in their contacts with foreigners.

Eisenstein, the famous motion picture director, came often, and until shortly before his death he rarely missed the showing of an American motion picture, although his criticisms of most of them were biting and sarcastically contemptuous. He spoke excellent English, was worldly-wise, and was an attractive and welcome guest. His pupil and successor, Aleksandrov, also came occasionally with his beautiful wife, who stars in most of his pictures. Another frequent and interesting visitor during those days was Lieutenant General Ignatiev, probably the only surviving member of the pre-revolutionary aristocratic officer corps. He had been a page of the last Czar, and then an officer of the Chevalier Guards, with much active service to his credit. He was Military Attaché in Paris at the time of the Revolution, and he disappeared from sight for several years with the records of his office. After things quieted down, he offered his services to the new Bolshevik Government, and they were accepted. Now, well past seventy, but looking ten years younger, he is an instructor in one of the military schools.

We carefully avoided any political discussion with these people, and we thoroughly enjoyed knowing them until worsening relations and the promulgation of the Soviet State Secrets Act, which makes it a grave offense to speak to a foreigner of anything which, by the most remote flight of imagination might be considered state information, terminated our association.

Every foreign official in Moscow has one Russian acquaintance who entertains him socially. The generally accepted belief among the foreign colony is that this is done so it cannot be said by foreigners that they were never invited into a Soviet home on a personal basis. Our "non-official" host was the head of the art department of Burobin, M. Alexandrov. He and his cultured and attractive wife, who was an instructor at the University of Moscow, entertained us a number of times, not, as we found later, at their home, but at an apartment which was available to them in their official capacity. There was usually music and singing, and occasionally the preview of a new Soviet motion picture. We exchanged small gifts on appropriate occasions and came to know them and like them well.

Unhappily, toward the end of my tour, both were arrested. I heard that Madame Alexandrov was liberated, but that her husband was given a long prison sentence. Through the Alexandrovs, we met and came to know the ballet star, Golubin, and his wife, who taught Russian to some of the Embassy officers. The Golubins, I heard, were also arrested, and I was glad to see him, shortly before my departure, in the lobby of the Bolshoi Theater. I did not embarrass him by speaking, and we passed each other without recognition.

In Moscow the diplomatic corps was by no means one big, happy family. It was a cosmopolitan group, ranging from the one extreme of multilingual career diplomats of long experience and easy social graces, to the new kind of workers' representative, the hard-boiled Communist veteran from the satellite states, some of whom had spent years in political prisons within their own countries. The war, too, had produced a certain number of soldier-diplomats of whom I was one, along with General George Catroux of France, a distinguished officer who previously had been Governor General of Indo-China and of Algeria, and General Popovic of Yugoslavia, a doctor turned soldier in the Spanish Civil War and later a partisan fighter of distinction in the guerrilla warfare waged under the leadership of Marshal Tito for the liberation of Yugoslavia from the Nazis.

The doyen of the corps when I arrived in Moscow was Dr.

Foo, the Chinese Ambassador who had been in Moscow for about ten years and who was facing up to the difficult task of representing the Nationalist Government, with which the Soviet Union maintained formal relations while Chinese Communist armies in the north of China were preparing its overthrow. Highly intelligent, and cultured as only a cultured Chinese can be, Dr. Foo's long experience and knowledge of Russian and understanding of Russian characteristics aided me greatly during my first months in the Soviet capital.

General Catroux and his wife had been in Moscow about two years at the time I arrived, and because of our previous acquaintance and association in North Africa when he was appointed Governor General of Algeria after the American invasion had ended Vichy control in 1942, he went out of his way to be helpful, both professionally and personally. A tall, slender man, with a thin, almost ascetic face, General Catroux was the epitome of the cultured French officer with a distinguished military and governmental background. Our relations were of the best and our discussions frank. But he had a serious problem within his own Embassy which reflected the bitterness and division of French political life. Even among his career diplomats, there was a three-way political split—some loyal to the MRP faction then in power, some who backed the return of General Charles de Gaulle, and a smaller but ambitious faction of Communists. The presence of the latter made it almost certain that any dispatch which the Ambassador sent to his government would be known simultaneously in the Foreign Office and at French Communist headquarters, unless he or one of a few trusted subordinates personally coded the message.

Madame Catroux was the *grande dame* of the Moscow foreign corps, who enjoyed the affection and respect of the entire foreign colony. She had a liking for Americans as a result of her work with our troops during the first World War, when she headed the French Red Cross and received a citation from General Pershing. Cultured and charming, she also had a fiery temper, evident on such occasions as when she described her experiences in an uncomfortable Soviet guesthouse on the airfield at Minsk during one of her trips from Paris to Moscow. After hearing this story for the first time, I sent her a certificate designating her as "Miss Minsk of 1948," a title she retained during the remainder of her stay in the Soviet Union.

My British colleague, Sir Maurice Peterson, appointed to succeed Lord Inverchapel when he was moved to the Washington Embassy, arrived in Moscow about two weeks after I did, and we shared the experience of learning the ropes together. A career diplomat, a canny though somewhat austere Scot, tall, rather saturnine and reserved on first acquaintance, Sir Maurice had come to Moscow directly from the Embassy in Turkey, and his long experience there and at other posts in the Middle East had given him an unusual insight into the affairs of this troubled area where Western and Soviet interests clashed. This knowledge and experience he shared with me as we both faced similar problems in our dealings with the Soviet authorities. His second in command, Frank Roberts, who had the rank of Minister, is one of the outstanding younger diplomats of the British Foreign Office. He and his charming Arab wife came to be regarded almost as members of our family.

When I first came to Moscow, the Italian Ambassador was Signor Quaroni, who had faithfully served Mussolini both as a diplomat and an intelligence agent before and during the war. He had been stationed in Russia before—at Vladivostok, I believe—and had married a Russian lady. He told me that during the war when he was stationed in Kabul, Afghanistan, he had plotted an insurrection of border tribes against the British in India, and had submitted the plan through his government to the German high command for approval. The Germans, believing that Britain was about to collapse under the pounding of the Luftwaffe, vetoed his proposal on grounds that they "did not wish further to diminish white prestige in the Middle East or India." Signor Quaroni moved on to Paris later. I had the greatest respect for and confidence in his successor, Ambassador Brosio.

The able Canadian Ambassador, Dana Wilgress, spent little time in Moscow, as his government kept him busy on a variety of assignments at sessions of the United Nations and other international conferences, and finally decided to station him in Switzerland instead of Russia. Canada was represented for the most part by a Chargé d'Affaires, John Holmes, who was among our best friends. John and the members of his staff, including his Military Attaché, Brigadier Allard, and their pleasant and attractive womenfolk, were frequent and welcome visitors to Spaso House.

One of the more interesting couples was the Iranian Ambassador, Prince Farouz, and his beautiful wife. Personally rather attractive but, in my opinion, officially completely untrustworthy, Prince Farouz, at the time of my arrival in Moscow, was suspected of being actively hostile to the reigning house in Iran, and was believed to be playing the Russian line even in the ticklish situation which at that time existed and to a certain extent still exists on the Iranian-Soviet frontier. Farouz later left Moscow under rather mysterious circumstances, and when I last heard of him was living in exile in Paris. His successor was a likable little man, distinguished primarily for his overwhelming fondness for bridge, and it was alleged with some truth that if he could not assemble a bridge foursome during the afternoon when most other diplomats were working, he would resort to the expedient of crashing the ladies' bridge parties. But I could hardly blame him, considering the unhappy state of relations between his country and the Soviet Union. He had almost no contact with the higher echelon of the Foreign Office, and was treated with extreme coldness by all Russians.

The Soviet Government did unbend slightly during the brief period of a visit by the Iranian Princess Ashraf to Moscow. I had promised on this occasion to attend the reception given in her honor, but for some reason was delayed and arrived late, to find my Iranian colleague anxiously waiting for me at the door. Seizing me by the hand, he literally dragged me up the stairs and into a room where the Princess was standing, and I went through the formality of an introduction in the bright glare of floodlights, while still and motion pictures were taken. My first impression was of a typical fairy story princess with dark hair, enormous and beautiful eyes, and classic Persian features. She was dressed in a white satin gown, the bodice of which was solid with pearls, and hanging from her ears were two enormous emerald and pearl pendants, which I was told were a gift of the Soviet Government. When she turned to lead the way to a sofa for a private talk, I noticed that the omnipresent Russian flea,

no respector of royalty or any other person, had bitten the
Princess squarely in the middle of her back.

Among the other members of the diplomatic corps whom
we saw frequently was the Greek Ambassador, M. Politis, a
friendly, effervescent diplomat, who had married a Russian
girl but who was not permitted to take his wife with him when
he left the Soviet Union. New Zealand was represented by
Minister Boswell, a sincere, honest, likable man. All of the
Dominion representatives, and especially the extremely capable
Australian, Alan Stewart Watt, were valued counselors and
true friends. We saw a good deal of the Scandinavian contingent, headed by Ambassador Solman, of Sweden, Ambassador Berg, of Norway, and Ambassador Doessing, of Denmark.
All the personnel at the Netherlands and Belgian missions were
close friends, and we spent a good deal of time with them, both
on business and socially.

Quite naturally, it was impossible to have really close relationships with the Russian satellite states, but we were on
moderately amiable terms with General Popovic, the Yugoslav
Ambassador, and we met the others from time to time at
official functions. Some were pleasant, some indifferent, and a
few were obviously and undiplomatically antagonistic. We took
them all as they came and, I hope, showed them all the same
imperturbable courtesy.

We were a divided city, with the Western diplomats and
those from the satellite states mutually suspicious one of the
other and the neutrals sitting on a fence trying to maintain
friendships in both camps. We maintained the closest relations
with some, friendly relations with others, and formal contacts
with the rest. But we all shared in common, whether satellite
Communists or Western capitalists, the same difficult problems
of attempting to do business with a vast bureaucratic machine,
where all policy emanated from the Kremlin and where a
subordinate official, or even a Cabinet minister, found it safer—
both professionally and personally—not to give the slightest
indication of his reaction or possible action until the most
precise orders had been received *in writing* from the men at
the top of this monolithic structure.

I had interesting proof of the fact that even relatively minor
matters, which with us would be handled directly by a junior

officer, must in the Soviet Union be passed on by a very senior official. One day, the Foreign Office, replying to one of our memoranda on a routine unimportant matter, sent by mistake with their memorandum the carbon copy which was intended for file. The margin of this copy bore penciled notations of half a dozen Foreign Office officials, in increasing order of importance, and at the bottom an official OK by no less a person than Vice Minister Vishinsky.

I found, also by experience, that it is a great mistake to attempt to delineate the Communist official as a free agent in terms of Western individualism. As a generalization, it is safe to say that in a Communist, and particularly in a Soviet, official there is no such thing as an independent point of view. There is only a party government point of view, to which all must adhere or else cease to be officials. Thus, while other statesmen can legitimately be described as entertaining varying official attitudes, it would be very misleading so to depict Communist statesmen. The best one can do is to say that so-and-so appears to be in a position to make minor decisions on policy without reference to the Politburo (as in the case of Molotov), or that he dares not move without reference to his government; that he is pleasant and even sociable, or that like Gusev and Gromyko, he is correct and reserved in his relations with foreign colleagues; or that he has small personal foibles, such as a childish aggressiveness with regard to his position.

I now realize that any Soviet and most Communist officials are immune to feelings of personal liking or gratitude toward any individual foreigner, and indeed would receive immediate and severe disciplinary punishment if they betrayed such feelings. The Communist Party operates on the theory that every foreign representative is acting solely in the interest of his own government, and that whatever he does may be explained by this fact. If he does a kind or obliging act, it is because he finds it in the selfish interest of his government to do so. It follows from this that no foreign representative can be considered objectively capable of an act of kindness or generosity, and therefore no Soviet official need feel himself under obligation to a foreigner. To do or say anything in deference to a personal relationship which one would not have done or said in the rigid performance of official duties would be considered by the

Soviet authorities as equivalent to acting in the interest of a foreign state. This is particularly true if the act or the statement is one favorable to the foreigner. If unfavorable, it can, unfortunately, be more easily defended.

These characteristics explain why my own initial callow but honest offers to present sympathetically to my government the official Soviet viewpoint on difficult questions were coldly received by the Russians. They also explain the only plaintive note I ever heard from General Marshall, who wired me from China that on an important question of Japanese repatriation he had received no reply to his repeated inquiries directed to the Soviet Ambassador, Petrov, "in spite of having loaned him a jeep." At the time, it was somewhat comforting to realize that Soviet practice was no respecter of persons, and was applied as rigidly to our most distinguished representative abroad as it was to me.

VI

MECHANICS OF A POLICE STATE

Nothing is more striking to an American, on his first arrival here, than the rigor of the police. It would seem that the capital was in a state of siege. And among all the astringents put into requisition for the preservation of peace and order, none is so abhorrent as the censorial power. As a proof of the extent to which it is carried, I may mention that the late message of the President of the U. States, was not regarded in all its parts as a safe document for Russian readers, and came to their hands scathed with the censor's knife. All that part on page 7 (commencing with "but it is now said by some") which states the views of those who desire our intervention in the affairs of Europe, was erased, while the views and doctrines of the President were suffered to pass; thus excluding the text while they admitted the sermon. It is difficult in many instances to see the reason of the application of this power; and no doubt it is often capricious.

—Excerpt from a dispatch of the American
Minister to Russia, Neill S. Brown, dated
St. Petersburg, January 27, 1853

"THE Soviet state determines the behavior and activity of Soviet citizens in various ways. It educates the Soviet people in a spirit of Communist morality of the system which introduces a series of legal norms regulating the life of the population, imposing interdictions, establishing encouragements, naming of punishment for the violation of these norms. The Soviet state stands guard over these legal norms with all its power. The conduct and activity of the Soviet people is also determined by the force of a public opinion which is created by the activity of numerous public organizations. In creating public opinion, the decisive role is played by the Communist Party and the Soviet state, which, through various media, formulates public opinion and educates the workers in a spirit of Socialist awareness."

I am rather impressed by this introductory paragraph, because I think it is the suavest definition of national regimentation I have ever read, especially considering the source. I copied it verbatim from Issue No. 4 of Moscow *Bolshevik,*

1947, and it thus constitutes a Soviet description of the all-pervading police state—a system under which the state begins to determine and regulate the behavior and activities of its citizens almost from birth, continuing as long as they live. The Communist leadership disbelieves profoundly in the ability of the people to regulate their own lives or to govern themselves. I was startled by the evident sincerity with which individual party members subscribe to this theory, and to the police state methods by which the people are educated "in a spirit of political awareness." During the early days of our association, when personal relations were friendly and rather frank, Marshal Sokolovsky spent a week-end with me at my quarters in Frankfurt, Germany. During our conversation I spoke critically of the methods of political repression which the Communists already were employing in the occupied areas of Central Europe. Sokolovsky, who is an intelligent man and honest according to his principles, looked at me in surprise and said, "I don't see why you should criticize. We aren't doing anything there that we don't do at home."

In his *Spoon River Anthology*, Edgar Lee Masters has an epitaph of a man who rose to power from one suspender. Part of this reads:

> . . . a nation can never be good,
> Or achieve the good,
> Where the strong and the wise
> Have not the rod
> To use on the dull and weak.

This is such an accurate thumbnail description of the Communist theory of dictatorship of the proletariat that it might well be carved on the cornerstone of the Palace of the Soviets, if this projected tallest building in the world ever rises from the great hole on the bank of the Moscow River which has for years marked its intended site.

The Communist Party of the Soviet Union still subscribes officially to the Marxian theory that as socialism develops, the state, which is an organ of class rule, will wither away. Since the contrary is obviously the case and the Soviet state is more robust than ever, Communist theoreticians explain the contradiction by pointing out to the Soviet people that they are

living under the dangerous conditions of capitalist encirclement. Stalin was quoted in *Izvestia* in 1947 as saying that the
state will continue to exist under communism unless capitalist
encirclement is eliminated, unless the danger of armed attack
from the outside is destroyed, and that the state will disappear
and wither away if capitalist encirclement is eliminated and
replaced by Communist encirclement. Thus the state is necessary just so long as the land of communism lives and develops
in the conditions of capitalist encirclement. However, Stalin
said last year that capitalist encirclement was no longer possible;
yet the state continues to broaden its police authority. Party
theoreticians haven't explained this yet. The words "police
state" bring at once to mind the secret police organization itself. Actually the term means much more. In the Soviet Union,
state control starts with the child, at a very early age. Soviet
children are brought up as ideological Communists, and general education is a secondary consideration.

The Soviet child learns that the Soviet Union is the only
nation which represents democracy and which stands for right,
justice and peace. He is taught that the United States is an
imperialistic, aggressive nation, where a small group of selfish,
predatory millionaires dominate all capitalistic trusts, which in
turn dominate the country, that workers are subjected to complete exploitation and literally kept in chains. When Anne
O'Hare McCormick visited a Moscow school, one child asked
her why the Americans kept their workers locked in dark
cellars.

The child is told continually that the destruction of Soviet
democracy is the primary objective of the capitalistic West, and
that the attainment of this objective is frustrated only by the
glorious Soviet Army and the strong and united determination
of the great Soviet peoples. The educational system is designed to insure the perpetuation in power of the Communist
Party and the exclusion of all political thought except that
dictated by the party line.

The teaching of nationalism is intimately connected with
political education. Its purpose is to arouse a boundless devotion to the Soviet Union in its struggle to establish the Soviet
regime.

The Soviet child enters the Red Pioneers at about the same

age that our boys and girls become Cub Scouts and Brownies. From the pioneers the children graduate into the Komsomol, or Communist youth organization, which admits young people from fourteen to twenty-six years of age. The Komsomol is the training school for future party members. The boy or girl receives a moral and political "shock group" training which at twenty-six will graduate the individual into the Communist Party if he or she has the intelligence, ability and response to discipline to qualify as a party member. Thus, from a very early age, Soviet youth is placed in an atmosphere which develops his "Socialist conscience" and the belief that he is above all a fighter for the defense of the Soviet regime, always menaced by capitalism.

Higher education is reserved for those who develop a "political consciousness" to a very high degree, or for the offspring of the new Soviet aristocracy. Indeed, the economic future of the Soviet young man or young woman depends to a large extent upon his political progress.

Aside from the evils inherent in its political aspects, there is nothing wrong with Soviet education in its primary stages that time and the constant attention given it by the government will not cure. In a country where work is obligatory for both parents, children become part-time wards of the state at an early age, and the Soviet state is a careful guardian of its most precious commodity. If the national average were taken as a basis of comparison, I believe that with certain clear exceptions the welfare of younger children in the Soviet Union would not be behind any other country in the world. The Soviet educational system is producing generations of serious-minded young people with a highly developed sense of responsibility, and illiteracy is being eradicated. In 1939 only 18.8 per cent of the total population of the Soviet Union was illiterate. Today's percentage would undoubtedly be appreciably less. The tragic thing about police state education is that all these young people are taught lies about the Western world, and there is no chance whatever for them to find out by observation and comparison that they are not being told the truth. The police state system molds the developing minds of its children for the loyal and enthusiastic support of a political regime that is basically evil.

When the young Soviet citizen leaves the direct supervision

of his teachers, he comes, in one way or another, under the omnipotent eye of the secret police.

Russia has had a secret police for centuries, in one form or another, and for centuries it has been a hated institution. Destruction of the Okrana, the Czarist secret police organization, was one of the most popular slogans of the Communist Party during the revolutionary period. Immediately after seizing power, however, the Bolsheviks established as an agency of the young Soviet state the "All Russian Extraordinary Commission" which soon became known to the Russian people and the world as the "Cheka" from the initials of the Russian words for "Extraordinary Commission." The word still conveys the impression of the terror of which it was the instrument and of which Lenin said bluntly, "The purpose of the terror is to terrify!" It may be that the memories of nameless dreads that inevitably attach themselves to the secret police organization have been one reason for its nomenclatural evolution from "Cheka" through GPU, OGPU and NKVD to the present MVD and its twin, the MGB.

The Communists did not establish a secret police without apologies to the people, whose lives they intended to regulate. An early issue of the *Soviet Encyclopedia* states:

"The apparatus of compulsion, the GPU, courts and prisons, is retained temporarily, only while the resistance of the bourgeois continues, but these instruments of struggle will wither away in proportion as the resistance declines. The state will disappear together with the division of society into classes."

And as long ago as 1939 no less a person than Stalin declared, "The function of compulsion inside the country has ceased, has withered away. The exploiters are no more, and there is no one to suppress any more."

But there is no slightest indication that the secret police are about to "wither away." On the contrary they have steadily increased in strength and power under Stalin's regime, and the organization has become a permanent and even a traditional feature of Soviet life, as it was in life under the Czars. The violent contradiction that involves between early Communist ideals and current Stalinist practice has had to be "resolved" dialectically. Therefore, the party line depicts the secret police of today as the guardian angels of the Soviet people against foreign machinations and enemy agents, foreign and domestic. The "organs of state security" are depicted as a beloved and benevolent feature of Socialist culture. But what colossal effrontery the writer must have had who described in *Pravda* recently the dread secret police organization in the following affectionate phrases:

> For three decades the organs of Soviet intelligence have faithfully served our people. Soviet intelligence is surrounded by the well-deserved respect and confidence of the people of our country, and is called upon to stand guard over the historic achievements of October. The workers of the Soviet Union know very well that, reared and directed by the Bolshevik Party, the workers in the organs of state security, whom the Soviet people traditionally call Chekists, devotedly defend the vital interests of the people and vigilantly safeguard the security of the Socialist motherland. For this reason the Soviet people not only trust the iron talons of the Chekists but also help it actively every day in its noble work of protecting the creative activity of millions from the subversive activities of agents of the imperialist countries.

Such nonsense might convince some of the starry-eyed Communist sympathizers in this country who live far from the "iron talons" of the Cheka, but the Soviet people are well aware that the thousands of inmates of Lubianka and other prisons, and millions of laborers in prison camps, are Soviet nationals, many of whom have never seen a foreigner in their lives. So this must be explained, and the Moscow paper *Izvestia* undertakes to do it. "The attempts of world reaction have strengthened in recent times," says *Izvestia*. "American imperialism has turned to an aggressive, frankly expansionist course. The juridical trials which have taken place in Bulgaria, Rumania, Hungary and other countries, conclusively show how capitalist espionage makes use of the forces of *internal* reaction for its infamous, undermining purpose."

Thus the permanence of the secret police as a Soviet institution becomes undeniable, even to the easily deceived Soviet people, just at a time when the concept of capitalist espionage is becoming especially useful to the aggressive foreign policy of the rulers of the Soviet Union.

The fact is, of course, that the Soviet Government would find it practically impossible to operate without its security organization, which is the cement that holds together the whole structure of the Communist state. It is not only the agency of political control, but actually is the cornerstone of the Soviet economic structure. Beginning with a first camp on the Solovetskie Islands in the White Sea during 1923, the Soviet Government has expanded the Old Russian system of hard penal labor into an enormous economic organization for the exploitation and development of those areas of the Soviet Union where life is unusually hard and difficult and where even the greatest inducements would not attract free labor. By this means the Soviet Government extracts from millions of human beings the unpaid labor which enables the Soviet system to concentrate on the expansion of its heavy industry without providing the consumers' goods incentive necessary to the use of free labor. The MVD administers this vast labor force, renting some workers out to other industries and using the rest itself in a nationwide network of enterprises.

Many books have been written describing life in Soviet concentration camps and the summary forms of justice practiced in the Soviet Union, but they have not, I fear, entirely convinced the people of other countries of the lack of personal liberty in a police state. One of the most recent, and by our observation, the most accurate studies of the Soviet slave labor system, that by David Dallin, has been challenged because the statistics seem to exceed American credibility. Actually, from our point of view, whether there are one million or ten million political prisoners in the Soviet Union is relatively less important than is the simple fact that under the Soviet regime numbers of individuals are deprived of their liberty and sent to concentration camps solely for political and economic reasons.

Louis Fischer, in his book, *The Great Challenge,* repeats a story told him by his son, Captain George Fischer, who was one of our officers stationed at our shuttle bombing base at Poltava, in the Ukraine. Captain Fischer tried to explain to Soviet officers the purpose of the balloting conducted throughout our forces during the Presidential election of 1944. "I don't understand," said a Red Army lieutenant. "You mean that Roosevelt is a Democrat, and he has been President for several years, and there are still Republicans in the American Army?"

It is the objective of the Soviet security system to remove the "Republicans" from circulation and to employ them in the best economic interest of the state. Any individual who deviates in his political views from the party line is in constant jeopardy of arrest and sentence, without public trial or basic legal rights, to hard labor for a prolonged period of years in remote parts of the country.

To an American who knows this, it is at first a surprise that the Soviet people show few outward signs of consciousness of omnipresent police surveillance or of the repressive activities of the agencies of internal security. I had lived in Moscow for some time before I began to appreciate the fact that the Soviet citizen is conditioned mentally to the chances of arrest and of "being sent away" just as we in this country are conditioned mentally to the chances of being struck by an automobile while crossing the street. His protective reactions to the one type of danger are as automatic and unostentatious as ours are to the other. For the true picture, one must look under the surface and this is hard to do. However, from a few among the stream of people who passed through the Consular Section of the Embassy, claiming American citizenship or seeking to enter the United States, I could at times get a glimpse of reality.

There was, for example, the man we called "The Beekeeper." He had lived for years in the United States, but returned to the Soviet Union in 1923. In May of that year he openly expressed sharp criticism of conditions in the Soviet Union and was arrested by the Cheka. After questioning on charges of espionage, he was sentenced "in closed session" (which means without a formal trial) to an indefinite period in the Solovetskie Islands. After ten years he was released and exiled to a small town in Siberia from whence, after a few months, he illegally came to Moscow. Apprehended there, he was sentenced to three years for breaking exile, and sent to a concentration camp near Khabarovsk.

After two years here he again escaped and came to Moscow in an effort to reach the border. On this occasion he confided his plans to a friend, and before the day was over he was again in the Lubianka prison. This time he was sent to the Kolyma region for an indefinite sentence and remained in camps there until June, 1945, when he was exiled to a small town about six hundred kilometers from Novosibirsk. Here he feigned feebleness and insanity, wandering about the tundra aimlessly and occasionally failing to make the daily registration required of exiles. When he managed to kill a deer, or other game, he sold the meat for a small fraction of the prevailing price. Gradually, the authorities became convinced that he genuinely was mentally unbalanced, and paid no attention to his activities. One day in August, 1946, he went to the river as if to bathe, and leaving his clothes by the bank to create the impression he had drowned, began the long journey from Siberia to Moscow, almost half of which he covered on foot. At the time I saw him, this man had spent twenty-three years in prison camps and in exile.

The stories of such men as these—all the same whether they came from long years in the Solovetskie Islands in the White Sea, in the Khabarovsk and Komsomolsk areas, the Kolyma gold fields or the Magadan Camp—create a composite picture of wretchedness, poor food, coarse living conditions, hard, exhausting work, rigid discipline and an extremely high death rate. Those who survive their prison term are usually sent to live in one of the more remote areas of the Soviet Union, such as Tarukharsk, Yenisei, Tashkent, Karaganda, Bokhara and Kazakstan. Rarely is a former "politically dangerous" exile allowed to return to life in any of the larger cities of the Soviet Union. This system of prison camps and forced labor seems to satisfy in part both political and economic requirements of the Soviet system. As one former inmate said to me, "No free men would do the work assigned to prisoners. So long as there is work to be done under sub-human conditions, so long will there be prison labor in the Soviet Union."

To me one of the most tragic aspects of the police state's political forced labor policy is the fate of the children of exiled parents. These children seem to some extent to share the odium of political deviation attached to their parents. I had personal experience with several cases of this kind, where a claim to American citizenship was involved. Often these children are left to the care of grandparents, or other aged relatives to whom they constitute an added burden, another mouth to feed. When artificially orphaned, mere existence for such children becomes a struggle. At best, they are placed in an institution. The state provides a small pension for those who do not go to state institutions, but from the pitiful circumstances of the cases that came to my personal attention, this can be little more than a token gesture.

Since such children often come from the households of intellectuals, they are, if old enough to think of the future, ambitious to obtain an education. For this reason they are reluctant to place themselves in a state institution since under normal conditions only one out of a hundred from these institutions ever gets to a university because of competing demands for labor as opposed to education. And, of course, the children of political prisoners are discriminated against. The fatalistic attitude of the intellectuals toward political arrest is remarkable. One, a very well-known critic, anticipating and predicting the intellectual purge of 1947, said to a friend of mine, "The new Siberian railroads will be built on the bones of people like me." This man was arrested in January, 1948.

The Soviet Union has always denied that it used masses of forced labor. As early as 1931, Molotov was compelled by the rising tide of foreign criticism to make a statement in connection with the use of slave labor in the production of export products. He said at this time:

"We have never attempted to conceal that in certain municipal and road operations we use the labor of prisoners who are healthy and capable of labor. We have done this in the past, we are doing it now, and we shall do it in the future. It is in the interest of society. It is good for those undergoing punishment, because it accustoms them to work, and makes them useful members of society. In a number of northern districts about which so much is written in the bourgeois press in connection with the campaign about forced labor, we have employed and are employing more prison labor, but this has nothing to do with the export of our products. These fables about forced labor have got to be put to an end."

This sounds frank and reasonable, if it were true. But it is not. While exact figures cannot be obtained, it is apparent that this involuntary labor drawn from four main sources is employed on a very large scale. The sources are:

1. Labor extracted from persons imprisoned without due judicial processes, that is by the secret police and other organs of state "security" directly and without trial.
2. Prisoners of war.
3. Persons imprisoned for labor in the Soviet Union from areas of Europe overrun by the Soviet Army during the war.
4. Labor performed by the so-called "Free Labor Force" (both industrial and agricultural workers) under conditions of partial or complete absence of freedom to choose occupation or place of work.

Estimates have varied greatly as to the strength of this involuntary labor pool, ranging from a few million to as high as twenty million. My own estimate, after examining all possible sources, is that the strength of the entire involuntary labor force is equal to about eight per cent of the total population of the Soviet Union, that is, about fifteen million.

A great deal has been written about forced labor in the Soviet Union, and most of it pertains exclusively to the first three categories I have mentioned. Few outside the Soviet Union know of the existence and extent of the fourth category, the so-called "Free Labor Force."

The Soviet Government established by law in 1940 a labor reserve. This law created a system for the mobilization of youth for work in industry and transport, and for this purpose it set up three types of trade schools: vocational schools, which give a two-year course for the preparation of skilled workers; the railway schools, giving a two-year course for the preparation of skilled railway workers, and the factory plant schools, which give a six-month course for the preparation of "semiskilled workers of mass professions" in industry and construction.

The 1940 law provided for the conscription each year of 800,000 to 1,000,000 male youths fourteen to fifteen years of age for the railway and vocational schools and of sixteen to seventeen years of age for the factory plant schools. Those called up are exempt from military service during training and for four years following training, but during this time they are required to work wherever directed by the Chief of Administration of Labor Reserves. Living is provided at state expense during training, and regular workers' pay is given thereafter.

In June, 1947, this law was amended to permit the drafting of males fourteen to seventeen years and females fifteen to sixteen years of age for the vocational and railway schools and of both males and females sixteen to eighteen years of age for the factory plant schools. A separate clause provides that for underground work in mines of the metallurgical and oil industry, only male youths of up to nineteen years of age may be called up. Nothing is said about vocational training for this group.

While extensive provision is made for actual vocational education under the labor reserve system, this is of secondary importance to the major objective, which is to provide a regular flow of conscripted youth for four years' work wherever assigned by the Soviet labor authorities. Thus a boy or girl fourteen or fifteen, who has not yet shown marked aptitude for higher education, or who has simply lacked educational opportunity, is subject to hard labor assignments. After vocational training, which may be only nominal and which may last from nothing to two years, the draftee must work for four years wherever the state sends him. Moreover, and this is very important, the draftee is still compelled by Soviet law to remain on his job unless he can obtain from his factory director permission to leave and work elsewhere. Thus he may well be stuck on the job for life, and any latent ability which might have led to professional or creative work will never have a chance to develop. He may also have to do his military service —two to five years, depending on the branch to which he is assigned.

Factory plant schools are particularly unpopular for this reason, and since few volunteer almost the entire quota for this type of school must be obtained by draft. As far as I have been able to ascertain, there is no reclama. The boys of the free labor reserve that I have seen working were in military uniform and obviously under military discipline. Later they will become trade union members, but in the Soviet Union trade unions are not independent bargaining agencies, concerned, as are ours, with the welfare of their individual members, but are agencies of the state, to channel labor as a tool of

the state. Strikes are forbidden. Philip Murray, Jim Carey and
other American labor leaders have had the same rather amusing experience as I in trying to pin down Mr. Kuznetsov (the
name in Russian means Smith, by the way), the head of Soviet
trade unions, as to their actual relationship to their individual
members and their power to bargain or strike. On matters like
this the Russians and ourselves are simply without a common
language. On one occasion, however, Stalin put the Soviet
position to Harry Hopkins in five words. Mr. Hopkins told
me that during one of his early discussions with the Generalissimo on Lend-Lease, he answered a complaint by Stalin about
slow delivery of certain items which had resulted because of
strikes in the United States. Stalin raised his eyebrows.

"Strikes?" he asked. "Don't you have police?"

The most important function of the agencies of "security"
of the police state, however, is the neutralization of political
opposition, not only outside the party, but inside, and on the
highest levels. The public and private life of every party member is under continuous scrutiny by the MVD, and the higher
his position in the state, the more carefully he is watched. The
average Soviet citizen, on the other hand, is conscious of the
secret police only in a rather negative way, so long as he stays
where he is registered, does his work, and refrains from comment or criticism of the Communist Party or the Soviet regime.
But if he steps aside even the shortest distance from the routine
path he is expected to follow, he is arrested at once, and his relatives and friends are likely to be arrested at the same time.

Arrests by the secret police are usually made at night and in
an atmosphere of mystery that is terrifying, even to the foreigner with diplomatic immunity. A recurrent Moscow joke,
told by Russians with a wry smile, describes the janitor of an
apartment building walking through the halls at midnight
knocking at the doors, and calling out loudly at the same time
"Don't be afraid, comrades, it's only a fire."

A general "political crime" provision in Article 58 of the
Soviet Criminal Code provides that for any acts disapproved by
the Soviet authorities an accused can be tried *in camera*, and
on the basis of entirely unpublished standards, by special MVD
courts.

Two other provisions of Soviet law are particularly shocking to Westerners, but are essential to the operation of a police state system. The first of these, Article 58-1-c of the Criminal Code, enacted July 20, 1934, reads as follows:

> In the event of escape or flight across the border of military service personnel, the adult members of his family, if they in any way facilitate the preparations for or committing of the act of treason, or even know about it but did not bring this to the attention of the authorities, are to be punished by deprivation of liberty for a term of five to ten years and the confiscation of all their property.
> The remainder of the traitor's family, who were residing with him or were dependent upon him at the time the crime was committed are subject to deprivation of voting rights and exile to remote regions of Siberia for five years.

The term "military service personnel" in the Soviet Union applies to any person who has served in the armed forces at any time, or who has had military training, since such persons are all considered under Soviet law to be members of the active reserve of the Soviet armed forces. In Moscow, it was our considered opinion based on reliable information, that this provision of law is universally applied. It makes potential hostages of the families of millions of Soviet citizens, and its threat against the innocent seems particularly horrible to me. It also makes me very suspicious of escapers from the Soviet Union who leave wives and children behind them.

The second, a decree of the Central Executive Committee of the U.S.S.R. of November 21, 1929, published in the 1947 edition of the Criminal Code, concerns Soviet citizens who refuse to return to the Soviet Union. It reads:

> 1. The refusal of a citizen of the U.S.S.R., an official of a state institution operating abroad, of the request of the organs of state authority to return within the borders of the U.S.S.R. is to be regarded as flight into the camp of foes of the working class and peasantry and to be classified as treason.
> 2. Persons who refuse to return to the U.S.S.R. are outlawed.
> 3. Outlawing involves the confiscation of all the property of the outlaw, and the shooting of the outlaw within twenty-four hours after identifying him.

4. All such cases are considered by the Supreme Court of the U.S.S.R.

5. The names of those outlawed are to be reported to all executive commissions of the Soviets and to the organs of the OGPU [now the MVD].

6. The present law is retroactive.

Although this decree says nothing about reprisals against families, the crime involved, that is, desertion from a post of trust abroad, is so much more serious in Soviet eyes than a simple attempt to escape from the Soviet Union that it is hard to imagine that it does not involve the visitation of penalties against families. I found it to be the general understanding among Soviet citizens that there are, in fact, very severe penalties applicable to the families of those who desert from posts abroad. These are probably covered in the unpublished sections of the Criminal Code as applied by the MVD courts, the contents of which are made known to Soviet officials proceeding abroad prior to their departure.

The operations of Soviet law have a very different objective from the impartial administration of justice which is the ideal of the Anglo-Saxon jurisprudence. In his authoritative work on criminal procedure, Mr. Vishinsky says, "The primary duty of the Soviet judicial system lies in its protection of the class interests of the workers. Contrary to the bourgeois legal system which attempts to conceal its true nature of a class protection with only the pretense of independence of government policies, proletarian courts do not propose to disguise the fact that in their essence they are class protectors. The judicial system is the arm of the workers and peasants who dispose of the power of the state and use it to further their own interests against other classes." I agree with Mr. Vishinsky's definition of the Soviet law except for one thing. If he had substituted the words "Communist Party" for "workers and peasants" he would have been correct. They are not by any means synonymous.

Recently when two minor employees escaped from the Soviet Consulate in New York our people must have wondered at the violent efforts of the Soviet authorities to regain possession of them, just as I wondered, immediately after the war, at the sustained and active campaign to force the return to the Soviet Union of all Soviet nationals who had been displaced, many of whom refused to return and some of whom even killed themselves when they thought they would be forced to do so. I asked the question of Mr. Vishinsky, who replied blandly that the Soviet Union did not, of course, want unwilling citizens, but that most of the persons to whom we were giving asylum were traitors or war criminals.

I know better now. The Soviet Government is well aware of the dangers existing in the presence abroad of thousands of persons who can and will testify at first hand of police state methods. These people foster nationalist sentiment and are quickly drawn to Estonian, Latvian, Lithuanian and Ukranian nationalist organizations, which continue to offer a faint hope of future independence and liberty, and which fight communism abroad. During the Paris Peace Conference I discussed this with a Communist statesman who occasionally spoke more frankly than his colleagues, and he put the Politburo's position and apprehension regarding Soviet displaced persons with one pithy sentence.

"That's the way we got our start!" he said, and of course that was true.

During the events which preceded the great purge the Chief of the Soviet Police, Yagoda, allied himself with Stalin's enemies. When Stalin gained the upper hand, and began the extermination of his enemies, Yagoda was shot. Later Stalin put Beria, whom he trusted, at the head of the police structure. Beria renovated and expanded the agencies of state security beyond anything that had been known before, and under his leadership they have become increasingly efficient.

The exact strength of the organization is unknown, but I am sure that it must number at least a million men, half of whom are organized as picked military formations, with their own artillery, tanks and air force.

The agencies of state security have complete supervision of every phase of national life. The Foreign Office cannot even give out an entry visa to a diplomatic attaché without the approval of the men of the Lubianka, in the shadow of which the Foreign Office building stands. These men have a vested interest in insecurity, and the growth and influence of the police state machine have been directly proportional to the fears on which it feeds. The Soviet people have been for thirty years in what amounts, economically at least, to a state of siege. They have been called upon to work harder and get along with less in the way of material compensation for a longer period than any people will accept without protest, unless there is provided some powerful stimulus.

The state provides this stimulus in the form of a series of enemies. First, there were the bourgeoisie to be exterminated, then the Trotskyite wreckers, and then the actual and deadly threat of Germany. There has always been "capitalist encirclement," with the threat of sabotage, and lest this become shopworn, the new bogey of a warmongering United States now is brought out on parade daily. The statement that these threats existed has always necessitated strict and unquestioned obedience on the part of the population to the edicts of the state. Uncomplaining acceptance and hard work may bring the reward of a carrot in the form of a decoration or more material gain. Any other attitude is certain to bring the whip, and the whip is wielded by the secret police.

There is nothing that the people can do about it. They go to the polls and vote, but a Soviet election is simply a political puppet show, in which the masses dance to strings pulled by party bosses. Externally the purpose of elections is to conceal the reality of a police state behind the constitutional façade. Internally they constitute a gigantic organized demonstration in which the populace registers solidarity with the regime whether they like it or not. If any evidence of this is needed the Soviet election press provides ample quantity.

A good example of this is a pre-election editorial in *Culture and Life,* a copy of which I kept. This editorial contemptuously contrasts "bourgeois democracy" with that of the Soviet Union which is "based on genuine active participation of the people." This ideological hocus-pocus is followed by assertion that in the forthcoming election the Communist Party comes forth in "bloc" uniting "non-party people and Communists in one common collective of Soviet people." The paper then urges party agitators and the party press to redouble election propaganda work. It notes that 240,000 agitators are operating in Moscow, half a million in the Ukraine, etc. Tens of millions of political pamphlets have been published.

All this in a one-party election, where there is one ticket

and one candidate for each office—an effort far beyond the wildest dreams of Tweed or Tammany in the old days. The press emphasizes that agitators must discuss subjects connected with the most important economic political tasks facing the country.

"They must ceaselessly wage the struggle for raising labor productivity, for labor discipline, educate workers in a spirit of selfless devotion to the cause of the party of Lenin and Stalin." The entire press, the radio and meetings must "urge all voters to vote unanimously for candidates of the bloc of Communist and non-party people." The editorial states that "forthcoming elections will demonstrate with new force the vitality and indestructibility of the Soviet multi-national state." The interesting fact is that there are no other candidates to vote for.

It is obvious to the most casual foreign observers that Soviet elections are not a contest as in a democracy but a carefully staged spectacle. The ruling party which controls the government, police, press and radio, uses its millions of members and the entire state machinery to get out one hundred per cent votes for its picked slated candidates. In these elections the public has no choice either on candidates or issues. Dissent from the party platform would of course be a matter for the secret police, but no Soviet citizen would dream of challenging publicly the party's choice of candidates or "issues." I say "no Soviet citizen," but occasionally there is the rare exception. During the 1947 elections we visited several of the polling places and the *Agitpunkt* or party agitation centers. At one of the former, late in the evening, a little old Russian woman, dressed in a padded cotton coat, a gray wool skirt and the usual felt boots, and with her head wrapped in a shawl, walked in, advanced purposefully to the official in charge and demanded, "How do you vote 'NO'?"

There was a moment's silence, all eyebrows went up, and then the official, who undoubtedly had a sense of humor and realized that one little old woman did not provide a very serious threat to the regime, took a blank ballot and carefully instructed her. She took the ballot behind the curtained booth, which is provided for those who wish to change a ballot in secrecy and which few voters ever dare to enter, recorded her

Boy drum corps on review in Red Square, Moscow.

The funeral of M. I. Kalinin in Red Square, Moscow, June, 1946.
Photo shows: J. V. Stalin, V. M. Molotov, L. P. Beria, G. M.
Malenkov and others.

One of the shops of the Stalin Auto Plant in Moscow, the first Soviet manufacturer of motor vehicles.

Celebration meeting at the Bolshoi Theater on the occasion of the Thirtieth Anniversary of the Soviet Army, February 23, 1948.

objection to conditions in general, and marched out with her head in the air. She had shown her independence and gotten away with it.

The foreigner who sees police state regimentation at close range might be able to regret it in a detached and impersonal way, return with relief and renewed confidence to his own democratic system, imperfect though it might be, and leave the whole thing for time and evolution, were it not for the sinister implications involved in a political religion that preaches hatred of all other political systems. It is this facet of communism that shocks Americans most. It is unwise and futile to disregard or to attempt to cheapen in any way a political ideology which, while it has in common with others the basic concept of overcoming the conflict of classes by transferring the means of production to national ownership, is unique in the profound belief that this end is attainable only by violent revolution, that subsequent to this revolution there must be a period of dictatorship based on open terror, and that the Socialist state can only be secure when capitalism is destroyed.

In 1947 the youth paper *Komsomol Pravda* featured an article on Leninism which contained this paragraph:

"Love for the Socialist Motherland is undoubtedly linked with fostering hatred for all imperialists and reactionaries throughout the world. Hatred for enemies of the land of socialism is an inseparable feature of Socialist ideology and the ideology of Leninism. What is reactionary bourgeois ideology? One may briefly reply, 'Look at the mighty armies of Hitlerite Germany.' That is bourgeois ideology in action. Whom has this ideology trained, and whom is it now training? People devoid of conscience and honor, detachments of wild beasts, hordes of barbarians, hangmen."

Well! This is us, and people like us, whom *Komsomol Pravda* describes in these unflattering terms to its youthful readers, and they are beginning to believe it. Lenin was right in more ways than one when he said that the establishment of socialism would require the sacrifice of two generations, for these young people whose minds are being shaped into a pattern of hatred for all the things which we believe to be indispensable to real democracy are as lost to the world of human freedom as is the generation which was liquidated to secure the Bolshevik regime in its present position of power.

This propaganda is effective. I cannot accept the picture some writers have given of seething resentment against the Communist regime. The vast majority of people now living in the Soviet Union, in my opinion, have no idea of personal liberty or of the processes of democracy as we in America understand these things. Those Russians who did understand such things don't live there any more. They are in exile, in prison or dead.

In fact, the Soviet citizen today believes he has the fruits of democracy. He can vote, and the fact that he casts his ballot for one candidate selected by the only existing political party is without significance to him. He can be elected to and sit on the legislative body of his state, or of his national republic, or of the Soviet Union. The fact that in this capacity he acts only as a rubber stamp for the party and, as I myself have seen, would pass a national budget without question or discussion in the short space of fourteen minutes does not impress him as unusual. He has no standard of comparison.

He has in Stalin the "little father" that the psychology of the Russian people seems always to have required—the demigod who represents all that is great and good in the national cosmos. Discontent exists, but I believe it is no more than the discontent which Lenin visualized when he said that "any regime that remains in power over a long period of time becomes unpopular."

Thus the Soviet regime is nailed in place by bayonets and held together by an omnipresent demonstration of force as well as by the psychological trickery of propaganda. The individual, his personal liberties and, to a considerable extent, his dignity as a human being, are submerged—all in the interest of the system as a whole, whose material achievements, particularly in vast stretches of backward territory, are ample evidence of impressive power.

VII

INDUSTRY AND AGRICULTURE

This is a hard climate, and an American finds many things to try his patience, and but few that are capable of winning his affections. One of the most disagreeable features he has to encounter is the secrecy with which everything is done. He can rarely obtain accurate information, until events have transpired; and he may rely upon it, that his own movements are closely observed by eyes that he never sees.

The Russian mind seems naturally distrustful; and this is especially so with the government officials. Everything is surrounded with ceremony, and nothing is attainable but after the most provoking delays.

—Excerpt from a dispatch of the American Minister to Russia, Neill S. Brown, dated St. Petersburg, January 27, 1853

A UNIFORMITY of poverty is being created across the vast Soviet-dominated areas of Eastern Europe and Asia. The Kremlin is milking the satellite states and demanding ever greater efforts from the long-suffering Russian people as it pushes forward a new series of five-year plans.

The standard of living average for the area as a whole is being lowered, not raised, as the Soviet Union concentrates upon building up its heavy industries—steel and machines—and gives only secondary consideration to the production of consumers' goods. Improvement in the Soviet economy is balanced by a decline in that of the satellite states as the entire Soviet orbit approaches a common level.

The Molotov plan is the Marshall Plan in reverse. The Soviet Union is not giving of its own strength and resources to help others recover; it is taking from the satellite states machines, raw materials and finished products designed to strengthen the Soviet Union.

In thirty years, the Soviet Union, by superhuman efforts of a regimented labor force, has performed a modern miracle by transforming itself from an economy in which the emphasis was overwhelmingly on agriculture into one in which already a small majority of the workers are in industry. Now the satellites are being told to go and do likewise.

The peoples of Latvia, Lithuania, Estonia, Poland, Czechoslovakia, Hungary, Rumania and, to a lesser extent, Bulgaria, have always enjoyed higher living standards than the residents of the Soviet Union. These were small capitalist states, with small farms and small industries predominating. Their pre-war economies were more agricultural than industrial, and their trade orientation generally was toward the West. They wore better clothes, lived in better houses, and had more to eat than their Soviet neighbors. Some of them are still better off, but going down. But now their newly established masters are beginning an intensive program of farm collectivization and a shift into industrial-agricultural economies. Already stripped of many of their resources by war damage and the loot taken by the Red Army as "war booty" or alleged Nazi assets during and after the war, they are forced to trade almost exclusively with the Soviet Union—and that is largely one-way traffic, Moscow-bound, as the embittered Yugoslav Communists have made so clear—and the result inevitably is a reduction in the availability of those necessities and luxuries for which free men toil in order to enjoy a better life.

There are, of course, the hard facts of economic reality to explain this reduction of living standards, but there are political reasons as well. The men in the Kremlin well remember the surprise of the simple Red Army man, as he marched westward into the "decadent" capitalist countries whose workers, he believed, were exploited and cruelly enslaved. There he discovered that the worker in even so backward a country as Rumania lived better than the skilled, hard-working Soviet factory employee. For the Rumanian or any other close neighbor to be better off than the Soviet citizen in the new pattern of post-war Europe would be intolerable to the Russians. The answer, therefore, is simple. As the Soviet standard of living gradually goes up, that of its satellite neighbors goes down. Soon a common level of economy will be established. Stalin said as much when he told Harry Hopkins that wider contact with foreigners and the outside world would be allowed for Soviet citizens as soon as the Soviet standard of living did not compare unfavorably with its neighbors'.

When Foreign Minister Molotov slammed the door on the Marshall Plan preliminary talks in Paris in 1947, he finalized the existence of two worlds, not only politically but economically as well. Little did he realize, I think, the far-reaching consequences of that brusque refusal of a generous American offer of assistance and the concomitant organized Communist effort to defeat Western recovery by strikes, sabotage and boycotts. The Marxist view has always been that the flag followed the dollar, and not vice versa, and it was a shock to the Soviet leaders and the Communist satellites to discover that Americans would not sell, even for dollars, steel mills, machine tools and other necessities for industrialization to nations which sought the ultimate destruction of our way of life.

The realization must have shaken their belief in a fundamental Communist precept—one, in fact, on which they rely so much in their theory of the inevitable collapse of capitalism—that in a non-Communist society patriotism would always be secondary to profits.

The Soviet Government makes it difficult for any foreigner to get an accurate picture of its industry and agriculture, both for military and political reasons. Such statistics as it does permit to be published are inadequate and, I believe, unreliable. They consist of glittering but non-committal generalities, usually claiming that the production of a certain commodity exceeded by blank per cent the unannounced production total of that commodity in a previous year. And the State Secrets decrees of June, 1947 increased the severe penalties for the unauthorized disclosure of the most routine economic information.

However, I was able to obtain permission to see some farms and factories, and members of my staff visited others. Occasionally American and other foreign businessmen and engineers, some of whom had made extended trips, gave us the benefit of their observations and opinions. The Soviet press, which we read constantly, presents a generally flattering picture, but gives occasional strong criticism and is otherwise revealing in a negative sort of way. The business of living for some years in the Soviet Union results in accumulated observations which are reasonably accurate. Thus, in spite of the dearth of published statistics, it is possible to draw reasonable conclusions. The following are my own.

INDUSTRY: Since the war destroyed the German industrial plant, the Soviet Union now is the second greatest industrial power in the world. All Soviet economic planning is geared to the possibility of war; therefore the greatest emphasis is placed on further development of heavy industry, much of which is centered in the harder-to-bomb Urals region. Light industry which turns out consumers' goods for the people is for the present at least the "orphan" of economic planning, and there are shortages of nearly every required commodity. While the Soviet industrial plant is not efficiently operated, and while there is great wastage of both manpower and materials, the record of transforming an agricultural country into an industrial power in thirty years cannot be minimized, especially when one takes into account the fact that, with a large part of the industrialized area in German hands, Russian factories still produced the bulk of the weapons used by the Red Army in its victorious counteroffensive against the Wehrmacht. (Lend-Lease was a very valuable supplement, but Soviet industry did the main job.) The post-war period has produced many problems, but the announced goals of the new five-year plan are being substantially attained, at least as far as heavy industry is concerned.

One of the major problems is the continued productivity of the labor force. Soviet labor, although completely regimented through the agencies of a police state, including trade unions which are agents of government rather than of the workers, is war-weary and caught in a vicious cycle of low wages, high prices and insufficient food and supplies.

AGRICULTURE: The food situation is still precarious. The country is fortunate if it has two good crop years out of five. Labor is wastefully used; most of the sowing and reaping is still done by hand because of lack of machinery. Nearly half of the Soviet labor force is still employed in agriculture, whereas twenty-three per cent of the population of the United States not only feeds this country lavishly but feeds half the world as well. Efforts to introduce collectivization into newly acquired territories, such as the Baltic states, are being resisted. There can be no doubt that the power of the Soviet Government will succeed in overcoming this resistance in the long run, but the cost will be high in terms of human misery.

About the time I arrived in Moscow, the newly elected Supreme Soviet met to hear Voznesensky, who headed the State Planning Commission, outline the main features of a new five-year plan. (Voznesensky was later to be purged from the Politburo, but at that time was heralded by the foreign press as its bright young man.) This plan was to be the prelude to at least two others and possibly more in an unending procession which began in 1928 and was interrupted only by the war. As described by Voznesensky, the current five-year plan had five primary objectives:

Soviet economy was to be completely reconstructed, with the chief emphasis on railway transport and heavy industry. By 1950, the over-all level of industrial production must exceed that of 1940 by fifty per cent.

The material welfare of the Soviet people was to be advanced so that by 1950 there would be an abundance of basic items of consumption in both food and industrial consumers' goods.

Soviet science was to catch up with and surpass the achievements of foreign science.

The rate of investment in the national economy was to be accelerated.

The Soviet armed forces were to be provided with the most modern weapons.

These specific targets for industrial capacity by 1950 were set up: Steel, 25.4 million metric tons; pig iron, 19.5 million tons; coal, 250 million tons; petroleum, 35.4 million tons; aluminum, 172 thousand tons; electric power generating capacity, 22.4 million kilowatts; truck industry, 430 thousand trucks; tractor industry, 112 thousand tractors; 2,700 locomotives, 146 thousand railway cars and 103 thousand tons of metallurgical equipment were to be produced.

One of the more interesting features was the provision for new construction to meet a desperate housing shortage which existed in every city of the Soviet Union, large or small. The new five-year plan called for the construction or rehabilitation of 240 million square meters of housing space. Russian housing standards, perhaps because of their acute problems and perhaps because of the historic lack of concern for the individual citizen, are very low. Under Soviet law, a person has a theoretical right in areas of acute housing shortage to a minimum of six square meters, *excluding* corridor, bathroom, kitchen and toilet space, which is normally shared by all the tenants of an apartment or house. This allowance would entitle a family of four to a single, normal-sized room in an American house. The huge total visualized in the five-year plan would, under minimum conditions, provide accommodations for more than eighteen million persons.

The problem is graphically illustrated by a letter which appeared in the newspaper, *Baku Worker*, in 1948, which declared:

> My family and I, consisting of six people, live in a damp room of fourteen square meters. In 1946, I applied to the Baku Housing Administration for another apartment. The Administration, in accepting my petition, recognized my right to "special" treatment. Two years have passed since then. Several times I have applied to the Director of the Administration and the Baku Ispolkom [Supreme Town Council] and asked that my family be speedily removed to new quarters. There are now on my petition more than ten injunctions: "Speed Up!", "Investigate!", "Take Measures!". Four of these belong to the Acting Chairman of the Baku Ispolkom, Comrade Kasumova. But strangely enough, none of these injunctions has yet been fulfilled by the workers of the Baku Housing Administration. When, at last, shall I be granted an apartment?

The law courts of Moscow daily are jammed with people fighting the battle for adequate housing, clearly demonstrating that the Baku complainant was talking of typical rather than exceptional conditions.

As we studied Voznesensky's figures, later to be expanded by Stalin's goals of 60 million tons of steel, 500 million tons of coal, 50 million tons of pig iron and 60 million tons of petroleum at the end of three five-year plans, we wondered whether the totals were realistic and attainable. We knew that previous pre-war five-year plans had been fulfilled to a great extent as far as heavy industry was concerned, but had rarely been fulfilled in those parts which bore a direct relation to the scale of living of the Soviet people.

By the middle of June, 1946, it became apparent that history was repeating itself, at least to the extent that during the last six months of that year the government introduced several far-reaching decrees, designed to increase the production of consumers' goods.

Early in 1947 it began to seem clear to us that there was a realization on the part of the government that those responsible for drawing up the five-year plan a year earlier had seriously miscalculated the ability of the Soviet people to accept continued hardships and further sacrifices. The Kremlin, eager to reconvert and reconstruct heavy industry and thus increase the military-economic potential of the Soviet Union, had made insufficient provisions for the production of consumers' goods to satisfy a people worn down by pre-war and wartime sacrifices, who hoped that peace would bring a higher standard of living. The resulting disappointment had a demoralizing effect on the productivity of labor.

The farmers were also affected. While they continued, of necessity, to deliver up the grain and food products required of them by the government, they either consumed themselves or diverted to the free market a considerable portion of their produce, particularly that part produced outside the collective farm system which, under normal conditions, would have found its way into government channels.

Food shortage affected labor production still more. Serious economic difficulties began to arise, and the Kremlin's actions to restore the situation set in train a series of events that revealingly highlight some very interesting features of Soviet economy and the factors which influence its development.

The government's first reaction to the serious production lag was to renew the old stimulus of a threat from outside. The Soviet propaganda machine went into high gear to depict the United States as an aggressive, hostile power, actually preparing for and intending to wage war against the Soviet Union. This time, the old formula backfired, not because the propaganda picture failed to convince a large part of the Soviet people, but because they were so war-weary and longed so fervently for peace that the prospect of revived hostility was too much to bear.

Russian peasants began to buy and hoard salt, something that they have done for generations when a great national calamity threatened. Industrial workers generally experienced a further drop in morale. Production lagged still more. To make matters worse, the symptoms of a food shortage compelled the government to put off the promised removal of food rationing.

During the latter part of 1946 and the early months of 1947, the government moved rapidly to remedy the situation. Stalin made reassuring statements to Soviet, satellite, and foreign press representatives, minimizing the danger of war. Steps were taken to force idle persons into industry by refusing to give food rations to several categories of dependents. A large number of employees were dismissed from administrative jobs, and were faced with loss of their ration cards, unless they sought factory work. When these measures did not prove sufficient in themselves, the government was forced to provide additional incentives for work by changing its production plans to increase the amount of consumers' goods available for purchase. The mass punitive measures employed in earlier years to meet similar situations were not resorted to because the Kremlin apparently realized that anything resembling another purge at this time would reduce the already limited number of competent personnel and would be completely demoralizing.

These measures gradually improved the production situation to the point where the government finally felt able to act drastically to lower the purchasing power of the Soviet people in order to reduce the general demand for consumers' goods and relieve the pressure on light industry. The currency reform undertaken in December, 1947, accomplished this. The existing ruble currency was declared obsolete without warning and new currency was issued which was exchanged at the rate of one new ruble for ten old rubles. State bonds were devaluated by two-thirds. Bank deposits, however, were exchangeable at equal value, but only up to 3,000 rubles with a smaller return on larger amounts. Food rationing was removed at the same time.

The farmers were wiped out, as their money was not in banks but in state bonds and currency. To pay taxes and meet current expenses, they sold food, so that for a brief period immediately after the monetary change, there was a flood of food in city markets for the first time in years. This lasted only a short time, and thereafter the industrial workers found that an even more drastic form of rationing actually existed, since only a limited quantity of each kind of food was sold to one person. After another brief interval, the number of food stores was reduced substantially. These steps prevented raiding and hoarding.

Except for bread, and a few other staples, prices remained at the same high level as before the currency reform. Thus, the ability of the individual to acquire more food or more goods hinged on his ability to earn more money, and to earn more money he had to turn out more work.

Few persons in the United States realize how hard a Russian already had to work for the little he received, and what a great strain was put upon his physical and mental resources in being forced to increase the duration and speed of his labor. At the time the currency was changed, we calculated that a Soviet worker had to work 4 hours and 57 minutes for a dozen eggs, 14 hours and 5 minutes for one pound of coffee, 1 hour and 10 minutes for one pound of wheat bread, 2 hours and 34 minutes for one pound of sugar, 2 hours and 4 minutes for a package of cigarettes, 104 hours and 30 minutes for a pair of men's shoes, 107 hours and 30 minutes for a pair of women's shoes, 580 hours and 15 minutes for a man's wool suit, and 252 hours for a woman's wool dress. His counterpart in the United States worked 38 minutes for the dozen eggs, 22 minutes for the coffee, 6 minutes for the bread, 5 minutes for the sugar, 9 minutes for the cigarettes, 7 hours and 15 minutes for the men's shoes, 5 hours and 32 minutes for the women's shoes, 28 hours and 4 minutes for a man's wool suit, and 12 hours and 52 minutes for a woman's wool suit.

This vicious cycle of wages-prices-rations-productions had a serious effect on labor, and revealed itself in the form of substandard production. From this there developed great pressures upon industrial management, particularly in the light industries. During the spring of 1948, *Pravda* reiterated almost daily the news that the Prosecutor General's office had instituted proceedings against various plant managers for producing poor quality goods or for failing to reach their production goals.

I made note of the following examples:

For systematically producing low quality bicycles, the chief
engineer of the Girdum Plant of the Ministry of Local Industry has been called to account. He has been sentenced to five
years' loss of liberty for his crime.

The chief of the technical control department of the Khramt-
sorski section of the "Kirovugol" trust, Ministry of Coal Industry, Mommisarchuk, and the chief of loading, Sukomel, have
been condemned to six years' loss of liberty for dispatching
coal below standard. The deputy chief of loading, Khokhlov,
has been sentenced to five years' loss of liberty.

In Leningrad, the chief engineer of the felt factory of Local
Industry, Makhnovski, has been sentenced to two years' loss
of liberty for producing low quality footwear.

In Oaklov Oblast, the director of the Totskaya Bakery has
been sentenced to five years' loss of liberty for systematically
producing low quality bread.

The director of the sewing factory in Moscow, Yashunin,
the technical director, Smirnov, and the chief of the technical
control branch, Nikitin, have been brought to trial accused of
producing low quality goods, as have also a number of employees in other plants.

Sewing factory of the Frunze District Industrial Combine,
Moscow, continues output of men's clothes that proved to be
unwearable. Director Tarachkov sentenced to five years' loss
of liberty.

In the Makeyeva Industrial Combine, Stalin Province, out
of 7,770 cultivator wheels delivered to the Mariupol Metal
Products factory, all save 217 were defective. Chief Engineer
Chrdakov and chief of the technical control department, Rad-
chemko, have been sentenced to five years' loss of liberty.

Tobacco factory, Saratov. Cigarettes found to contain dirt,
stalk and rubbish. Badly filled, often torn, owing to faulty
machinery. In six months, this factory alone produced over
1.4 million packets of faulty and bad quality cigarettes. Director V. K. Orchinsky has been sentenced to seven years' loss of
liberty. Chief Engineer P. V. Kireyev and chief of the technical
control department, V. I. Podshivalin, have each been sentenced to five years' loss of liberty.

Obviously there are certain mental hazards common to the
"management classes" in a Communist state which do not yet
exist in a capitalist system. It will be noted, also, that most of
the sufferers represent the management element of light indus-

try. Part of this is explainable by the Soviet policy that there must be scapegoats when things go wrong, thus pointing the fault-finding finger at individuals and turning it away from the government itself. But the major reason is that heavy industry gets the cream of industrial ability, and light industry has to take the dregs. The Soviet Union is, I believe, the only country in the world where in time of peace heavy industry, which produces fuel, metal and machines for consumption by industry itself, is larger than the light industry which produces consumers' goods for the population. Heavy industry is also the basis of a nation's war potential, and the Soviet Union is acutely aware of the fact that her voice in post-war world councils has carried such great weight because of the demonstrated power of Soviet arms. She does not intend that the weight of her words shall grow less.

In 1947 I visited the great Moscow plant of the Stalin Auto Works, but I was not permitted to see many sections of this plant. I was told they were "not in operation" for some reason, or that the workers were having lunch. I was told the same thing about the motor assembly plant, although at that moment I was looking through a twelve-inch gap in a pair of large sliding doors, and could see that motor assembly was proceeding at full blast. Nevertheless, having myself once worked in an automobile factory, I saw enough to know that the truck production line could compare favorably with similar plants anywhere. One and one-half ton trucks were coming off the line at the rate of one every three minutes. The director of the plant, who had spent some time in Detroit and who had seen everything we had to show, was obviously a first-class production engineer. He told me that the Moscow plant had a large subsidiary factory in operation in the Ukraine, and that it was also the parent of another big factory in the Urals, where a large number of skilled workmen from the Moscow plant had recently been sent to get things started.

Eric Johnston, who visited this same plant six or eight months later, and who knows much more about factory management than I do, confirmed the excellent impression I carried away after my own visit.

Visits to other heavy industrial plants by Americans, and conversations with the few American engineers and industrialists who have been in the Soviet Union recently reflect the same good impression. There are weaknesses, to be sure. One of the most common is the extreme shortage of such highly trained technicians as shop foremen, master mechanics and maintenance men. American engineers report that insofar as theoretical training is concerned, the young product of Soviet engineering schools is as good as any that we turn out. On the other hand, they say that these highly trained young men are remarkably deficient in practical mechanical knowledge and ability. One's first thought is that surely this is something that will be acquired by experience. My engineer friends were pessimistic. The fact is that Russian youngsters do not possess the mechanical aptitude with which most American boys seem to be born, and they gain practical mechanical knowledge with difficulty. At Spaso House, we employed a Russian mechanic, who was very good at diagnosing and correcting the motor troubles of our small fleet of antique motor vehicles. One day, however, I asked him to take the lawn mower apart, clean it, and adjust the cutting blades. Here he was completely lost. He was trained as a motor mechanic, and there his mechanical knowledge and comprehension ended.

I do not mean by this that the Soviet Union does not have first-class men in every field of engineering and production. The best Soviet engineers, like the best Soviet scientists, are second to none. But beneath this top stratum of ability is a large gap which will not be adequately filled for many years, owing to the shortage of skilled foremen and middle-grade engineers. German engineers, scientists and technicians, imported since the war either willingly or unwillingly, have helped, but are far from being numerous enough to do more than provide a leavening.

Another factor of weakness which particularly affects heavy industry is the inadequate transportation system of the Soviet Union. Russia's railway system is less than a third of that of the United States, and it serves an area three times as great as ours. The roadbeds are in poor condition, by our standards, and passenger train speeds of thirty miles per hour are about the average.

Strenuous efforts are being made to improve this situation. Within the past year and a half almost two days have been cut off the former twelve-day rail trip from Moscow to Vladivostok, but this is exceptional. The Soviet Union has acquired by capture, indemnity and plunder a large number of locomotives and railway cars to help replace their wartime losses, and rolling stock production has a high place in the current five-year plan, but it is still in very short supply.

The same shortages are apparent in long distance water transport. The Soviet shipbuilding industry has always been relatively insignificant, and during the war her large shipbuilding centers were heavily damaged. She has partially reimbursed herself by retaining all the merchant vessels obtained from us during the war (without, incidentally, reimbursing us), but a large merchant marine is still remote. Moreover, the northern coastal routes are very difficult and limited to about four months of navigation per year, although their importance is great.

One of the most interesting trips I made during my stay in the Soviet Union was in July, 1947, to the collective farm, "Kolos" (the Russian word means a head of wheat). Kolos lies seventy-eight kilometers north of Moscow in the Dmitrov region on the northwestern slope of the Smolensk-Moscow Ridge in the watershed of the River Yakhromy. John Hickerson, then head of the State Department's European office and now an Assistant Secretary of State, was visiting us at that time, and he went along, as did Joe Bulik, our Agricultural Attaché. As interpreter, we took Philip Bender, one of our oldest Soviet employees, who has since been arrested—a fate that sooner or later awaits all Soviet citizens who are employed for long periods by foreigners. Mr. A. I. Kubyshkin, an English-speaking officer of the Soviet Foreign Office, was our official escort, but my journal notes too that we were accompanied also by six "employees" of the Ministry of Internal Affairs, who followed us in the usual black car.

The road followed the Moscow-Volga Canal, which links Dmitrov, the county seat, with Moscow, and which passes through the entire length of the *raion* (county). I was again impressed with the solidity of the lock construction, and the importance of water traffic in this country of poor land communications.

At the town of Dmitrov we left the paved highway, and after a few miles on a dusty road arrived at the collective, where we were met by its chairman, Mr. Bakaikin, a tall, middle-aged man with a strong, honest face. He led the way to his office, where we met his two assistants, the *agronome,* or agricultural expert, and the secretary of the collective. Both were good peasant types. The *agronome,* I gathered in conversation, was the technical man of the farm, and the secretary was its book-keeper.

The office was a small room with bare, plastered walls and wooden floor. The walls were covered with photographs of the farm, charts showing its progress, and several citations for high production. In an adjoining room, similar to the office, were portraits of Stalin, Malenkov, and Kosygin. Mr. Bakaikin showed me the formal "deed in perpetuity" which gave the farm title to its specified land area for use for all time, and which made provision for any approved changes in the size of the farm. This collective was organized in 1931, Mr. Bakaikin told me, and he has been chairman ever since. Its total land area is 1,151 acres, of which 477 acres were in cultivation. On it lived 370 men, women and children in eighty-four households. I did some rapid mental arithmetic and calculated that the total land area per household was about a little over thirteen-and-a-half acres, but that the plowed acreage per household was about 5.7 acres on the basis of 477 plowed acres. The total labor force was two hundred adult farmers of working age, sixty-five per cent of whom were women. This means about two and one-half acres of plowed land per farmer—man or woman. This labor force is divided into four "brigades"—a vegetable brigade, two field brigades, and a livestock brigade. Mr. Bakaikin said with obvious grief that of the 110 people who had gone into the Red Army from this collective farm village, forty-one of them had not returned. In a more cheerful vein, he observed that the farm was doing well and added that he expected its money income that year to exceed one million rubles.

I asked him what procedure would be followed if the collective decided to cultivate more land, and wanted to enlarge the size of the farm. He replied that in this case a formal request would be made to the state for the additional land desired, and if approved, adjoining lands from the state land fund could be turned over to the collective farm. In this event, these lands would be entered in the act of perpetuity.

A large state farm adjoins the collective farm, and this gave me the opportunity to compare the two. The collective farm seemed to me to be much the better, and I thought this must be due to the personal incentive, since the members of a collective farm receive a direct benefit from increased production, while a state farm is cultivated under state management by paid agricultural laborers who receive a fixed wage without regard to output.

Both of these farms, and others in the neighborhood, were probably once part of a large estate, and the village of the collective was only one of the villages on this estate. It consisted of about twenty-five houses, of from one to three rooms, along one side of a dirt road. Several other homes of similar type were somewhat removed from the main group. The typical impressively large Russian village church, now used as a schoolroom and for storage, stood at one end of the village street. In front of the church was the little village store, which in size and construction was very much like a Midwestern American small-town hot dog stand. Each house was surrounded by its own vegetable garden of about an acre. These plots are cultivated by members of the household on their own time. Of the eighty-four households, fifty-five owned a "private" cow, and about forty-five owned one or more hogs. Most of them had a few chickens. In addition, the farm itself owned sixty head of cattle, forty-five horses, thirty hogs, and sixty sheep.

This farm, I found, was rather highly specialized. It was primarily a grain seed farm, with livestock production a secondary operation. It received select seed from the state seed fund for the purpose of enlarging the supply for distribution to other collective farms.

The chairman told me that the farm averaged to the acre about thirty-nine bushels of winter rye, forty bushels of winter wheat, thirty bushels of spring wheat, and 268 bushels of potatoes. These yields, which were a good deal above the average of the Moscow area, were undoubtedly the result of better than average seed and farming.

I was most interested in knowing how the farm did business, and I asked how its crop was marketed and how the proceeds were divided. Chairman Bakaikin replied that he would take wheat as an example, since that was the main crop.

In 1946, he said, the farm had produced seventy metric tons of wheat and a fixed percentage, amounting in this case to nineteen metric tons, was sold to the government at the fixed government price (which, incidentally, was very low and amounted, in fact virtually to a token payment). Payment then had to be made in kind to the machine tractor station, which did the tractor plowing as well as the threshing, and this amounted to seven metric tons. The farm committee had decided to set aside fifteen tons for seed, three tons for the crop insurance fund, two tons for the children's nursery, and to sell another two tons to pay for other production requirements. This left a little more than half of the wheat crop for distribution among the collective farmers, each of whom received grain on the basis of the total number of "work days" earned during the year.

He went on to explain that an average farmer, man or woman, was credited with a "work day" for each day of actual work. Children, who helped with the animals and poultry, were credited with less, usually half a "work day" for each day's work. Specialists got more, some receiving credit for two, or even three "work days" for a day's work. The average farmer on "Kolos" earned about 350 work days annually. If he did not exaggerate, this is an unusually high figure, as other "showplace" collective farms in Moscow Oblast reported the average earnings of collective farmers to be between 200 and 250 work days annually.

For each work day, the farmers of Kolos received 4½ pounds of grain, 11 pounds of potatoes, 2 pounds of other vegetables, 2½ pounds of straw and 3½ rubles in cash—which was a large income, by Soviet standards. If the total income in kind of any family was greater than its needs, the surplus could be sold. The farm owned two trucks, which hauled its own surplus and that of its members to the local market or even to Moscow.

I asked if the amount of grain required for delivery to the government remained the same each year, or if it varied from year to year. Mr. Bakaikan replied that the government quota is based on the grain acreage of the farm and on probable yields. The authorities, he said, are familiar with the potentialities of the farm, its performance in past years, and with the allocation to the farm of additional machinery, fertilizers and other items that tend to increase yields. The amount of grain to be delivered is assessed on estimated production. The government also sets up a scale of payment in kind for the various operations performed by the local machine tractor station. The amount of these payments depends on the yield obtained by the farm, so that if the farms it services have a good year, the machine tractor station and its personnel also have a good year. As a check on the performance of the machine tractor service, the chairman of the farm and the brigade leader concerned make a joint assessment of the quality of its work, which they report to the director of the machine tractor station and also to the ration agricultural authorities.

Kolos had a brick-making plant, which had just begun production. The bricks were made by hand, with the aid of a wooden form, and the chairman said the capacity per man was five hundred per day. He had high hopes for this little project, which he intended to expand. He also showed me a simple sawmill which was in operation, making shingles at the time. I was very much impressed by the primitive effectiveness of the home-made machine in which billets of birch wood, almost fifteen inches long, were being shaved to shingle thickness by a manually operated cutting blade placed in a pole which was hinged at one end for proper movement, and weighted for ease of motion. The process was quick and ingenious, and it produced shingles of fairly uniform quality. The chairman was proud of it, and I thought he had a right to be. Yet my Foreign Office escort, Mr. Kubyshkin, was apparently embarrassed because a primitive method was being used, and when he saw one of our party taking a photograph of the little machine he brusquely forbade it. Later on, he approached the farm agronome, who was walking with me, took him by the elbow and spoke to him, apparently under the impression that my limited knowledge of Russian made his conversation unintelligible. I understood enough, however, to realize he was telling the agronome that I had asked to see the interior of an average peasant's house, and that I was not to be shown such a house.

Instead, I was taken to the chairman's house for tea. The three-room log building was simple, clean and neat. There was

one bedroom, a larger room for living and eating, and a rather
rudimentary kitchen. The table was spread with the farm's
own black bread, wheat bread, hard-boiled eggs, cucumbers,
honey, currants, milk and tea. The usual vodka was conspicu-
ously absent. We contributed the sandwiches and coffee we
had brought from Spaso House. Our hosts were friendly and
cordial, but their attitude reflected a certain amount of restraint
due to the presence of a uniformed Foreign Office official inside
the house and a covey of plainclothes MVD agents hovering
about outside.

The chairman asked a good many questions about agricultural life in America, and was interested in my explanation of
cooperative buying. He explained that in the Soviet Union
each county had an organization with the unpronounceable
name of Selskokhozaistbennor Snabzhenie, which made bulk
purchases for all collective farms.

After eating, we had a look at the chairman's acre of personal
garden, which I complimented, although personally of the opinion that it didn't touch my own at Spaso House, and then went
to the farm's day nursery.

A separate house, one of the largest in the village, was devoted to the care of small children while their mothers worked
in the fields. More than twenty little people were there under
the watchful eyes of two young women, who received their
"work day" credit for this duty. The children, most of whom
were sleeping, ranged in age from a few months to possibly five
or six years. The noon meal for most of them was prepared in
the nursery kitchen, but four of the smallest, who had not yet
graduated to kasha, were getting their lunches direct from the
natural source and their smiling, unembarrassed young mothers
were obviously well up to the collective's norm in milk production. They return from work as often as necessary during the
day to nurse their babies.

The nursery was bare and unelaborate, but clean and obviously well-managed. I noticed that while the windows were not
screened there were individual net or cheesecloth screens to
keep flies from the faces of the sleeping children.

I left this farm with a good impression of it. True, the whole
establishment would have been laughed at by an American

farmer who would handle more cultivated acreage with two or three men by machine methods, and whose employees would scornfully reject the living conditions which the Soviet collective farmers accept as perfectly normal. But I had come from Moscow, with its food shortage, and these people had enough to eat. They always would have enough to eat, and a roof for shelter, and fuel and warmth, and this is a great deal in the Soviet Union at the present moment. Time was when the farmer could not count on beating starvation. This was during the bitter days when the collective system was being forced on the resisting farmers, many of whom scorched the earth rather than give it up, and when more than two million peasants starved in the Ukraine after the government seized their crops. The peasants, who demanded land during the Revolution, received it. The great estates were divided into small farm plots of a few acres each and given to those who had formerly worked them for landlords. The results were intolerable to the Communist leaders. The individually operated small farms produced small surpluses in good years, enough to feed the factory workers in the cities, but not enough to build up a reserve. In bad years, the surplus production was inadequate to feed the cities, and the farmers hoarded. Gradually the inefficient and improvident among them began to sell or leave their land to more efficient neighbors, and there grew up again a new class of more prosperous farmers who began to employ labor. These, and even their less prosperous neighbors, had all of the independence of men who own their own land, and thus constituted a class of small bourgeoisie in the Communist state. During the early and difficult years of the Soviet state, Lenin tolerated these kulaks as he tolerated private trade in other lines of industry, in order that the state might survive. But as soon as the state was strong enough, liquidation of both classes of "small capitalists" began. The small, independent farmers were destroyed as a class and the small farms were combined with large collectives and state farms. Thus food production was concentrated in large units, which the government could control in order to drain off the surplus to feed the workers of the rapidly expanding Soviet industry.

As of this writing, the food position throughout the Soviet Union as a whole still is precarious. The last three crop years have been good, but this is exceptional in the Soviet Union, which is lucky to get two good crop years out of five. The 250,-000 collective farms, however—the cornerstone of Soviet agriculture—are insurance against positive famine, even if there are several bad years.

Later, I found that the Kolos collective was far above the average. Its percentage of women workers, high though it was, was lower than most collectives. Many of them run as high as eighty and ninety per cent. When John Strohm, the Associate Editor of *Country Gentleman,* was in Moscow, he was told by the Minister of Agriculture, Benidiktov, that by 1960 or 1970, "when things get back to normal," about fifty-five per cent of the farm work would be done by women.

In spite of the machine tractor stations, Soviet agriculture is still primarily a matter of manpower (or womanpower), of hand sowing and hand reaping. It is, as Strohm remarked, "three parts biblical and one part twentieth century." Lenin was fully alive to this fact, and he said on one occasion, "Give us twenty thousand tractors, and we will have socialism."

Granting that this is an over-simplification, the fact remains that heavy industry and agriculture are inter-related in such a way that they pose a difficult problem for the Kremlin. There isn't enough food to go around. It is hard to produce more food without more, much more, modern farm equipment. The workers who produce this farm equipment are underfed and overworked. So production lags.

There is still a good deal of collectivization to be done. In the newly acquired territories, and particularly in the Baltic states, collectivization has only been started. Here the stubborn descendants of a hundred generations of small landholders are putting up a game but losing fight. I talked to two of these while I was in Moscow, and they told similar stories. One, a Lithuanian, had seventeen hectares. He owned one horse, one cow, and her calf. Of course he does not employ help, for that would subject him to the charge of being an exploiter of labor. He gives the government 6,600 pounds of grain, 5,280 pounds of potatoes, 37 pounds of butter, and 170 eggs per year. If he is short of any of these things, he must buy or trade for them with another farmer. He is required to sell all surplus products above the rations allowed for himself and his family to the government at extremely low prices as compared with the open market. He said bitterly that the government paid him 4½ rubles for 2.2 pounds of butter, which was about one-tenth of the market price, and 2.75 rubles for 110 pounds of potatoes, which would cost 50 rubles in Moscow. He expects to get about 80 rubles from the government for his calf, which he will sell to help pay taxes, although the market price of veal in Moscow is about 12½ rubles per pound. Thus he is literally being taxed out of existence.

The other, a Latvian, told almost the same story. This man, who is young, intelligent and independent, farms an area consisting of 11½ hectares of arable land and 4½ hectares of pasture. In this district, collectivization had just begun and was being opposed. This farmer also owned one cow. He was required to sell to the government 176 pounds of meat per year at a price which varies according to the type of meat, but which averages about 17½ kopeks per pound. (On the Moscow market meat averages 17 rubles per pound.) In his own district he can get 10 rubles per pound for beef and 20 rubles per pound for pork. He must also sell to the government 9 pounds of butter and 220 liters of milk per year at correspondingly low prices, and must give up to the government more than 300 pounds of rye and 750 pounds of potatoes, which are paid for at about one-one hundredth of their market value. This farmer pays 600 rubles per year land tax, and he is required to pay a premium of 300 rubles per year for insurance on his home and barn.

I asked him how the government justified the demand on his one cow for milk, butter and fresh meat at the same time. He laughed and said that the government did not explain these things. He and his neighbors, who were trying to hold onto their land, had pooled their resources for these contributions in kind—in other words, two farmers might each contribute a calf or a hog to make the meat contribution for themselves and two of their neighbors. The two neighbors would provide the milk and butter for all four.

He must have known his struggle was hopeless. If he and his neighbors do not succumb, the tax will be increased and the prices paid by the government for their forced contributions will be lowered until they go under and either join a collective farm or work for the state.

I saw a perfect example of state tactics on the agricultural front shortly before I left Moscow. The press announced that the Council of Ministers of the Moldavian Soviet Socialist Republic (in which there still are some independent farmers) had issued a decree requiring the compulsory delivery of potatoes to the state during 1948. This decree established a quota of two kilos per hectare of land for collective farms, but it required from each *individual* peasant homestead the following:

15	kilos	per	hectare	from	farms	of	1	to	5	hectares
20	"	"	"	"	"	"		5.1 to 10		"
25	"	"	"	"	"	"		10.5 to 15		"
30	"	"	"	"	"	"		over 15		"

These amounts must be delivered regardless of whether potatoes are grown, and if they are not, the farmer must buy them at the high prevailing open market price and sell them back to the state at the low fixed price for quota deliveries.

Under Stalinism, the doom of the independent farmer is sealed. From the beginning of forced collectivization in the Ukraine to the present date, this has been so unmistakably evident that it cannot be questioned. And since the farmer is essentially an individualist and a landowner, it has been amazing to me that Communist parties have grown in strength in the agricultural areas of Western Europe.

Apparently, like everyone else, the farmer only learns the hard way. He overlooks the example, already given in such full measure, that it is impossible for a Communist state to permit the existence of a large number of "small capitalists," and that no matter what promises are made to the contrary, agriculture must ultimately and inevitably be collectivized and brought under the complete control of the state. The farmers of Western Europe particularly have been influenced by young intellectuals and by actual Communists who penetrate farmers' associations, especially in countries where a non-Communist government, through stern necessity, has been forced to take unpopular measures.

When M. Thorez, the French Communist leader, was visiting Moscow, I stood near his elbow as he was discussing the

Communist situation in France with a group of his Soviet colleagues. He said that while Communist publications had gained increasing circulation among French farmers, they (the farmers) were conservative in their response and that the Communist gain in voting strength among them had been slower than expected. One of his Soviet listeners, a true Old Bolshevik in appearance, remarked impatiently, "Treat them like the kulaks."

The Communist has never trusted the peasant, and last year, even the collectives felt the pruning shears with the revision, on July 14, of the Law of Agricultural Taxation. The new decree, as published in *Pravda* and *Izvestia,* begins with the statement that "In view of the increased income of collective farmers from industrial supplementary sources such as household gardens, cattle and non-agricultural products, the rate of the agricultural tax is increased as of 1 July." The act then goes on to provide for increases of from thirty to thirty-seven per cent; requires that aged persons, who had previously been exempt from taxation, must now pay fifty per cent of the computed tax; and revokes the fifteen per cent reduction previously allowed for dependents. It provides, however, that income either in money or in kind from collective farm "work days" is not subject to this tax. Obviously, too many collective farmers had discovered that with the high price of food on the "open market" they could make more money by devoting more time to their individual acre gardens than from "work days" spent on the collective. The government therefore decided to eliminate this "remnant of capitalism."

However, regardless of its effect on the individual, the drive to eliminate the independent farmer and centralize agriculture under complete state control has produced satisfactory results from the government's point of view. Crop production has been largely restored to its pre-war level as the result of constantly increasing mechanization, and production continues to go up in spite of the fact that now, for the first time in history, slightly less than half of the Soviet population depends on agriculture for a livelihood.

This does not mean that the utilization of the farm population is as yet by any means as efficient as in some industrially advanced countries. But Soviet farm methods are progressing.

Trade agreements concluded during the past two years by the Kremlin have included the export of limited quantities of wheat and coarse grains to Great Britain and Belgium, as well as to the various satellite states, and the supply of foodstuffs in the Soviet market was greatly increased during 1948, although food is still far from plentiful. The fact that the Kremlin was willing and able to export grain under conditions of shortage and high prices at home is very significant.

I have often been asked, since my return to the United States, whether, given time for development, Soviet industry may become one of our great competitors for world markets, especially in the undeveloped areas of the Middle East and Far East. It is difficult to make predictions about a dictatorship and its probable course of action in a fluid situation.

Answering this question from the viewpoint of one accustomed to an economic system under which domestic demands must be met before exports can be made, it would be natural to say that the Soviet Government is so far from filling the needs of its own population that it could hardly be considered seriously as a potential rival in the markets of the world. Answering the query from the standpoint of a businessman who must show a return on his investment, it would be logical to reply that Soviet industry is at present so inefficient and so wasteful of both manpower and labor that it could never compete on a cost basis with the efficient mass production methods of the United States.

But the fact which should never be forgotten is that the Soviet Government is neither democratic nor capitalistic. It can, if necessary, disregard for considerable periods of time the unfulfilled desires of its own regimented people, and it need not concern itself with costs as opposed to selling prices if political considerations are involved.

If Communist Party strategy so dictated, the Soviet Government might indeed become a competitor of the West in areas where the inauguration of substantial trade promises high political and ideological dividends. In such a case, it need not worry about costs—who could call it to account if it sold a $3,000 automobile for $1,000, or if it withheld textiles from its home market and exported them at less than cost in order to exploit through foreign trade a promising political situation? This is certainly possible, but I think it is very unlikely for some time to come. Heavy industrial development is considered by the Politburo to be of such vital importance that nothing short of a major crisis could cause a revision in present plans, or divert facilities to the production of merchandise for export, except on a very limited scale, and then only when exports would result in a direct material or political benefit to the Soviet economy, as for instance the recent export of tractors to the Balkans. When the projected series of three five-year plans has attained its objectives, more attention can be given to raising the standards of living of the Soviet people and improving the products of Soviet light industry. Meanwhile, the Russian consumer will continue to echo the sentiments of a ruefully critical article published late in 1948 in Moscow *Bolshevik* under the heading "A Heart-to-Heart Talk":

"Recently after a long time I again met Ivan Ivanich Khrompromdrevshvein. His face was sour, sad and he looked hurt. In answer to my question he only waved his hand:

" 'What's the good of talking about it! The buyer is not the same as he used to be—that's all there is to it. You can't do business with him!'

" 'And what is there about him, Ivan Ivanich, that you don't like?' I dared to be inquisitive. And received the categorical reply:

" 'Caprices! Well, the artel, The Moscow Chemical Combine, has accumulated at least 2,000,000 roubles' worth of shoe polish, but the customer, whatever happens—he won't buy it! Surely that's monstrous?'

"I tried to object moderately: 'But this shoe polish, they say it's rubbish?'

" 'But the tin's got a picture on it!'

" 'They say your boots become still more muddy when it's used?'

" 'But you can get as much as you want! There's no restriction on it!'

"Thus we parted, without either of us having succeeded in convincing the other. Where he went, I don't know. But I went to the artel, Children's Toys. I went in, looked around, and asked: 'Perhaps an undertaker's office has moved in here now?'

" 'No,' they said, 'everything's the same as before. We're making toys.'

" 'Well, why are you looking so miserable?'

" 'Because of these skipping ropes. We made 150,000 of these ropes, but the girls won't buy them.'

" 'And they have not been buying them long?'

" 'From the very beginning. They say they don't like them.'

" 'Then you should have given them up at the very beginning! You ought to make what the girls like.'

"Please make what the consumer needs. Make it conscientiously. Take an interest in the demand, and don't ignore critical opinions. And you will see that it is all for the general good.

"I give you my word, you can do business with us."

VIII

WAR OF WORDS

I had a good deal last winter to try my patience, for this Government possess in an exquisite degree the art of worrying a foreign representative, without giving him even the consolation of an insult. I was apprehensive for some time that there would be a breach of diplomatic intercourse. But the occasion that gave rise to this suspicion having passed off, nothing remains of a tangible nature to excite any disquietude.

—Excerpt from a dispatch of the American Minister to Russia, Neill S. Brown, dated St. Petersburg, May 27, 1852

NOT very many people have had the dubious distinction of being used to start a "peace offensive" in the middle of a "cold war," with the Soviet Foreign Office mobilizing all its resources in a full-scale propaganda campaign designed to disrupt the diplomatic unity of the West.

Although this particular Soviet venture failed, the incident remains important because it taught all of us, the hard way, that the men in the Kremlin had carried over into peace the tactics of breaking confidence, of indulging in practices of deception, falsification and evasion which we had always hitherto associated only with relations between enemy states in time of shooting war. For us, it was the clinching evidence that propaganda as employed by the Soviet Union was a full-scale aggressive device which shifts its emphasis with the greatest flexibility from one to another of the political and psychological fronts in the struggle for men's minds now being waged around the globe by the great powers.

The occasion was the now well known, but supposed-to-be-confidential series of talks which I had with V. M. Molotov, then Soviet Foreign Minister, in May of 1948. I had sought an interview with Mr. Molotov, on instructions from the State Department, to emphasize to the Soviet leaders the firmness and continuity of the bipartisan foreign policy of the United States Government and its intention to contain further Communist expansion by aggression, lest they be led astray by the sound and fury of American campaign oratory. This was at a time when at least a three-way race for the Presidency was assured in the 1948 elections, with Henry A. Wallace bidding for the pacifist vote in a Communist-supported attack upon the leaders of both the Democratic and Republican parties, whom he accused of courting war by being "too tough" with Russia. Neither the Republicans nor the Democrats had picked their candidates yet, and many men of varying opinions on domestic and foreign issues sought preferment. As the campaign developed, it was certain, regardless of the general agreement of an overwhelming majority of the American people on the fundamentals of foreign policy, that the conduct of international affairs would be debated; certain policies which the Administration had adopted and acted upon, and other proposals which it had rejected would be challenged and discussed. The men in the Kremlin are isolated and, because their own elections are rigged, cut-and-dried affairs, have no real conception of the interplay of opposing forces in a free election such as America holds every four years. We did not want them to get the idea that America was divided on basic issues or that its people were so concerned with domestic politics that they had relaxed their vigilance toward the tension spots of the international scene. We also did not want them to accept too blindly their own Marxist propaganda that an economic collapse was so inevitable in the United States that its strength as a world power could be discounted. The Soviet authorities had mistakenly attributed to Mr. Wallace far greater strength and significance than his campaign deserved. As a result, pressure on the Iranian and Turkish frontiers, and Communist support for the Greek guerrilla movement, had greatly increased.

These were the considerations which were in the minds of the President and the Secretary of State when I was instructed to call upon Mr. Molotov and to differentiate for him—and through him for the Politburo—the distinction between campaign speeches and statements, and the definite, firm, bipartisan character of the foreign policy of the United States, which had not and would not be changed however the election resulted. I was carefully prepared for this interview, and the State Department approved in advance the notes from which I made my principal statement of American policy.

My first meeting with Mr. Molotov, in this series, took place on May 4. I told him that I had been instructed to communicate to him informally, frankly and confidentially the position of my government. Our talk was courteous but grave. We discussed for several minutes the value of such informal and confidential communications in establishing a mutual understanding, as compared with the more formal conferences where publicity was unavoidable. There was no misunderstanding whatever of the confidential nature of this communication between an Ambassador and a Foreign Minister.

I then read from notes the following declaration, which has been published before, but which remains important today because it still represents the basic policy of the American Government:

"Two years ago, during my initial conversation with Generalissimo Stalin and yourself, I stated as clearly as possible my estimate of the inevitable reaction of the American people to the continuance of a policy by the Soviet Government which would appear to have as its purpose the progressive extension of the area of Soviet power. At that time I pointed out that it would be a grave misinterpretation of the fundamentally pacific character of the American people to believe that they would not react strongly and vigorously to the progressive domination by one country of its neighbors and the clear threat to the world community which such actions would imply.

"I emphasized at that time that the United States had no desire whatever to see the world divided into two major groupings, nor to divert a large part of its income to the maintenance of a military establishment which such a world situation would necessitate in elementary self-defense. It seemed apparent then that such a line of policy as that described would lead inevitably to a crystallization of the non-Soviet areas of the world, whose people would quite understandably feel themselves progressively threatened by such developments. It seemed also inevitable in such a case that the United States, as the strongest nation in this community, would be forced to take a leading part in this movement and to divert a large portion of its energy, which by preference our people would prefer to utilize for assistance in the reconstruction of the ravages of the war, to the maintenance of a military establishment adequate to meet the developing world situation.

"Unhappily, the apprehensions I felt at that time have been realized.

"Since that date, Soviet policies in Eastern Europe have produced the reaction which was predicted. The situation which has resulted is obviously one of great seriousness.

"The European community and the United States have become alarmed at the implications of Soviet policy, and are drawing closer together in mutual self-protection, but only in self-protection.

"It is for this reason that my government desires me to outline to you with complete clarity and frankness the position of the United States Government.

"There should be no mistake about the determination of the United States to play its part in these cooperative movements for recovery and self-defense. The concern and the determination of the people of the United States have been intensified by the inexplicable hostility of the Soviet Government to the European Recovery Program—a measure which in its inception and subsequent development is so obviously only a measure of American assistance for reconstruction on a cooperative basis without menace or threat to anyone.

"The tense situation which now prevails has been produced by the policies of the Soviet Government or by the actions of political groups apparently under its control, and there has followed a natural and inevitable reaction on the part of other countries, including the United States.

"My government has no idea what conclusions the Soviet Government has reached concerning the present attitude of the United States. It has noted that the picture of this attitude given by the Soviet press is dangerously distorted and erroneous. Whether, or in what degree, the members of the Soviet Government themselves believe this distorted version, my government has no means of estimating. For this reason I wish to make plain certain points on which my government considers it ex-

The kitchen at Spaso House. Hungarian, Russian, Czech and Polish are the four nationalities represented.

Dinner at the Greek Embassy showing Ambassador Smith, Secretary of State Marshall and Mrs. Smith.

tremely important that there be no misunderstanding at this time.

"1. The policies of the United States Government in international questions have been made amply clear in recent months and weeks. They have the support of the overwhelming majority of the American people. They will continue to be vigorously and firmly prosecuted.

"It would be a grave error if others were to assume that domestic considerations, such as the forthcoming elections, would in any way weaken the determination of the United States to support what it believes to be right. The American people have always known how to separate domestic and foreign policy at the proper moment.

"Similarly, my government is aware that Communist organizations here and there have been disseminating propaganda to the effect that a forthcoming economic crisis in the United States will soon produce a radical change in American policies. It is hoped that no one will be so foolish as to forfeit the chances of progress toward world stability for the sake of an economic prognostication which has been proven wrong time and time again. Even those who persist in believing such a prognostication must, at the very least, realize that an economic crisis would not affect in any way our basic productive capacity nor our concept of the basic factors underlying our foreign policy.

"It must be emphasized that the present state of world affairs involves issues which the people of the United States consider to be vital to United States national security and to world peace. No one should deceive himself as to the seriousness of United States policy with respect to these issues.

"2. On the other hand, my government wishes to make it unmistakably clear that the United States has no hostile or aggressive designs whatever with respect to the Soviet Union. Assertions to the contrary are falsehoods which can result only from complete misunderstanding or malicious motives. United States policies have been so devised that they cannot possibly affect adversely the interests of a Soviet Union which seeks to live at peace with its neighbors and to refrain from attempts to exercise undue influence, directly or indirectly, in their affairs.

"In fact, many of the elements of United States foreign

policy to which the Soviet press takes such strong exception today would never have come into existence if it had not been
necessary for the United States to aid other countries to defend
their own political integrity from attempts, on the part of
Communist minorities, to seize power and to establish regimes
subservient to foreign interests. Should these attempts cease,
the necessity for some of the manifestations of United States
foreign policy, which are apparently unwelcome in Moscow,
would cease with them.

"The present state of United States-Soviet relations is a
source of grievous disappointment to the American people and
to the United States Government. As far as we are concerned,
it represents a painful and undesired alternative toward which
we have been driven, step by step, by the pressure of Soviet and
world Communist policy. We still do not despair by any means
of a turn of events which will permit us to find the road to a
decent and reasonable relationship between our two countries,
with a fundamental relaxation of those tensions which today
exercise so unhappy an influence on international society everywhere. As far as the United States is concerned, the door is
always wide open for full discussion and the composing of our
differences.

"My government earnestly hopes that the members of the
Soviet Government will not take lightly the position of the
United States Government as here expressed. They have it in
their power to alleviate many of the situations which today
weigh so heavily on all international life. It is our earnest hope
that they will take advantage of these possibilities. If they do,
they will not find us lacking in readiness and eagerness to
make our own contribution to a stabilization of world conditions entirely compatible with the security of the Soviet
peoples."

When I had concluded, Mr. Molotov, as we had anticipated
he would, immediately moved to the counter-attack, blaming
the United States, instead of the Soviet Union, for the worsening of relations between the two Allies since the termination of
shooting hostilities between the Axis powers, but said the new
statement of American policy would be carefully considered by
the Soviet Government—meaning the Politburo—without
whose authorization he could not speak. I told him that if it

would be of any assistance to him and the Soviet Government I would be glad to provide him, informally, with a copy of the notes from which I had spoken. He accepted, and a copy was sent to the Foreign Office as soon as I had returned to the Embassy on Mokhovaya Ulitsa, just across the street from the north wall of the Kremlin.

Five days later, the Soviet Foreign Office telephoned and said that Mr. Molotov would receive me to give his government's answer to my statement. When I reached his office, Mr. Molotov, grave and unsmiling, began, as I had done before, to read from notes the statement of his government.

He said, first of all, that the Soviet Government "shared the desire expressed by the government of the United States of America to better these [Soviet-American] relations," and would agree to the American proposal that the two governments should begin "a discussion and settlement of the differences existing between us."

That was the only harmonious note in the long statement that followed, and that single note of harmony was based upon a misinterpretation, unconscious or deliberate, that we were willing to discuss with the Soviet Union alone and without the participation of France, England, China and the other great powers the issues of transcendant world importance which I had stated to Mr. Molotov earlier were the causes of worsening relations between his country and mine.

In any event, it became clear as Mr. Molotov proceeded that the leaders of the Soviet Government had missed or deliberately ignored the principal points I had sought to make—that the American public was overwhelmingly united in support of a bipartisan foreign policy of containing aggressive Communist expansion and would not change nor relax its vigilance, whatever might be the superficial indications of a heated domestic election campaign.

The remainder of Mr. Molotov's statement was and is so familiar from its constant repetition that it need not be reproduced textually here. It was devoted entirely to the theme that Russia is always right, the United States is always wrong; that Russia was blameless for international tensions, and the United States must bear all the blame for division and discord between the wartime Allies; that Russia never interfered with the sovereignty of its neighbors, that the United States extended its interference in the internal affairs of other states from its own continent to Europe; that the American Government was building up bases and forming or sponsoring military alliances directed against the Soviet Union; and that, while Russia lived up to its trade agreements with the United States, my country discriminated against the Soviet Union in the shipment of essential goods, already contracted and paid for, as part of a policy basically unfriendly to his government.

When Mr. Molotov had concluded, I made the following brief reply:

With regard to remarks about "development of United States bases, our policy of encirclement and our war-like threats," I had only to say that our entire history was refutation of any suspicion of a policy which involved aggressive war. As I stated during our previous conversation, the drawing together of the Western European countries and the support which was being given them by the United States was a direct reflection of the apprehensions and fears which had been aroused by the expansionist policy of the Union of Soviet Socialist Republics, and that while I had no right to disbelieve his statement, I could not refrain from paraphrasing Mr. Vishinsky's comment that facts spoke for themselves.

The United States was secure in its honesty of purpose with regard to ERP. Our people were, as stated previously, completely unable to understand implications placed on that program by the Union of Soviet Socialist Republics. The United States appreciates and fully understands the desire and indeed the necessity of close and friendly relations between the Union of Soviet Socialist Republics and its neighbors, but that here again facts spoke for themselves, and I was fully familiar with events which followed the acceptance by Czechoslovakia of the invitation to the ERP conference in Paris and subsequent reversal of this acceptance during the immediately following visit of Mazaryk and Gottwald to Moscow. A country like my own which permitted complete freedom of political thought and expression did not oppose communism because of its Marxian ideology, but purely and simply because we had seen repeated instances of Communist minorities coming into power by illegal means and against the will of the majority of the population in the countries referred to. The United States remained convinced that these minority coups d'état would have been quite impossible without the moral and physical support of the Union of Soviet Socialist Republics.

With respect to trade agreements, there was nothing the United States would like better under conditions of reasonable and honest understanding than to participate in expanding trade with the Union of Soviet Socialist Republics and to contribute to the economic recovery of the Soviet states, which had suffered during the war. If proof were desired of our previous feelings in this respect, it could be found in fact that under Lend-Lease we had shipped to the Union of Soviet Socialist Republics enormous values in basic industrial plants which when shipped obviously would not be in production in time to contribute to the war effort. Our change in views with regard to trade was again a direct reflection of the Soviet expansionist policies referred to in my previous conversation.

I did not wish to indulge in a contest of words which might be interpreted as the "pot calling the kettle black," but I had recently reviewed some of our past agreements with the Union of Soviet Socialist Republics, particularly the Roosevelt-Litvinov agreement, and that I would remind him of what I am sure he already knows, i.e., that the only provision of this agreement which had not been violated by the Union of Soviet Socialist Republics was that permitting the presence of an American clergyman in Moscow.

However, these were matters which it would be profitless for us to pursue to the exclusion of the major issues. I had, I believed, made completely clear the policies of the United States and the reasons which prompted the adoption of these policies. I appreciated Mr. Molotov's statement of the policies of his government, which I would communicate at once to Washington.

The interview then terminated, and, so far as I was concerned, there still was no question of the confidential character of the conversation between us. It had not been the purpose of the American Government to seek or to conduct bilateral negotiations with the Soviet Government on these major problems, and the best proof that this was so is that my long-standing plans for a fishing vacation in Normandy, to begin the day after my second conversation with Mr. Molotov, remained unchanged by the nature of his answer, which had been passed along by me to the State Department in Washington.

Early the next morning, I left in the Embassy airplane for France, via Berlin, and no sooner were we in the air than I heard Radio Moscow broadcasting the text of Mr. Molotov's reply alone, without any reference to the substance of my statement of the American position. I was surprised and ashamed, because there had been in the Department of State some who, when the original proposition of stating the American position frankly and confidentially was first considered, had anticipated the possibility that the Soviet Government might violate diplomatic confidence in order to seize the opportunity to renew its propaganda "peace offensive." My opinion had been asked, and I had replied that in matters of this kind the Soviet Government always had been meticulously correct, had never to my knowledge violated diplomatic confidence, and that there was, therefore, no reason to think that it would do so in this instance.

But as the airplane roared toward Berlin, I knew that I had gravely underestimated the ruthlessness of Soviet propaganda, and I could foresee the confusion and uncertainty which this misinterpretation of the American approach would cause in all the capitals of Europe, and the furor among the American electorate over such a development.

As it turned out, Secretary Marshall was ready to move swiftly with a statement that we had "no intention of entering into bilateral negotiations with the Soviet Government on matters relating to the interests of other governments" and that we expected from the Russians deeds, not words, to prove their devotion to world peace and the settlement of acute current problems.

The Soviet Government thus achieved, at best, only a temporary propaganda triumph, but it did so by such highly unscrupulous methods that the world in general learned another lesson about the impossibility of attempting to deal with the Russians as we do with other members of the world community.

I have dealt at length with this incident because I think it illustrates the totality of the Soviet propaganda approach, and that propaganda for them is a major instrument of internal and external policy of the government, surpassing in technique and volume the expert efforts of Dr. Goebbels and the Nazi Ministry of Propaganda.

Soviet propagandists are versatile and flexible. They draw on the experience of half a century of revolutionary practice. They mastered, long before the Nazi did, the tricks of deception and confusion. At any time they can change their level of appeal, change sides, or contradict a previous campaign. In the European satellite countries, they now are using every device to suppress national patriotism and subordinate it to the emotional ties with the Soviet Union. At the same time in Indonesia and in other colonial areas, nationalism is heavily emphasized, and, in the sessions of the United Nations and in every other international conference, the Soviet delegations stress their support of national sovereignity. That this is completely inconsistent with the Soviet position that Marshal Tito of Yugoslavia is an enemy and must be removed by the people of his country bothers them not at all.

The foreign policy of the Soviet Union and the aims of international communism have become so closely related that they are indistinguishable one from the other. International communism has its homeland in the Soviet Union, and operates with the resources of the Soviet State. The financial and moral resources are always available, and, where geography permits and Western vigilance does not prevent, the physical authority of the Soviet Government also is brought to bear as a fact or a threat.

As a result, there has been a blending of the Lenin-Stalin interpretation of the theories of Karl Marx with the centuries-old Russian imperialism to produce the hybrid doctrine the world now knows as "Stalinism," since it certainly is not communism as Marx visualized it.

For an American to appreciate the volume and effect of Soviet propaganda, it is necessary for him to remember that the government owns and controls *all* media of information—newspapers, books, magazines, radio, ballet, theaters, motion pictures, and, just recently, television, since video broadcasts were started last January in Moscow and Leningrad, and television sets can be purchased in both cities. The government uses these media without limitation to create and change public opinion, both at home and abroad, and to these have been added, since the war, all media of information in the satellite countries.

Communist parties outside the Soviet Union are considered by the Kremlin to be the first line of attack against all other political philosophies, but more than this is demanded.

"Support of the Soviet Union is one of the chief tasks of all Communists," said Stalin in 1925.

Non-Soviet Communists have responded loyally. Fajon, speaking for the French General Confederation of Labor, said to the Cominform in 1947: "We promise to defend with all our strength the Soviet Union."

At the same time, Louis Saillant, the French General Secretary of the World Federation of Trade Unions, said: "I am more than ever convinced that it is more and more necessary to understand, love, and defend the Soviet Union." Bitossi, representing the Italian General Confederation of Labor, pledged "the forces of Italian Democracy to render determined opposition to the provocators of a new war, who are conducting an unbridled campaign against the Soviet Union." And the leaders of the American Communist Party declared their members would not fight on the side of the United States in any war against the Soviet Union.

During the Paris Peace Conference in 1946, I lunched alone one day with Dr. Vladimir Clementis, at that time the Communist Deputy Foreign Minister of Czechoslovakia, who wanted to discuss with me why the United States should modify its position on the withdrawal of a credit previously granted to Czechoslovakia.

I spoke of "Comintern" activities, to which he replied that "the Comintern has been disbanded."

"After all," I said, "it is not necessary to use fictions when we are alone together. You know as well as I do that the Communist parties outside the Soviet Union get direction and support from the Kremlin."

Dr. Clementis asserted that the U.S. Communist Party did not receive either support or direction from the Kremlin.

"Would you be willing to say the same at this time about the French Communist Party?" I asked.

When he looked at me, without answering, I declared that "the real fact is that the Politburo, which carries on the mission of the Comintern, gives support and direction to Communist parties outside the Soviet Union as the international situation and the policies of the Kremlin indicate as desirable."

This, then, is the vast propaganda machine available to the Soviet Union directly—and which receives a powerful assist from fellow-travelers throughout the world—and which, since the spring of 1946, has made the United States and Great Britain, in particular, and Western civilization in general, the object of a campaign which in viciousness and intensity is without any parallel in time of peace. As directed against the United States, this campaign has grown in intensity until today it has reached the state where we are depicted as the virtual heirs of what the Soviet propagandist calls "the maddened, rapacious Fascist beast."

This is a matter of grave concern to every American. We are not so much worried because the Soviet attitude is grossly unfair and unjust in its deliberate misinterpretation and falsification of United States motives, its deprecation of our contribution to the war effort and to post-war rehabilitation, its disdain for American democratic institutions, ridicule of the American press, contempt for American cultural and scientific attainments and denunciation of our leaders, both in the Administration and in Congress.

We don't like this, of course, but it is not the falsehoods and infamies which alarm us. We know that our way of life does not suffer by comparison with that of any other nation in the world, if comparison were permitted. We are alarmed because the Soviet propaganda line has been devoted to international obstruction and intimidation, and because it is fraught with danger. The United States is pictured, on the one hand, as a reactionary monopolist, imperialist nation, bent on the establishment of world domination, and on the other as decadent, strife-ridden and incapable of real strength, no matter what the emergency. Our economic system is depicted as breaking down, with unemployment mounting rapidly, industrial strife growing to the point of open warfare, the wealthy becoming wealth-

ier and the masses impoverished and enslaved. The President
and the leaders of Congress in both foreign and domestic policy are said to represent only reactionary monopolists and to be
without the support of the people, who are pictured as ruthlessly exploited, frightened at the aspects of the future, and
yearning for the "democracy" of the Soviet Union as their ultimate hope.

The circumstance which makes especially dangerous this
propaganda picture of a United States Government with vicious
designs but without the strength necessary to carry out those
designs in the face of staunch opposition is the fact that it is a
possibility that, just as the uninformed masses of the Soviet
Union are deluded by it, the small group of policy-makers
themselves seem, at times, to be hypnotized by it, and to become
drunk with the liquor of their own brewing. It is a very strong
drink.

At the end of the first month of the 1948 session of the
United Nations General Assembly, the newspaper *Izvestia*,
which even Mr. Molotov acknowledged to me on one occasion
to be the official mouthpiece of the Soviet Government, published under the headline "Struggle for Peace" this account of
the progress of the session:

> Representatives of the U.S.A., Britain, France, Canada, Aus-
> tralia and others seized the weapons of slander and malice
> against the warriors for peace. It is naïve to think that Mar-
> shall, Bevin, Schuman, or even the excessively zealous McNeil
> or Shawcross, would openly defend the preparations for the
> new aggression. They attack the principle of unanimity in or-
> der to isolate the Soviet Union and other countries of the
> people's democracy, to turn the United Nations into an obe-
> dient tool of the American aggressors. They talk expansively
> about the rights of man, to mark their horrifying arbitrariness
> and their narrowly egotistical aims. They devised scores of cun-
> ning maneuvers and set in motion machinery voting.
>
> But the voice of the Land of the Soviets is heard everywhere.
> To all these wiles and maneuvers the Soviet delegation has
> opposed concrete and clear proposals for the prohibition of
> atomic weapons, reduction of armaments and the establishment
> of international control over these activities within the scope
> of the Security Council.
>
> By closing one's eyes and listening to the speeches of the

Anglo-American orators, one might think that there had been
no Nuremberg trials, that Ribbentrop had not been hanged
and Goebbels had not committed suicide. One would think
that, having altered their appearance and their passports, they
were again preparing to attack peaceable countries, and were
defending the right of atomic bomb production and a mad
armaments race.

Together with the Soviet Union, life itself unmasks the warmongers. While the Anglo-Americans attempt to deceive public opinion with empty general phrases about love of peace,
their papers report a new armaments race, new military taxes,
new U.S. military bases in the Pacific and Greenland, and the
equipment of twenty-five tank divisions by Americans for the
Western Military Bloc.

The Brazilian delegate asserts that man is made in the image
of God, but opposes concrete Soviet proposals to obviate death
from starvation and to abolish the death penalty.

The United States wants to command the world. Her representatives emphasize that America is superior in everything.
While forcing their will roughly on other states, the representatives of the U.S.A. try to represent their country as the noble
protectress of small nations or as the savior of Europe from the
"red menace."

It is an extremely interesting spectacle. The chairman calls
for voting, and scores of obedient eyes are turned toward the
American delegation. An American slowly raises his hand, and
the hands of the representatives of Cuba, Australia, Brazil,
Belgium, Turkey, Greece and the other countries dependent
on the United States are raised like shadows. Others vote with
their legs, not having the courage to raise their hands against
the unjust demands of their American masters.

Whatever the result of the voting, the first month of the
General Assembly has signalized a moral victory for the
U.S.S.R. The peoples of all countries have seen who is defending the cause of peace and security and who is kindling
the campfires of war.

This is a very mild statement by comparison with the attacks
which appear daily in the Soviet press and are broadcast constantly over the Soviet radio network. The wealth of vituper-
ative adjectives which the Soviet propagandist has at his
command is simply amazing. In one brief article in the *Vchi-
telskaya Gazette* I made note that American and British "bour-

geois morality" was referred to as "cannibalistic," "treacherous," "cruel," "deceitful," "inhuman," "bestial," "hypocritical," "venal," "false," "nourished by vice" and "formed under the influence of evil passions."

We have become so habituated, during a relatively few years, to the violent character of Communist invective that we are in this respect like the farmer's dog, described by Vice President Barkley, which became so accustomed to having tin cans tied to its tail that whenever it saw a can it backed up to it. Thus we are prone to overlook two important facts.

The first of these is that Soviet propaganda invariably accuses other states violently for allegedly doing those things which the Soviet Union itself is doing, or which it intends to do in the future.

The second is that the Soviet Union has, in its international relations, carried over into peace the propaganda tactics of deception, falsification and evasion which we have always hitherto associated only with war. Millions of Americans have wondered why. The answer can be found by evaluating Soviet propaganda in terms of what we know to be the major objectives of the international strategy of the Soviet Union. This is, in the words of Stalin himself, "to consolidate the dictatorship of the proletariat in one country, using it as the base for the overthrow of imperialism in all countries."

A remarkable characteristic of Soviet propaganda has been its appropriation and perversion of words and phrases which express the highest ideals of Western democracy. "Democracy" is an example. It is applied by Soviet statesmen and propagandists to political regimes which to us are in every way the complete antithesis of democracy. "Liberty" and "freedom" are employed in the same way. So is "national sovereignty," a slogan on which the Soviet Union has based its blockade in the United Nations against any effective cooperative action for the international control of atomic energy.

In Moscow, our greatest concern was not with the foreign propaganda offensive of the Kremlin, but with its efforts within the Soviet Union. These were devoted largely to destroying the reservoir of good will for the United States that was created in the Soviet Union during the war, and the long-standing admiration felt by the Russian people for American industrial and scientific progress. Press and radio were reinforced by the theater. Even the clowns in the Moscow Circus gave at least one anti-American skit at every performance after an article in *Pravda* castigated them for their "apolitical attitude." The anti-American play, *The Russian Question,* was produced in five hundred theaters throughout the Soviet Union. It was followed by others in the same vein but progressively stronger. One of the most recent, *Zakon Chesti,* (*The Court of Honor*), honored us by featuring our Russian-language magazine, *Amerika.*

This play deals with two Russian scientists who have prepared a new medicine. They believe there should be free exchange of scientific knowledge between countries; consequently, their article on the new preparation is published first in an American magazine. A Red Army General, while leafing through a copy of the magazine, *Amerika,* in the office of these scientists, notices an article with the heading, "States Have Boundaries—Science Has None." The article describes the work of the two Russians and mentions the fact that their article was published in an American magazine. The General, infuriated at such disloyalty, decides to investigate the case. Several American scientists appear in the laboratory for an interview with the Russians. Their objective is to learn the formula for the medicine, sell it to an American company, and thus earn a large sum of money. Although the Russians give them permission to watch the manufacture of the preparation, the laboratory assistant breaks the machine in order to keep the process secret. A party man arrives and says the Soviets are also interested in learning the formula for a new medicine these Americans have discovered; therefore, he requests them to exchange information. The American throws up his hands and says that unfortunately he has sold his formula to an American firm, and they own the complete rights to it. Thus he cannot give the information. (This scene was particularly enjoyed by the audience.) It finally develops that one of the American scientists is a spy for the U.S. Army. The case of the disloyalty of the Russians is brought before Stalin, who orders the Russians to be tried before the Court of Honor. The result is that the one recants; the other does not, and in the future he is to be refused admission to the laboratory. The curtain falls with the former saying that henceforth his scientific findings in the field of medicine will be published in the Soviet Union, and used to heal the Soviet people first.

Children's magazines, especially, gave much space to anti-American features. I condensed the following article from the August 12, 1947, issue of the children's paper, *Pionerskaya Pravda*, because, though very restrained by comparison with others of a similar nature, it was such a perfect example of the "little steps for little feet" by which the children of the Soviet Union are taught to hate and fear the United States:

The United States of America is the richest capitalist country. She profited particularly at the time of the two world wars: 1914-1918 and 1939-1945. These wars laid waste almost all the countries of the world, carried off millions of human beings, resulted in enormous destruction. But they did not touch America. To the United States fell the remunerative role of supplier of weapons and other goods to the belligerent armies. Production in the U.S.A. expanded, the profits of the capitalists doubled, many countries incurred debts of hundreds of millions of dollars to America.

In the second World War the U.S.A. lost on the fronts no more people than ordinarily are killed in America . . . in automobile accidents. America came out of the war with a large army, with an industry which had not suffered but which on the contrary had expanded.

After the war the heads of many American politicians simply swam with a sense of the U.S.A.'s power. In America there are many people—including prominent Secretaries, Senators, Generals and Admirals—who consider that now the United States is world master and can dictate its will to other states. Whoever doesn't want to submit can be compelled to submission by force, by the atom bomb.

However, the American people itself has not been made happier as a result of this situation. Strange though it may seem, people in America now are living at a lower, poorer level than they lived before. Surprisingly, in the United States production has increased but the workers receive less than before the war!

A Soviet man, living in conditions of socialism, knows that the more our whole country produces, the better the people live. In proportion to the reconstruction and expansion of our industry and agriculture, the more goods will each of our families receive. With every year, with every month, we will now live richer, better lives.

It is not so in America. Capitalism exists there. Moreover, it is the very last stage of capitalism, namely, imperialism. All the plants and factories there belong to a very small group of millionaire monopolists. One such monopolist owns all automobile factories, another all textile factories, a third is complete owner of the footwear industry. They do not even have competitors.

The whole wealth of the U.S.A. belongs to fifty to sixty families of millionaires. They gain new billions. In 1946 they raised all prices on an average of forty per cent. But wages did not increase. Industry is working at full capacity, but there isn't a market for all the goods because the population doesn't have enough money. With the piling up of merchandise, the owners have begun to close plants and factories, to discharge workers and employees. Millions of unemployed are appearing, and in consequence of this the purchasing power is falling still lower. A crisis means poverty and hunger for the national masses, a lowering of production, the ruin of workers, farmers, employees.

The population of America awaits this disaster with trepidation and alarm.

The big capitalists are in power in the United States. Cabinet members, Senators, Members of Congress know of the terrible crisis, but it never even enters their heads to curb the monopolies, to curtail their appetites, to force them to lower prices in order to better the position of the people and more quickly sell off merchandise.

The capitalists reason according to their own logic. In the first place, they do not fear a crisis very much: it will strike millions of workers, but it will not ruin the big capitalists. In the second place, they hope to escape the crisis in their own imperialistic way: to force other people to buy American goods at the same high prices.

The United States has become complete master in South America, where with its support reactionaries who obediently execute the will of American capital are in control of almost all the countries. But now this is not enough for the American Imperialists: they want to possess the whole world. How are they to bring to submission other, free states?

President Truman has announced the following principles

of American foreign policy: The United States will everywhere support with weapons and money reactionaries, Fascists who are hateful to their own people, but who on the other hand are ready to place their country under American control. Two countries suitable for this were found at once: Greece and Turkey. Now they have both in fact come under American domination. Americans are building their military bases there, American capitalists are opening businesses and buying up all that seems to them profitable. For this the Greek and Turkish reactionaries, who are in power, are receiving from the Americans money and weapons for the struggle against their own people.

But Greece and Turkey are too small, and American appetites are great. American expansionists are dreaming of all Europe or at least of Western Europe.

Directly to propose that the European countries become American colonies such as Greece and Turkey is somehow inconvenient. And so the "Marshall Plan" emerges in America. It was announced that the United States wants "to help" the European countries to reconstruct their war-destroyed economies. Many believed this.

But it was soon evident that the "Marshall Plan" was simply a cunning way of subjecting all Europe to American capital.

This is what was disclosed:

In the first place, the Americans want to decide themselves what each country has the right to produce and what it is obliged to buy in America.

In the second place, the Americans will give their goods on credit only to those countries where capitalism is preserved. All must renounce a planned economy. In this way, European countries actually are forfeiting their independence.

In the third place, the Americans wish first of all to reconstruct not those countries which were ruined by the Hitlerites, but Germany. They believe that Germany must again become a strong industrial country.

In the fourth place, in their opinion, American and German capitalists should be complete masters in Western Germany.

Many European countries—first of all the Soviet Union, but after it Poland, Yugoslavia, Czechoslovakia, Bulgaria, Hungary, Rumania, Albania and Finland—immediately rejected this plan of American intervention in their internal affairs.

Some other countries were tempted by Marshall's proposal, but even they were immediately disillusioned and confused.

They saw that the Americans wanted to take advantage of their need in America's own interests. Everywhere—in England, in France, in Italy and in other countries—the people are criticizing the Ministers who had swallowed the American bait.

Faced with this vast array of propaganda mechanism, all designed to make the people of the world hate and mistrust America and the generosity of its post-war assistance programs, our government was confronted with the counter-measures it could adopt to tell our own positive story abroad.

"One grain of truth dropped into Russia is like a spark landing in a barrel of powder," De Custine had written 110 years ago.

Every report by our observers throughout the Soviet Union stressed the same line, and it was this view that led the American Government to act in a far more positive way, in February, 1947, than it had ever attempted before in peacetime. Before that date, we had, of course, published the Russian-language, *Life*-like, slick paper magazine, *Amerika,* which had a recorded circulation of fifty thousand, but whose every word had been censored in advance by the Soviet Government, which also controlled the distribution inside the country. It was valuable, but it obviously had its shortcomings.

Yet *Amerika* magazine has many readers, despite the restrictions of governmental distribution. Worn and dog-eared copies are seen in every corner of the Soviet Union that has been visited by Americans, and, incredible though it may seem, *single sheets* of the magazine are sometimes sold on the black market at prices ranging up to a ruble (12½ cents at the diplomatic rate) per sheet, depending on the interest of the subject matter it contains.

In time, we could hope that we would be able to reach the Soviets in many ways—through the circulation of American books, the showing of American films, systematic exchange of students and professional personnel, as well as through short-wave radio and wider distribution of the Department's magazine, *Amerika.* However, and despite extensive efforts on our part, we had been unable to make much progress in such fields as exchange of students or free circulation of American books and films. We intended to keep working in these fields, but future possibilities remained uncertain.

The need for a Russian-language broadcast through "Voice of America" facilities had been recognized both by the Moscow Embassy and the State Department long before it was begun. A great deal of preliminary planning was required, however, because of such problems as provision of a satisfactory radio relay point; collection of a staff which could voice and write modern, idiomatic Russian and still meet rigid security tests; and working out a program content which would get across to the Russians information about the United States and its policies in an interesting attention-holding fashion. In all the preliminary planning and preparation, the Embassy worked as closely as possible with the State Department in Washington. We all sought as detailed guidance as we could get from American and British experts on Russia, from experiences of BBC Russian-language broadcasts, and from practices of Soviet domestic broadcasting systems.

The "Voice of America" first spoke in Russian on February 17, 1947. Several days before this, I officially notified the Soviet Foreign Office, and wrote letters to the newspapers *Pravda* and *Izvestia*, asking them to publish the date, time and wave-length of our initial program. These letters were ignored.

We did not expect the first programs to be finished products. We all expected serious flaws, but we believed that once actual broadcasting had begun we could quickly iron out our shortcomings.

In the Embassy, arrangements were made for close monitoring of the broadcasts and for obtaining as extensive reaction from Soviet listeners as possible. Detailed reports and criticisms were sent back to the Department on all phases of the program.

From the first, we were pleased with the language and voices and handling of the news. Reception, however, was poor; subject matter was not sufficiently light and entertaining; much of the music was bad for short-wave; and the pacing of the various parts of the program (news, technical features, light features, dance music and serious music) was off. These constructive criticisms were reported to the Department with suggested changes.

As we had anticipated, once broadcasting had begun and an opportunity had been given to study it in actual operation, improvement was rapid and steady. The broadcasts quickly demonstrated their value as a means of getting into the Soviet Union full facts about American developments which were of immediate policy importance.

For example, it enabled us to give to the Soviet people President Truman's speech announcing our intention to give support to the governments of Greece and Turkey. We received a report that Soviet engineers working at the Dnieper Dam were "amazed" at the President's speech and that they asked an American to make a check at the Embassy to find whether the President really made such a speech or if they had heard an underground station. They said they had not heard such things for thirty years.

A Russian connected with Radio Moscow, after admitting that he heard the President's speech and on being asked if he had heard it plainly, stated with slow emphasis: "That speech was plenty plain." He made it clear that he was referring to contents as well as reception.

For obvious reasons, the Embassy has never been able to make a systematic check of the extent to which our programs are heard by the Russians.

In May, 1947, I was able to tell members of the House Committee on Foreign Affairs, with reasonable assurance of accuracy, that there were probably more than half a million radio sets in the Soviet Union capable of receiving our broadcasts, and that the number might exceed one and one-half million. Later, we became convinced that this was an underestimate. Subsequent articles in *Pravda* and *Izvestia* emphasized that in recent years "large plants have been built providing all necessary equipment for radio development," that "many broadcasting stations have been constructed," and that "a radio set has become the normal thing in every family." The articles added that by 1950 the Soviet radio receiving network will have increased by seventy-five per cent as compared with pre-war.

From bits of conversation here and there, members of the Embassy staff were able to piece together extensive indications that "Voice of America" programs were being heard not only in Moscow but also in a number of provincial areas. A Soviet executive from an industrial city near Moscow stated that he and many of his acquaintances listened regularly; a traveler in Byelorussia found that half of the persons he talked to on the train knew of the broadcasts; a farmer from the Caucasus discussed the program content in some detail with an American Army officer whom he met on the street; a United States naval representative at Odessa reported that in Odessa "our broadcasts are apparently now receivable and are being listened to by most Russians having seven-tube sets or better"; visitors returning from Leningrad reported that the program was being listened to there just "as in Moscow."

Our first evidence of the impact of our broadcasts came on April 10, 1947, when Ilya Ehrenburg, an outstanding Soviet writer noted for the bitterness of his attacks on America, denounced the "Voice" in the strongest terms in an article in the magazine *Culture and Life*. I wrote the State Department:

"That a top-flight commentator like Ehrenburg should be assigned the job of lambasting our broadcasts is the most encouraging reaction we have seen. It shows that the program is on the right track. Our hearty congratulations."

Ten days later Mr. Ehrenburg renewed the attack. In a long article published in *Culture and Life* he again denounced the program, his central theme being that "it does not speak for the American people, but for American reactionaries." On April 30 the Soviet humor magazine *Krokodil* paid us the compliment of a featured cartoon attacking the broadcasts.

For a while we welcomed these attacks. They gave us free advertising and expanded our audience.

It may have been the Kasenkina affair that caused the Kremlin to decide to eliminate this source of truthful news. This incident afforded an excellent demonstration of the effectiveness of our broadcasting, for our true version of the story of Madame Kasenkina's escape from the Soviet Consulate General in New York was current news in Moscow almost simultaneously with Radio Moscow's propaganda version of her "kidnapping by White Guards and bandits," with the implied connivance of the United States Government. Most Russians accepted our version, for the very sound reason that they were familiar with the methods of their own government and secret police. There was much covert laughter among Muscovites over an incident which the Soviet Government took very seriously.

It certainly enhanced the reputation of the "Voice of America" broadcasts, and increased their audience. Russians from outside Moscow who were not aware of the danger of visiting the American Embassy, and occasionally even a resident who was willing to take a chance, began to visit our Information Office, which was at a different location and less conspicuous than the Chancery, and to offer comments.

One of these spontaneously offered the opinion that the principal audience was "youth." He then gave a more precise definition: "The young, cultured working class, aged from twenty-five to thirty-five, without higher education but having a lively interest in a variety of subjects." He cited himself and his friends—a printer, a barber, a lathe operator and a shoe factory worker—as typical examples of members of this youth group. There were a very large number of such young cultured workers, he said. Their interest in America was not the result of war contacts, but was a long standing one, arising from the fact that "America represents progress—it has authority." This interest is strong, he continued, and it persists in spite of current attempts by the Soviet press to blacken and slander America. Asked directly for his estimate of what percentage of Soviet citizens believed the "Voice of America" and what percentage believed the Soviet press, he gave a direct answer. He said that, although there are a good many "thoughtful, skeptical people," that over fifty per cent believed the Soviet press and less than fifty per cent believed the "Voice of America." He then remarked acutely that the technique of endless repetition as employed by the Soviet press is of tremendous importance.

When asked to comment on specific items in our programs, he singled out, particularly, President Truman's message on the occasion of a Jewish holiday, a feature commemorating the Negro scientist, George Washington Carver, and a news item stating that Communist Party meetings were permitted in the United States. The first two, he said, had impellingly suggested the thought: "How can there be race discrimination in America to the extent suggested by Soviet propaganda?" All three he described as "concrete examples of democracy in action—things which we will remember, which 'got home.' "

Several Soviet citizens told us that interest in the "Voice" was intense in Moscow, and that every day the subjects it discussed were spread by word of mouth through the greater part of the city's population. I believe this, because of the immediate spread of our version of the Kasenkina case.

One visitor informed us that when his family moved from one city to another they turned their radio on the "Voice of America." A senior Soviet Army officer, who was living in the same building, asked them please to stop listening, declaring that "if it were known that I was exposing myself to the 'Voice of America' my career would be completely ruined."

Gradually, the evidence multiplied that the effect of these broadcasts on Russian thought was very great. The Soviet Government evidently thought about this also. These sparks of truth could not be allowed to fall among a people who are being taught that they are hated by the external world, which is always striving for their destruction.

The outstanding characteristic of our broadcasts was truth as opposed to falsehood, and it was a continual source of speculation in Moscow, among Russians as well as among Americans, how long it would be before the Soviet Government took some sort of really effective action to interfere with them. I was surprised that the Kremlin waited until the spring of 1949 to begin the extensive program of jamming, which has, at least for the time being, almost completely silenced the "Voice" in the Soviet Union and reduced its audibility by about fifty per cent in many of the satellite countries. There was, of course, a reason for this tolerance of the truth for so long a time. The Soviet Union, in complete disregard of known facts, had stated so loudly and so often that it did not suppress the truth that the Kremlin delayed as long as possible before giving to the world this added proof of the naked power with which it controls all media of information.

Concurrently with its campaign of propaganda and suppression, the Politburo has acted to discredit as much as possible the character and standing of foreigners, particularly of American and British individuals and officials, in the eyes of the Soviet people. The Foreign Office and the MVD cooperated in this phase of the cold war, the line of action being either to "uncover" cases of espionage or to induce Americans to leave their posts and attack the policies of their government and the character of its representatives abroad.

The first was comparatively easy, as it involves playing upon a centuries-old Russian characteristic.

"Here in Russia," wrote De Custine in 1839, "friendship itself partakes of police surveillance. How is a man to feel at ease with people so circumspect, so discreet in whatever concerns themselves and so inquisitive in what concerns others? The excessive suspicion with which you are looked upon here by people of every class is a warning which keeps you on your guard. This Byzantine government and, indeed, all Russia, have always looked upon the diplomatic corps, and Westerners in general, as envious and malevolent spies."

This is as true today as when it was written. Though the officers of the American Embassy were under the strictest written orders to confine themselves to recognized and legitimate channels of information, and otherwise to act so that they would be above reproach, we were all suspect. The Soviet Major General Ilia M. Sarayev, an old acquaintance of mine who had served in the United States with the Soviet Military Mission, said quite frankly in an official conversation that all foreign officials "were considered potential spies." This is revealing for two reasons. It shows how the Soviet official conducts himself when abroad and it confirms the fact that the simplest items of current interest are considered by the Soviet Government as state secrets.

We had two "spy" cases while I was in Moscow, and the British Embassy had one. Our first involved one of our young naval officers, formerly stationed at Odessa, who went to the Moscow Customs Office to help clear a shipment of furniture and rugs intended for the Embassy. A former Odessa acquaintance, who was in charge of the shipment, which had been routed through that port, offered some comments on recent shipments of heavy material through the Port of Odessa. Since that came from an official, our young officer noted them down with pencil in a notebook, whereupon MVD agents entered the room, confiscated the notes, and accused him of espionage.

The affair was so obviously pre-arranged that I felt certain it was done for propaganda purposes. Consequently, when, two days later, Mr. Vishinksy asked me to call at the Foreign Office, I took with me a copy of the telegram I had sent to Washington reporting the incident. This report stated bluntly that in my opinion the incident was a frameup, and that now, having a "spy" case, the Soviet Government could be expected to exploit it to the limit to counter-balance the unfavorable world-wide publicity which had been given to the espionage trials involving the activities of Soviet agents in Canada and the United States. When Mr. Vishinsky opened the subject, as I expected he would, I showed him my telegram. He could do no less than deny officially that any propaganda considerations were involved, and the result was that the story actually did not appear in the Soviet press until many months later, after our own and foreign newspapers had given wide publicity to the escape of Madame Kasenkina. By this time, it had become rather stale and attracted little attention.

One of our correspondents, Robert Magidoff, was the next victim. No American in Moscow was more meticulously careful to observe the letter and spirit of Soviet laws and regulations than was Mr. Magidoff, and I will never know why he was selected to be a "spy," unless it was because he and his Russian-born wife, Nila, had many Soviet friends, some of whom still clung to him. The McGraw-Hill Publishing Company in New York had written, through the regular Soviet mail system, asking for some data on Soviet industry which, anywhere except in the Soviet Union, would have been entirely routine. One of his Soviet employees, a Miss Nelson, read the letter and filed espionage charges against Mr. Magidoff in a letter to the newspaper *Izvestia*. The incident was given the widest publicity in the Soviet press and propaganda in a story which alleged that he had received instructions for and had transmitted the results of his espionage through the American Embassy's diplomatic pouch. It was also asserted that he regularly communicated information to the U.S. Military and Naval representatives in Moscow. Mr. Magidoff and his wife were placed under police surveillance and his credentials were withdrawn. At that time I issued the following statement, which, needless to say, never saw the light of day in any Soviet publication:

During the more than two years that I have been in Moscow, no correspondent has ever sent news stories through the diplomatic pouch, nor would this be permitted. Neither Mr. Magidoff nor any other correspondent has ever received documents or instructions through the American Embassy in Moscow. I talked with Mr. Magidoff this morning and confirmed the fact that the "documents and instructions" referred to in Miss Nelson's letter came through the regular Soviet mails. The news items asked for are quite obviously of a type which in the United States and most other countries are considered newsworthy and are given general newspaper publicity as matters on which the public is entitled to information.

Mr. Magidoff, like other American correspondents in Moscow, has close acquaintance with American Embassy personnel, including the Military and Naval Attachés. There are few Americans here, and during recent months, through no desire of our own, our contacts with Soviet citizens have been limited purely to official relations, and we depend on each other for companionship and normal social relations. Mr. Magidoff's relations with our Military and Naval personnel have been entirely of a social nature.

I have insisted and have insured that diplomatic, Military and Naval personnel of this Mission restrict themselves implicitly and exclusively to legitimate and authorized sources of information. Mr. Magidoff informed me that the allegations made by the Soviet citizen, Miss Nelson, and published in *Izvestia* are entirely false. I can confirm the fact that they are false (insofar as they relate to American Embassy personnel).

Mr. Magidoff also informs me that he is answering these allegations, and I sincerely hope that his answer will be given publicity equal to that accorded his accuser.

I am reporting all the facts and circumstances in the case, together with my statements, as above, to the Department of State in Washington, and I assume that they will be made available to the press of the United States.

The British Embassy also had its troubles. The British Military Attaché, General Hilton, used a monocle. One winter day, as he was taking his daily constitutional and looking for a slope, within walking distance of the Embassy, on which he might practice skiing, he screwed the monocle to his eye. This unusual gadget attracted the attention of an enthusiastic Communist worker in a near-by factory, who assumed that the single lens must be some sort of camera with which the foreigner was photographing the strategic industry of the Soviet Union. He immediately summoned the police. The situation was complicated by the fact that the General was wearing a rather well-worn British military issue felt coat, and thus, as Mr. Molotov stated in the subsequent exchange of notes, "from his outward appearance did not at all resemble a cultured person, but was dressed as an ordinary worker."

The Soviet Minister of Foreign Affairs thus declared it his opinion that it was impossible for one to be both a cultured person and an ordinary worker, and coincidentally that "clothes make the man." It would have been difficult for any enemy of the Soviet Union to have phrased a more complete negation of the principle of the rule of the working classes on which the government of the Soviet Union allegedly is based.

Nevertheless, the Soviet propaganda machine plugged the "Hilton affair" for weeks. The favorite clown in the Moscow Circus quickly produced an act in which, loaded with cameras and field glasses, he impersonated the General "looking for a ski-site." The intensified police surveillance and the embarrassment to which he was subjected made poor Hilton's life miserable, and we were all glad for him when his tour in Moscow ended. But Soviet anti-foreign propaganda had reaped a rich harvest.

Another fruitful source is the occasional foreigner who can be persuaded or coerced into "deserting the capitalist camp." We had two incidents of this kind during my tour in Moscow, both resulting from emotional involvement. The one most publicized both in the Soviet Union and the United States was Miss Annabelle Bucar. Miss Bucar, a well-liked and rather attractive young woman attached to the Cultural Information Section of the Embassy, fell in love with a Soviet citizen named Lapschin, an operetta singer whom we knew best for his reputation as having courted, at one time or another, almost every unattached young foreign woman in Moscow. A post-war Soviet law categorically prohibits the marriage of Soviet citizens and foreigners, and I believe that since Miss Bucar wanted very much to marry Mr. Lapschin she hoped, by repudiating her Embassy connection and declaring her opposition to U.S. policy, to obtain an exemption from this law.

For a while after her letter of resignation was published, she was employed by the Soviet Government in lecturing to factory workers on the beauties of the Soviet system as compared with the economic slavery which exists in the United States. Later there was published over her name a book entitled *The Truth About American Diplomats,* which presented us all in a most unflattering light. Miss Bucar did not write this book, since though presumably based on her own observation, most of it was devoted to officers who had served in and left Moscow before she arrived there. Aside from the viciousness of the propaganda tissue of lies and half-truths, this book had another interest. Examination of the gaps in the narrative lent credence to the local rumor that the dossier files of the MVD actually had been lost or destroyed during the period of the German advance on Moscow. We were all sorry for Miss Bucar, for we could understand the pressures to which she was and will continue to be subjected, but this does not excuse her actions.

A much more flagrant, but less publicized, case was the desertion of one of our Army code clerks—Sergeant James M. McMillin. This young man is the son of an Army officer of my acquaintance. He became involved with a young Soviet woman of the minor-agent type formerly so active in their attentions to foreigners in Moscow, and under her influence he deserted from the Army and his post in Moscow. Less intelligent than Miss Bucar, he has been of comparatively less propaganda value. It is possible that the MVD hoped to obtain some code information from him, but our codes are so unassailable that the only information a deserter of this type could give would be from classified messages which he remembered, and there were few messages which we exchanged with the Department of State that I would not willingly have shown on request to the Soviet Foreign Minister. The fact is that on this score the unreliable employee is dangerous only while at his post—not after he deserts from it.

Most of the Western embassies in Moscow have had similar incidents during the past three years, and even careful advance selection is no real assurance of stability when the emotions become involved.

There will continue to be disaffections for various reasons, including real ideological convictions. The counterfeit currency of the Soviet version of "freedom," "equality" and "democracy" will continue to be circulated, and will be accepted at face value by a great many people. Fortunately for us, Soviet propaganda has some decided shortcomings. The propaganda machine is unwieldy—a vast bureaucracy, which though swift and effective in attack on any given line, lacks flexibility when it loses the initiative.

Soviet propaganda in general aims low on the cultural scale, yet even in those countries where a Communist minority has seized control and has almost a monopoly of all communication channels, it has rarely achieved the real mass support necessary to make communism a true people's movement. The "people" as a mass consists of individuals who hunger for the freedom of choice which communism disallows. Soviet propagandists are finding it more and more difficult to peddle their wares to the people of the Western nations. They have abused their credit and cannot depend any longer on having their declarations accepted at face value. As the Western nations become more sophisticated politically, they are warier and less susceptible to the "big lie" technique, and they are increasingly aware of the difference between Soviet words and Soviet action.

We cannot expect the present hostile Soviet propaganda line to change until the aims of the Soviet Government change, or until that day which now appears far off when the Soviet people learn the truth about the world community and act on that knowledge. For the present, we must accept the Kremlin's long-range hostility as a working premise, and avoid the mistake of seizing upon the lastest Soviet tactical maneuver as proof of a genuine change of heart.

IX

COMINFORM AND TITO

In our Party, we Leninists are the only Lefts. Therefore, in our Party we Leninists are neither Lefts nor Rights. We are the Marxist-Leninist Party. And in our Party we fight not only those whom we call open opportunist deviationists but also those who want to be more Left than Marxism, more Left than Leninism, and conceal their Right opportunist nature behind high-sounding Left phrases.

—Stalin: *Leninism* (1933), p. 96

VIEWED from the American Embassy in Moscow, the Cominform struggle to unseat Marshal Tito of Yugoslavia created visible and ever-widening political and economic repercussions throughout Eastern Europe and, indeed, among inquiring minds susceptible to Communist influence all over the world.

It breached the Iron Curtain and violated the principle of Kremlin omnipotence. The wall the Soviets have erected around their part of the world can be visualized as a dike holding in check the churning torrents of the pent-up emotions of Eastern Europeans, who may know little of real democracy at home but who historically have resisted every kind of foreign rule. This breach, like any leak through which angry waters find an outlet, threatens to grow larger with every passing day and, if unmended, eventually to destroy the entire structure of control and inundate the surrounding area.

The Men in the Kremlin have stated it, just this bluntly and without equivocation: the first loyalty of Communists everywhere is to the Soviet Union; their devotion to their own countries and their peculiar national interests must be secondary. Moscow said, in terms impossible to misunderstand, that it expects every Communist Party of every nation to obey without question the dictates of the Communist Party of the Soviet

Union (Bolshevik) and that, if and when one of them comes to power, it must apply in its own country the exact system of regimentation and collectivization now in effect in the Soviet Union.

Tito said "no," and the Kremlin said he must recant or be overthrown.

That was eighteen months ago, as this is written, and neither has happened. Tito is still in power, and, judging by available evidence, probably politically stronger than when the fight began.

Since Moscow is the political, economic, military and psychological headquarters for world revolution, it quite naturally was one of the primary tasks of the Ambassador and his staff to keep in the closest possible touch with every phase of international communism, both before and after the "Cominform" openly took the place of the "Comintern," which had been disbanded in 1943 as a sop to the public opinion of the Western Allied world in the middle of the war against Hitler. We followed, therefore, with increasing interest, the step-by-step development of the Tito controversy.

Just as they have never put a time limit on achievement of the world domination by Communists which they consider inevitable, the Soviets likewise have never established any time schedule for eliminating the heretical Yugoslav Marshal. They believe, quite obviously, that time is on their side, but this may not necessarily be so.

It would not be wise to make any prediction at this stage as to whether Tito eventually will win or lose, recant or lose his job, if not his head, but I believe it would not be without value to total the particular advantages thus far accruing to the West from Tito's continued successful defiance of the Kremlin.

On the basis of my experience in Moscow, I would list these major gains:

Any totalitarian system lives to a large degree on the myth that its leaders are infallible. As long as Tito lives, unrepentant and still in power, he is a negation of this principle.

The Communist drive directed from Moscow has been stripped naked of any internationalist pretense and exposed to the world as nothing more or less than "Great Russianism." The theories of Marx and Engels, who were most interested in how to make a revolution and almost not at all concerned with operating a revolutionary state, have been revised to fit Russian organizational concepts, which are a modernization of the age-old Czarist practices of despotic power and absolute control.

Because nothing is more contagious than independence in a totalitarian state, the so-far successful Tito revolt already has shaken the structure of the Communist Party leadership in Poland, Hungary, Albania and "Free" Greece by the admission of the Communists themselves. There is every reason to think it may have been behind less-publicized party troubles and purges in Bulgaria, Rumania and Czechoslovakia.

In the Balkans, the Cominform-Tito split created differences among the major leaders of the Greek guerrillas, and when control was handed to anti-Tito forces, Yugoslavia ceased its once considerable aid to the Greek rebels and made easier the American-supported task of crushing the Communist Army in Northern Greece. Albania, as an anti-Tito Soviet satellite, is now separated from any friendly neighbors and shaken by an internal political crisis, brought on in part by the fact that most of its trade since the war had been with Yugoslavia or routed through Yugoslavia. The Communist-supported plan for a South Balkan federation, upon which Yugoslavia and Bulgaria had agreed, was dropped when Bulgaria aligned herself against Tito. And, without Soviet support, Yugoslavia has had to reduce its pressure on the Free Territory of Trieste, which its troops jointly occupy with American and British forces—an area ardently desired in full by both Italy and Yugoslavia.

Internationally, the controversy furnishes further evidence of the mendacity of the Soviet claim that it respects treaties and the sovereignty of small nations. By its own words in a series of angry notes to Yugoslavia, the Soviet Government has made it clear beyond a shadow of a doubt that it is in fact interfering directly in the international affairs and national sovereignty of Yugoslavia in complete violation of the United Nations Charter.

Inside Yugoslavia, it has strengthened Tito among middle-class groups previously opposed to the regime, who by their Balkan heritage and even their enlightened self-interest are more anti-Russian than anti-Tito.

Inside the U.S.A., it certainly has caused at least a small decline in the enthusiasm and support of fellow-travelers who found it difficult to regard Tito as an international Communist hero one day and an enemy the next.

Because this unexpected development has had and continues to have such world-wide repercussions, it is worth while and illuminating to delve a bit into its background.

Despite his Russian character and outlook, Lenin was one of a band of genuine international revolutionaries. There is no doubt that he visualized Russia immediately after the Bolshevik coup as an instrument of world revolution. He did not wait until the Soviet victory in Russia had been stabilized, but instead moved promptly to create the international mechanism he believed would stir revolts in other capitalist countries. In January, 1919, while the newly established Soviet Government was still in a very precarious position, with much of its area in the control of hostile forces and with starvation widespread among its population, he called other Communist parties to meet in Moscow. There, on March 4, 1919, the Communist International, which became known in abbreviated form as the Comintern, was formed. Though he had some difficulties in imposing his will on his associates, Lenin was able to give to the Comintern the same type of dictatorial domination which he had saddled upon the Russian Communist Party itself.

While the specific rules of the Comintern organization were embodied in long resolutions, too lengthy and involved to be analyzed in any detail here, the essentials can be summarized briefly. The Comintern was based on the Leninist conception of "Democratic Centralism." This meant that each national Communist Party was entitled to elect members to the Comintern Congress which met in Moscow under the thumb of the Soviet Government. This Congress elected an executive committee, authorized to take action binding on the lower bodies. Representation was roughly in accordance with the number of party members, a formula which gave the Russians immediate preponderance. Theoretically, discussion was allowed on any matter at any conference until a decision had been reached by the higher organs. This was allegedly the "democratic" aspect of "centralism"; but of course no Communist would be foolish enough to stick his neck out, as the penalties for "devi-

Threshing crews at work at a collective farm in Kiev region. Note preponderance of women.

A street in the village of the Molotov Collective Farm in the Altai.

Sovfoto

Election meeting at Moscow Electrical Equipment Plant.

Sovfoto

A Currency Exchange Point in Moscow.

ationism" extended to death. After a decision was reached, blind obedience was demanded and an iron discipline enforced. The Central Secretariat, which included a secret police type of control, kept close check on every Communist Party member in the world. This was the result of developments during the nineteen twenties. Police control became absolute after the accession to power in the Comintern of Georgi Dimitrov in 1934.

In practice, the organization was run by the Kremlin, with the aid of a group of specially selected international Communists, working and residing in Moscow and almost completely Russianized. These included such expatriate types as Thorez and Duclos of France; Dimitrov of Bulgaria; Bierut and Gomulka of Poland; Pieck of Germany; Gottwald of Czechoslovakia; Togliatti of Italy, and Ana Pauker of Rumania. Hundreds of other Communists throughout the world were brought to Moscow for intensive training in Communist theory and practice.

National Communist movements were directly subsidized. Under these conditions even the original pretense of democratic procedure soon melted away. International communism was ruled by a handful of men in and around the Kremlin, and even the party congresses were discontinued as the years went by, despite the fact that they had become little more than rubber-stamp affairs, approving past actions of the men in control.

After Stalin rose to power, there developed a rather subtle change in emphasis. Basically a nationalist, Stalin brought the concept that the world revolution must be an instrument of the Soviet state rather than the Soviet state an instrument of world revolution.

"In present conditions," Stalin said in 1922, "one cannot call oneself a Marxist unless one openly and devotedly supports the first proletarian dictatorship in the world."

The Comintern had its ups and downs. The capitalist world passed through a major economic crisis after the first World War and, though severely shaken by the great depression which began in 1929, held together and began to work its way back toward prosperity in the nineteen thirties. Despite these strains, the Kremlin was unable to use its international agency to accomplish revolution in other countries. Indeed, there were many observers of the Soviet scene who believed that Stalin actually feared a real revolution in a major foreign state which might rival that of the Soviet Union and get out of the Kremlin's control, and that, for this reason, he deliberately imposed a restraining influence.

However, during these years, the Comintern was developed very successfully as an effective agency of Soviet world policy, specializing in subversive activities and espionage for Moscow. Extremely clever psychological conditioning was applied to the membership of Communist parties throughout the world to make them believe that in serving the Soviet Union they were serving a great and noble cause to which their national patriotism was secondary. These methods have been well described in such publications as the confessions of the American ex-Communist, Ben Gitlow, and in the report of the Canadian Royal Commission on the Soviet spy ring in Canada.

Through the tactics of the Popular Front and of the infiltration and seizure of control of reformist and humanitarian organizations, the Communists, in fact, multiplied many times their nominal numerical strength. During the years between wars, they were particularly active in opposing military training and supporting movements which had a decisive effect in undermining the morale and undercutting the defense preparations of the Western nations.

The Comintern itself underwent a major strain when, in August, 1939, the Soviet authorities suddenly signed the non-aggression pact with Hitler, which gave the Nazis the go-sign for the invasion of Poland—an act which surprised and shocked Communists all over the world because there had not been time to prepare them in advance for this shift in tactics. But, while the party lost members in many countries, and many liberals who had been inclined to go along with Communist efforts in United Front crusades were revolted, it is a tribute to Russian organizational methods that the Comintern remained intact without the deviation of a single national party organization. The Communists who stayed in fought any preparation for war against Hitler or aid to England as imperialism, but they were due for another shock, on June 12, 1941, when the Wehrmacht suddenly invaded the Soviet Union and the party line had to shift rapidly again. As England and the United States rushed to the aid of the Soviet Union, on the theory that they would help anybody who fought against the Germans, the days of the Comintern as an open instrument of world revolution were numbered, because Stalin and the other leaders in the Kremlin well knew the resentment and suspicion which would be aroused in the West by efforts of a wartime Ally to undermine Western governments.

Consequently, on May 22, 1943, Moscow Radio made the dramatic announcement that the Executive Committee of the Comintern had just met in that city and decided to dissolve the organization—an act which brought immediate and favorable reaction throughout the Western countries, whose people were anxious to believe anything good about their Russian Ally. Although the Soviet Government always had maintained the pretense, which no informed person took seriously, that it had no responsibility for the Comintern, Stalin himself seized the opportunity to make some more good propaganda by answering some interrogatories posed by Harold King, the tough, sharp-questioning Moscow correspondent of Reuters, the British news agency. Dissolution of the Comintern, Stalin wrote to Mr. King, "puts an end to the lie" that "Moscow allegedly intends to intervene in the life of other nations and 'Bolshevize' them." He asserted also that it ended the "calumny" that Communist parties in various countries "are allegedly acting not in the interest of their people, but on orders from the outside."

It is important, I think, to emphasize again the fact that the old Comintern, despite two great depressions, had not been able to produce a successful revolution in even one country outside the Soviet Union, and that it had not, ideologically, been able to win enough members in any country to constitute a major parliamentary force.

Its dissolution, I think, marked an adaptation of Kremlin tactics to the new circumstances which had developed during the second World War. By 1943, it was clear that the Allies eventually would win, and the Kremlin already was calculating how this victory could be exploited for the expansion of Soviet power. The overt Comintern organization obviously was not a practical instrument to use for this purpose. The time was approaching when expatriated Communist leaders, members of the Comintern Executive Committee, could return to their countries on the heels of Soviet armies, and assume the tasks for which they had long been trained and prepared in Moscow. The Dimitrovs and the Paukers and the Gottwalds could resume the mantle of nationalism as they prepared to take over their countries for the greater glory of the Soviet Union.

As we know, they did just this; although it is pertinent to observe that they were able to take control only in those countries bordering on the Soviet Union which were directly subjected to the power of the Soviet armies. While this fact should be reassuring to us in the sense of indicating that Communist double-talk ideology has not, in itself, sufficient strength to effect the conquest of any country, it is a reminder at the same time that the Soviet Union, in appropriate circumstances, will not fail to add the necessary element of Soviet military strength.

"Force," as Lenin pointed out long ago, "is the handmaiden of revolution."

Since the establishment of these trained Soviet puppets in power in the satellite states, we have witnessed a gradual process of remaking them in the image of the abject Soviet constituent republics.

I am satisfied that there never was the slightest intention on the part of Stalin and the Politburo to allow any other pattern to develop in the satellite area or to honor—at any point or in any way—the many agreements they had made with the British and ourselves to allow the people of Eastern Europe freely to choose their own form of government and to decide on their own futures. The Kremlin, from the very beginning, was determined to prevent us from having any role or any influence in Eastern Europe and, by preventing us from assisting the reconstruction of Western Europe, eventually to open the entire European continent for further Russian expansion and exploitation.

History does not record another instance where a program of aggressive expansion has attained its objectives with such rapidity. In less than three years of peace, the Soviet Union, by political infiltration and suppression, overran a great deal more territory than the Red Army had conquered during the entire war.

Meanwhile, the Western powers, whose people generally were reluctant to admit, even in the face of overwhelming evidence, that their hopes for a united world were being completely shattered, passed through a period of indecision and hesitation.

"Democracies," General Marshall used to say, "are slow starters, but when they do move they act with great force and resolution."

When it finally was apparent to the people of America that the Soviet Union and the Western democracies had widely divergent peace aims, and that the lofty agreements entered into so hopefully during the war were being given almost diametrically opposite interpretations, they reacted positively and effectively.

The Truman Doctrine, specifically promising aid to Greece and Turkey but in principle holding out the prospect of aid to any country resisting Soviet aggression, came in March, 1947, and was followed a few months later by the Marshall Plan for European economic recovery.

A very wise and experienced Western European statesman and diplomat said to me at this time: "The Marshall proposals were a stroke of sheer genius, and if coupled with a judicious political fusion of the Anglo-French-American zones of occupation in Western Germany, can provide an impact against present Russian strength and bring about Russian withdrawal to the East, short of war."

The first conference in Paris provided the final test of Soviet intentions. When the French Ambassador told me at the end of June that he had issued visas for Molotov and a group of sixty-odd economic experts to attend the Conference on European economic reconstruction at Paris, I wondered for a moment, despite all I had learned in the Soviet capital, whether it was possible that there would be a new cooperative shift in the Kremlin's tactics, even though in the preceding two years there had not been a single statement by any Soviet leader expressing interest in any common effort to restore European economic well-being.

But when Molotov walked out of the Paris Conference, refusing to cooperate with the plan, and when the Kremlin forced the withdrawal of Czechoslovakia, which had announced its acceptance, and Poland, which wanted to join the program, we knew that there would be no change—that the world was indeed divided, by Soviet decision, into two camps.

It is possible that the Politburo hesitated for a time to make this decision. Mr. Bevin told me that during the first two days at Paris, Molotov's attitude had seemed to him encouraging. During the third day's session, however, while Mr. Molotov was speaking, one of his aides handed him a telegram. He interrupted his remarks to read it and said nothing more during the remainder of the day's meeting. On the following day he denounced the plan. His final instructions evidently had been contained in this telegram.

I frequently glanced at the translation of the political columns in Soviet children's magazines. They were interesting and amusing, because they gave the raw propaganda line in words of one syllable, unseasoned by Communist dialectic. Here is how the Marshall Plan was described for the children of the Soviet Union:

ZOYA DAVIDOVA, MANSOUR KAYUMOV, MUKHAMET LETFULLIN AND OTHER CHILDREN ASK: "WHAT IS THE MARSHALL PLAN?" DR. OF ECONOMIC SCIENCE E. VISHNEV ANSWERS THEM.

Marshall is the Secretary of State of the United States of America (in this country he is called Minister of Foreign Affairs). Last summer Marshall made a speech in which he declared that in European countries there prevails at present economic chaos and that the United States are ready to help these lands restore their economies. Marshall proposed to the European lands first of all to consult among themselves how they could help one another. "Just let these countries," said Marshall, "calculate what resources they have themselves and what are their needs. Then America will decide how it can help them." The American papers immediately raised a great noise about this plan. In different terms, they emphasized "the magnanimity" of America which had decided to help war-stricken Europe.

However, actually, this cunning plan pursued entirely different aims. The American capitalists want to use the help of the Marshall Plan to overwhelm Europe and bring it into subjection to themselves. The government of the Soviet Union at once recognized the real meaning of the Marshall Plan and definitely refused to take part in setting it up. So also did the governments of the other democratic lands—Poland, Czechoslovakia, Bulgaria, Yugoslavia, Rumania, Hungary and also Finland. But sixteen European states adopted the Marshall Plan against the wishes of their peoples.

Let us see now how the U.S.A. is preparing to carry out the Marshall Plan and what it promises the European countries which have fallen for the American bait.

Representatives of these sixteen European states met together and calculated that they had to receive from the U.S.A. 29 billion dollars to restore their economies. The Americans answered that this sum was too high and asked for its reduction to 20-22 billion dollars.

The Americans, moreover, attached the following condition: they themselves will dictate to each European country what branch of economy it must develop and what it must curtail. For example, they say to Britain: "You Britishers, build fewer ships for yourselves; you will buy ships from us in America." They propose to the French a reduction in the production of automobiles—American factories can make automobiles for France.

It goes without saying that this was very useful for American capitalists. In America everybody is fearfully awaiting "the economic crisis," i. e., the time when many factories and industries suddenly close and millions of people are left without work. At that time it will be difficult for the manufacturers to get rid of their output. A man out of work has nothing with which to buy them. So the American capitalists are greatly concerned how to sell profitably their output in Europe. Further, the European countries inevitably will become dependent on America: once they make a few machines, tools and automobiles, it means that willy-nilly they must defer to the Americans.

According to the Marshall Plan the American capitalists want to restore all the great factories of Western Germany. In other countries they are hastening to close many factories, while in Germany, on the contrary, they are opening them up. Their purpose there, too, is quite understandable: clearly, the U.S.A. considers Western Germany as its colony. By controlling the big industries there which can also make armaments, it will be easy for the Americans to frighten the European countries dependent on them.

The American capitalists counted on using the Marshall

Plan to stir up trouble between the peoples of the democratic
countries and the Soviet Union. The Americans proposed to
these countries as follows: "We will give you dollars if only
you will abandon your friendship with the Soviet Union. But
if you don't, we won't give you anything." But the peoples of
these countries did not fall for the American capitalists' trick.
They answered the Americans: "We will not exchange our
freedom and independence for dollars."

In America and the capitalist European countries people
make a great fuss about the Marshall Plan, but to date the
Americans have not given anyone a single dollar of the sum
indicated in the plan . . . and meanwhile America is asking
that the European countries grant her the right of building
on their territory and in their colonies harbors for American
naval vessels and aerodromes for American planes.

Belgium has a colony, the Congo, in Africa. Rich deposits of
uranium ore exist there. This ore is needed for the production
of atom bombs. In the French colony of [New] Caledonia are
deposits of nickel. Nickel is a metal which is very important
for the making of armaments. The Americans are demanding
that Belgium and France hand over the uranium ore and nickel
to America.

But this isn't all. The American capitalists have still another dastardly aim. After using the Marshall Plan to reduce
the European countries, they want to unite them in a military
alliance for a future war against the democratic states. The
Marshall Plan is highly profitable to the United States. For the
European countries it brings only poverty. Any land which
wants to receive "aid" by means of this plan will be entirely
dependent on America. Its economy will not be assisted: on
the contrary, it will fall into greater ruin because the country
will have to close many of its industries and plants and hundreds of thousands of people will be out of work. That is why
both in America itself and in all other lands progressive people
are opposing the Marshall Plan with all their strength.

The Kremlin's answer to the Marshall Plan was the re-
establishment of the Comintern in the form of the "Communist
Information Bureau"—the Cominform—at a secret meeting in
Western Poland in September, 1947, and of the Eastern European Council for Mutual Economic Aid (CEMA) in January,
1949.

I am glad to report that neither of these steps came as a surprise to the Embassy or to the United States Government. Much as we were deliberately isolated from original sources of information in the Soviet Union, it is inevitable that when one lives there long enough to become thoroughly steeped in Russian history, Stalinist ideology and Communist double-talk, he develops a fairly accurate "sixth sense" for what the Kremlin is going to do and why.

Moscow had, for some time, been showing an inclination to tighten the bonds between the Communist parties throughout the world and, for this purpose, had adopted the procedure of organizing what were really big international Communist meetings around important national Communist congresses. Thus I find notes in my diary early in 1947, which were reflected in my reports to the State Department, to the effect that the British Communist Party conferences held in London at that time seemed to be the occasion for a secret, rather large-scale Comintern meeting. Visiting delegates of considerable importance in the Communist world were to be present from practically all countries in Europe and the Near East. We felt that this revived international Communist activity was probably a prelude to the overt re-establishment of an international Communist agency.

Furthermore, the recapture of the initiative by the West through the Truman and European reconstruction programs had put the Kremlin on the defensive and called for some dramatic new action. Consequently, while the actual time and place of the Cominform meeting in Poland was a carefully guarded secret to which we were not privy, it was no surprise when *Pravda*, on October 5, 1947, announced that the conference of Communist Party leaders from nine countries had taken place.

Actually, the public establishment of the Cominform probably added very little to the thoroughness or the effectiveness of the Kremlin's international organization which had been constantly and continuously in existence under cover. However, organization is not everything. The struggle for Europe is to a large degree a struggle for the minds and for the allegiance of men.

In face of the new positive program of the West, even the Communist faithful needed some kind of publicly declared program to which they could pledge allegiance. And this publicly declared program, at the same time, served as a public commitment, making it impossible for the Communist leaders in the satellite countries and in France and Italy to yield to any temptation that they might feel to secure American material aid for the reconstruction of their countries' economy. This was the official declaration of economic war confirming Molotov's action in walking out of the Paris Conference.

Like all such Communist documents of this nature, the Cominform declaration was filled with double-talk and featured by that particular Russian practice, often very revealing to us in the Embassy, of accusing others of doing what they are themselves doing or about to do.

It charged that the Truman and Marshall plans were "only a farce, a European branch of the general world plan of political expansion being realized by the United States of America." Then, in elaborating on this alleged world plan of political expansion by the United States, it offered, as applying to American imperialists, as good a short description as I have ever read of Russian Communist tactics:

"The arsenal of tactical weapons used by the imperialistic [here one should read Communist] camp is further very complex. It combines direct threats of force, blackmail and intimidation, all sorts of political tricks and economic pressure, bribery, the using for its own ends of conflicting interests and disagreements with the aim of strengthening its position, and all that is camouflaged by a mask of liberalism and pacifism in order to deceive and befuddle people not too dexterous in politics."

Even the title of the new organization was deliberately misleading. While it was described as an Information Bureau, the declaration specifically describes its tasks as including "an exchange of experience between parties and, in case of necessity, coordination of their activity." It said the lack of bonds between parties at that time was "a grave deficiency in the present situation."

And that was where the Communist leaders, led from the Soviet side by the late A. A. Zhdanov and Georgi Malenkov, made the big mistake that was to lead to the quarrel with Tito and the first break in the international Communist front. The pre-war Communist parties which the Comintern had bossed were groups which, outside of Russia, had been unable to come into power in their own countries; but the post-war situation was very different with the Communists in control of Poland, Czechoslovakia, Hungary, Yugoslavia, Bulgaria, Albania and Rumania.

Marshal Tito visited Moscow only once while I was there— in late May of 1946 to negotiate a commercial treaty with the Soviet Government. He was there at the time the ancient and venerated Mikhail Kalinin died, and was in Red Square next to the box allotted to foreign diplomats to witness the solemn ceremonial state funeral. Certainly there was no visible sign of the developing rift, for soon after Stalin and the other members of the Politburo who acted as pallbearers mounted Lenin's tomb, the Yugoslav leader was invited to leave his special box and join them on the reviewing stand as the ceremonies proceeded.

Certainly none of us in Moscow expected a revolt in Communist ranks led by one so important and so well trained as Tito, but I had recorded in my journal, two months before the Tito-Cominform split became public, my belief that Moscow's efforts to maintain the same kind of iron discipline over its disciples abroad as it had over the party leaders at home eventually must lead to trouble.

"A Soviet mistake has been a failure to realize the difference between the pre-war and post-war situations," my diary said. "The Politburo seems to think of the Cominform as a revived Comintern, which will enable it to impose its will on other Communist parties, apparently forgetting, or ignoring, the fact that while before the war these were only small minority groups without power, they now, though still minority groups, control nations and have obligations to their own countries. The undivided allegiance which the Soviet Government expects from foreign Communist parties can hardly be maintained, now that these governments have come into power."

But even so, we in Moscow were surprised at the sudden dramatic announcement on June 28, 1948, that the Yugoslav Party had been expelled from the Cominform, and that the people of Yugoslavia were being told to force Tito and his top lieutenants to recant or throw them out. *Pravda* published only the Cominform declaration, and the "Voice of America," in Russian, brought back Tito's angry defiance, which brought these comments from Russians on the street when asked for reaction by Embassy officials:

"The Americans made it up."

"Tito will come to heel, or be overthrown by loyal Yugoslav Communists."

"Once Stalin has it in for somebody, he can't let go and will stop at nothing."

"The communiqué contradicts itself. The first part accuses Tito of being too right, and the last part accuses him of being too left."

"The Communist Party in Yugoslavia cannot survive without the aid of the Soviet Union."

"Soviet troops will enter Yugoslavia through Rumania with Rumania's permission."

"It's all word for word from Stalin's book, *Problems of Leninism.*"

And most of the comment reflected more surprise at the fact that the rift had been made public before Tito had been dealt with than over the struggle itself.

One of our Embassy officials asked a Communist Party official from another Embassy what the attitude of his government would be toward the Yugoslav Communists, and received the reply, "They must be gotten rid of by force of arms." When the American observed that this would be proof of Soviet imperialism and aggression, the Communist said such a remark was hostile comment about the Soviet Union.

The basic issue in this struggle was the attempt by the Soviets at direct control of the Yugoslav Communist Party. All other matters of substance are secondary. The crisis was precipitated by Yugoslav resistance to Soviet espionage and subversion inside Yugoslavia and by resistance to unequal economic treatment by the Kremlin. The open break came when Soviet officials there found they could not cope with Yugoslav security organizations, when Soviet attempts to split Yugoslav leadership failed, and when Yugoslav officials, acting as Soviet agents inside the Yugoslav Communist Party, were discovered and arrested as traitors to the nation and to the party. Withdrawal of Soviet military and civilian specialists was its first manifestation.

It is now clear that the Soviet Communist Party demands the same authority over foreign Communist parties as it exercises over subordinate organizations inside the U.S.S.R., and that foreign governments, even though headed by national Communist parties, must submit to the same Soviet espionage infiltration and subversion as is carried on against the "enemy" bourgeois states. What the Soviets demanded in Yugoslavia was freedom to gather information independently, to construct intelligence nets, and to develop party cadres whose first allegiance was to the Soviet Union. This the Yugoslavs could not permit and retain independence of party or nation.

The Russian threats and pressures upon Tito have multiplied as the months have gone by since the initial denunciation of his regime by the Cominform. Angry notes without precedent in times of peace have been handed back and forth between Belgrade and Moscow. In the notes the Russians have referred bluntly to the Yugoslav regime as "an enemy," and have threatened, without recourse to the United Nations, to take more effective measures to protect citizens it claims are being mistreated in Yugoslavia. Russian armored divisions have openly maneuvered on the Hungarian-Yugoslav frontier, where they have a right to be under the peace treaty clause permitting the Soviet Union to protect its supply line to occupied Austria.

As the trusted Tito failed to obey his masters, the Russians became more and more suspicious of other satellite representatives, and especially of their diplomatic representatives in Moscow. It was quite obvious that these Moscow envoys were not the real channel of communication between the Soviet Government and the governments of their own countries, and it became apparent that they knew very little of what was going on. Most of my satellite colleagues in Moscow, hastily recruited when the old bourgeois diplomatic career staffs were liquidated immediately after the war, were acquiescent leftist professors or writers—high-minded people, yes, but trusted by no one. They did not dare to associate with the diplomatic corps in general, and they got no better reception from the Russians than the rest of us; in fact, I believe they were even more dis-

trusted than were we Westerners. Any Russian official has
been trained how to deal with a capitalist, but, apparently, he
has not been trained how to deal with a hybrid. In those circumstances, the Russian knows very well that his best bet is to
do nothing and say nothing, but remain on his guard. Occasionally these unhappy satellite diplomats would venture to
invite non-Communist colleagues whom they regarded as relatively neutral or safe, together with Soviet officials or other
satellite diplomats. I have heard amusing accounts of these
occasions. No one says anything. If some well-meaning individual, in an effort to be congenial, casually mentions the
weather, the whole company freezes, remembering that such
information was recently classified as an official state secret by
Soviet decree. The entire evening thus goes on, through an
infinite succession of courses, from vodka and caviar to Russian
pastry, in an atmosphere of melancholy silence or utter trivia.
Finally, at an early hour, the company disbands—the host completely exhausted and the others searching their souls to see if
they had dropped an incriminating word during the ordeal.

The mistake made by Zhdanov and his top lieutenants, when
they chose this open fight to show other national Communist
leaders they could never be more than "straw bosses" without
independent judgment under Kremlin control, was that they
miscalculated the real character of Tito. While Tito has had
some Moscow training, he was not one of the expatriate Communist puppets who stayed in Moscow during the war and who
were carried back to their own countries on the shoulders of
the Red Army. He spent the war years in his native hills, taking an active and courageous part in the struggle against the
common enemy. He was an independent, self-made man who
had not lost his national character; a vain, self-confident and
successful guerrilla leader. He was fully aware of what the Russians wanted to do to his country, and he could not stomach a
surrender to the Kremlin of the personal power which he had
won mainly by his own efforts.

All the hypocritical verbiage of the Cominform resolution
on Yugoslavia, which we found in our *Pravda*s on June 29,
1948, did not obscure the obvious fact that here was a pure
issue of power—of the individual power which, in the Soviet
mind, means one hundred per cent control from the top down.

And this resolution was but a formal and ostensibly multilateral confirmation of a decision already taken by the Kremlin with regard to a bilateral dispute which had been carried on between Moscow and Belgrade for months. Most of the accusations were farcical in that Tito was condemned for doing most of the things which are established practice in the Soviet Union, and which Tito had learned well during his Moscow training.

The Kremlin certainly did not mind Tito's establishment of a secret police, or of a strong military force. Indeed, the men of the Politburo would have criticized him for doing anything else. But they strongly resented his refusal to let them operate these agencies through Soviet "advisers." The Kremlin certainly could not validly criticize Tito for not having proceeded vigorously and immediately with the collectivization of Yugoslav agriculture. This step required both a thoroughly established regime and a lot of material things, such as tractors and other agricultural machinery. The Russian revolutionaries had, themselves, been obliged to postpone collectivization for nearly a dozen years after the Revolution, until they felt able to weather the destruction of millions of recalcitrant private peasant farmers. But the Kremlin vigorously resented Tito's independent decision to go slowly.

The Kremlin cannot risk the existence of a Communist Party abroad which is not an abject instrument of Soviet foreign policy, and to which other nationalistic forces in the Balkans or Eastern Europe might adhere. To do so would risk the formation of a Balkan bloc not under direct Kremlin control, another power center which the Soviet Union is determined to prevent.

Moscow must, therefore, attempt to destroy Tito and his machine and to install its own puppets, and will continue its efforts to eliminate him either by political maneuver, economic pressure or assassination.

The split between Tito and the Kremlin, and its Cominform, is profound, and it strikes at the heart of the Stalinist objective of Russian expansion through the instrumentality of complete Kremlin control of world communism. On the other hand, Tito's attitude toward the West has softened only slightly, in spite of his defiance of the Kremlin. He continues to attack the Western democracies as reactionary, imperialist and war-mongering. Neither he nor his principal lieutenants are likely to deviate from their Communist faith, and the Yugoslav Communist Party keeps Yugoslavia in line in the bloc of so-called anti-imperialist countries of the "new democracies." But in spite of our dislike of dictatorships, and certainly Tito's is an advanced form of Communist dictatorship, it is not to our interest to make his position more difficult; in fact, quite the contrary, for if a power-vacuum developed in Yugoslavia due to Tito's weakness, as a result of economic deterioration, this vacuum would inevitably be filled by a Communist regime completely subservient to Moscow.

It is our policy to do what may be possible to assist the people of the world who are now being held in slavery by Communist regimes to free themselves. The United States certainly desires that the Yugoslav people should be free to select the government of their choice. It follows, inevitably, that we oppose in principle the totalitarian dictatorship of Tito. The fact remains that Tito has defied the Kremlin, with its expansionist policy of world domination, and he has destroyed, at least for the time being, the myth of Stalin's infallibility. He does not feel under obligation to Moscow, and he refuses to become an instrument of Soviet imperialism. While he is, paradoxically, himself guilty of "Stalinism," his is a Yugoslav "Stalinism" and a nationalism with a patriotic focus in Belgrade, not in Moscow.

Nationalist tendencies in Communist-dominated countries, whose Communist parties themselves have only unwillingly accepted the iron control of Moscow, have been given hope by his so-far successful bid for independence, but his position is precarious. He has shown no signs of an intention to broaden the base of his power in Yugoslavia by negotiating with non-Communist elements; perhaps he cannot, because to depart from his present pattern of full control by the Communist Party quite probably might mean the beginning of the end of his regime.

The mass of Yugoslavs will back Tito against Moscow and the Cominform, but not against the West. Tito knows this. He and his lieutenants have a deep personal conceit, which most probably transcends their devotion to the Communist religion.

They are not prepared to relinquish their power, and they are now presented with a choice of readjusting their faith, of stepping aside, or of being liquidated. Faced with these alternatives, they are already beginning to rationalize their Communist faith and to invent new dogmas.

Many of Tito's leading lieutenants are not Communist theoreticians or idealists, but rather tough Yugoslav nationalists who have risen to positions of great power within the Yugoslav Communist movement through force, rather than through theory. They are realists, who hardly could be expected to face extinction for a Marxian tenet. It follows that the forces of political, economic and ideological attraction inexorably will draw Tito and his government toward the West. It seems to me that these forces should be encouraged and have free play. This will require an increase in our commerce with Yugoslavia, else the Soviet Union, by sheer economic pressure, will destroy the will to resist on the part of a cold, hungry population of fifteen million, over which Tito now rules, the large majority of whom hate the Communist system, whether it is of the Moscow or the domestic brand. We should ship goods to Yugoslavia which represent no threat to our national security, but which are vital to Yugoslav economy without Soviet support.

Tito's defection has been a profound shock to the Russians, and throughout the Balkans it has had repercussions which are now provoking ruthless and bloody repression. Nevertheless, while Tito survives, I cannot help but feel that the Soviet Union will have increasing difficulty in consolidating its complete control over the countries of Central Europe. In these countries there is entrenched a strong feeling of nationalism. In some of them, such as Czechoslovakia and Poland for instance, freedom is remembered, and international communism, with complete subservience to the boss of its party, will be hard-pressed where love of country prevails and where some individual liberty has been known. Even those Central European states with strong popular Communist tendencies will want to adapt communism to their own national characteristics, and this of course violates the "rule or ruin" policy of the Kremlin. Even in Russia, there is a conflict, although a less significant one, between nationalism and internationalism.

The Communist Party of U.S.S.R., through the agency of the

Cominform, is therefore now engaged in a long-range and thorough housecleaning of all dissident and dangerous elements. The major purpose is to produce as promptly as possible in the countries of the Soviet orbit a hard core of Communist adherents who are unquestionably loyal to the Kremlin, are in firm control of their respective countries, and are completely trustworthy in the event of war between the U.S.S.R. and the West.

As the Soviet position in the West has deteriorated, the U.S.S.R. realizes that it must use the precious time at its disposal to place its own house, and those of its satellites, in order. The Kremlin is fully conscious of the relative unpopularity of the Soviet Union among the nationalistic peoples of its satellite area, and that consciousness, plus its knowledge of the strong nationalism which has ever pervaded these peoples, whether resisting the Turk, the Teuton or the Russian rule, combine to make any nationalism, if opposed to Soviet imperialism, a cardinal sin among Communists. It is to be exterminated at all costs, since in time of crisis it might be synonymous with disloyalty to the Soviet Union.

X

THE MOSCOW CONFERENCE

Soviet war aims: "Equality of nations and inviolability of their territories; liberation of enslaved nations and restoration of their sovereign rights; the right of every nation to arrange its life in accordance with its own wishes; rendering economic aid to the nations that suffered losses; restoration of democratic liberties, destruction of the Hitler regime."

—Stalin: Speech, November 6, 1942

THE Moscow Conference of Foreign Ministers which opened on March 10, 1947, is remembered for its failures rather than for its accomplishments. I think of it as a very successful failure. This meeting of the Foreign Ministers, in spite of all the frustrations it produced, resulted in clarifying beyond any possibility of misinterpretation the Soviet attitude toward Germany and Austria, and this in turn resulted in unifying the policies of France, Britain and the United States to an extent which otherwise might have been impossible.

Early in January, we began preparations for receiving our delegation and facilitating their work. While the administrative section of the Embassy concerned itself with housing, food and transportation, the Chancery officers prepared, for the benefit of our incoming delegation, our own advance estimate of the course the conversations might take and the line of action we might expect from Soviet representatives. The main issue, it was already established, would be Germany and, with it, the future of Europe.

We believed that our experience in Austria was adequate indication of how the Soviet Government could neutralize the effectiveness of any strongly centralized government. We estimated that the Soviet Union would seek agreement now on a similarly centralized government for Germany in the hope of neutralizing its effectiveness by the same methods. The objective of the Kremlin, we believed, would be to restrain the rehabilitation of the Western zones and prevent the development of federalism unless it was bound by the rigid framework of its own Communist one-party machine. We also believed that the Russians demanded all of the privileges of the Anglo-American concept of democracy to forward their legal and underground organizations in the Western zones, but that they would continue to deny similar privileges in the Soviet occupied zone.

It was obvious that reparations would play a major role in the discussions. If the Soviet Union could win its fight for a high reparations figure, this would at once solve a very great economic problem at home and at the same time retard the growth of a healthy economy in the Western zones of Germany. We attached the same dual significance to the question of the Ruhr.

We recalled the extreme reaction of Moscow and the foreign Communist parties to the British and American plans for economic unification of their zones in Germany. This had been denounced as anti-Soviet, and as a direct violation of the Potsdam agreement which would promote federalism, facilitate the intervention of "monopoly capital" into Western Germany, and destroy the unity of the country, both political and economic.

However, by now we were entirely familiar with the Soviet tactic of accusing others of the very sins which they themselves were in process of committing. For this reason, we felt sure the Kremlin would continue to distort the Potsdam agreement in order to quote it against the West and in support of Soviet objectives. It seemed probable that the Soviet representatives would charge us with an attempt to split Germany in two, whereas in actual fact the increasing separation of that country was an inescapable result of the totalitarian economic and political methods employed by the Soviet Government in its own zone.

As to American policy for the future, it was our view that we should be prepared, if necessary, to accept temporary separation of the Eastern and Western zones, rather than to acquiesce in a hollow unification which would simply facilitate the achievement of Soviet objectives in Germany as a whole.

The only right thing for us to do, we felt, was to promote and support in word and deed all truly democratic and progressive forces in our zone, and in so far as we could to defend them from infiltration and subversion by totalitarian machinations from the East. I underlined the need for *active* support and defense as distinguished from the moral support and defense which I felt was all that we had so far provided.

Because of these fundamental issues, it seemed probable to us that the Moscow Conference would be tedious and prolonged. The Russians were at home and would find patience an easy virtue, but I felt that we must be prepared to match patience with patience, no matter how trying this might be. I hoped that our delegation would come to Moscow resigned to an indefinite prolongation of deliberation if this was necessary; and that arrangements would be made so that we could carry on "at the deputy level" if Secretary Marshall had to return to Washington for some important reason.

For the official delegation itself, there were no serious difficulties. In spite of the acute housing shortage all over Moscow, the Soviet Government emptied its best hotel, the Moscow, and several other smaller hotels, of their semi-permanent and transient guests to make room for the visitors. The buildings were given an almost complete cellar-to-attic renovation, with the refurbishing extending even to include brand-new uniforms for the doormen and attendants, who acted very self-conscious indeed in such unaccustomed finery. As the final touch, a fleet of Zis taxicabs appeared one morning in an impressive cab rank in front of the Moscow Hotel, which was just across the square from our Chancery building. To most Muscovites, whose previous experience with taxicabs had been limited to one and one-half ton trucks on which the word Taxi had been painted on the tailgate, this must indeed have seemed the beginning of the millennium.

Some time later I remarked to the director of the Stalin Auto Works that I would have thought the smaller Moskvich or Pobieda cars would have been more suitable for taxis than the expensive, handmade Zis. He replied that he thought so too, but that "Comrade Stalin wanted the others."

We could provide sleeping accommodations at Spaso House only for the Secretary of State and two or three of his staff. But we prepared to feed people at almost any hour, since we knew that sessions would be long and most of the staff members

would be working far into the nights. The ballroom again became, as in wartime, a workroom for the stenographic pool and
the indispensable battery of mimeograph machines. Parlors,
billiard room and halls were converted into offices and reference
libraries. The dining room and pantry became a cafeteria and
tray-service restaurant. To most American embassies around
the world, this would have been a tiresome chore, but to us in
Moscow, isolated as we were, the prospect of an extended visit
by old and new friends from home was delightful and exciting—
well worth any effort.

My only real difficulty during this preparatory period had to
do with the number of American correspondents who would be
admitted to Moscow to cover the conference. I was present at
the London Conference, when the decision was taken to hold
the next Foreign Ministers' meeting in Moscow. At that time,
the question of press representatives and censorship was raised,
and Mr. Molotov said that there would be no restrictions imposed on correspondents. The Americans and others had interpreted this to mean that there would be no restriction on the
number of correspondents who could attend, as well as no censorship of what they wrote. Quite naturally, almost every paper
in the United States wanted to utilize this opportunity to send
a correspondent to Russia. It was with some difficulty that the
State Department's press section in Washington reduced the list
to about one hundred, I believe, and there were roars of indignation and charges of breach of faith when the Soviet Foreign
Office announced that a maximum of twenty reporters and
broadcasters from each nation would be admitted. Telegrams
from the State Department and protests from the press began
to pour into the Embassy, and I went to see Mr. Vishinsky to
do what I could. He, of course, called my attention to the housing shortage. I had anticipated this, and I knew that it was a
valid argument—but I also was fully aware that it was not the
only reason. The Kremlin, quite seriously, viewed newspaper
and radio correspondents as spies, or, at the very least, as highly
undesirable observers who would have an almost free hand because of the unusually liberal conditions that were to prevail
during the conference.

Somewhat to my surprise, Mr. Vishinsky pointed up his argument about lack of space by remarking, "You must realize that
these people that we have put out of hotels are not exactly

shopkeepers!" You can imagine my surprise at such a comment from a leader of the "classless society."

When I recovered from my shock, I produced my carefully prepared space-saving plan. I told Mr. Vishinsky that in the interest of more adequate press coverage by U.S. newspapers, we would reduce our official delegation from one hundred to eighty-four. This would free sixteen hotel rooms. We also would place our delegation headquarters in the Embassy, thus freeing five more hotel rooms which had been reserved for this purpose. (This was easy, as we had no intention of compromising the secrecy of our intra-delegation discussions by holding meetings in a Soviet hotel.)

I stated that we would accommodate the Secretary of State and three others in Spaso House. This would free four additional rooms, or a total of twenty-five. The correspondents would double up, two to a room.

Thus, we could provide sleeping accommodations for fifty more reporters without any change in our present space allocation. It was hard to get around these figures, but Mr. Vishinsky did it.

With unfailing courtesy, he maintained his position, reluctantly granting permission for one reporter and then another, taking so long to do it that finally the State Department was as glad as I was to compromise for an additional sixteen. Most of the thirty-six radio and press representatives were top-flight representatives of their newspapers and radio networks, and both the conference and Moscow were covered very ably for this brief period of no censorship.

On March 8, the delegations began to arrive. Mr. Bevin and M. Bidault, both of whom I knew, came by train. I met them both at the railroad station, together with all the other Chiefs of Mission in Moscow, as is customary when the Foreign Minister or the Chief of State of one of the great powers makes an official visit to a foreign capital.

Secretary Marshall arrived by plane on March 9. The big C-54 touched down on the Moscow Central Airport at 3:30 P.M. in the frosty wind and clear sunlight of a Russian early spring day. General Marshall looked very fit, and his quiet dignity made an immediate impression as I introduced him to Mr. Vishinsky and to the foreign Ambassadors. Moscow's diplomats for some time had been speculating on how the Secretary of

State, without previous experience in international conferences, would be able to deal with what one of them called "this
group of tough, Middle-Eastern bazaar traders."

I had no misgivings whatever. I had seen General Marshall
under all conditions of stress and strain, and I had never seen
him fail eventually to dominate every gathering by the sheer
force of his integrity, honesty and dignified simplicity. Moreover, his whole service had been a preparatory course for high-
level negotiations. I knew that he would say little until he had
the situation and all the facts well in hand and that he would
make no mistakes. When necessary, he is patience personified,
and no one ever takes liberties with him.

My pleasure in greeting him was tempered by his obvious
lack of admiration for my diplomatic "bowler" hat, purchased
in Paris in a moment of desperation when I found I could not
reconvert my excess French currency into dollars, and worn for
the first time in his honor. When later I saw it in a photograph,
I understood his reaction.

The following morning, March 10, the conference opened
in the Hall of Aviation Industry, a handsome building that
stands on the site formerly occupied in Czarist days by the famous Yar restaurant.

This haunt of the wild and wealthy young nobility was im-
mortalized in a very old Russian ballad, which goes:

> Sweetheart, don't go to the Yar,
> Don't throw your money away.
>   Better to buy a guitar,
> And play on it all of the day.

With a few changes, I thought this might well have served
as a theme song for the forty-four protracted and frustrating
sessions that followed. The first action of the conference was
definitive enough, however, for it put a period to the brutal and
bloody history of the Prussian state, by an agreement of the
four ministers to liquidate this core of German militarism.
This took place so quickly that it left most of us rather breath-
less. Drew Middleton, then the *New York Times* Moscow correspondent, wrote, with tongue slightly in cheek: "This erasure
in a single minute of a state that for years has dominated Central Europe appears to be a happy augury for the conference of
the powers that battered the Third Reich to its knees."

Secretary Marshall renewed the United States proposal for a forty-year, four-power treaty to insure the world against German aggression. This treaty had been offered first by Secretary of State Byrnes at Paris in July, 1946, and, while not decisively rejected by Mr. Molotov, had been opposed on the ground of inadequacy. The sincerity of the Soviet Government was to be tested on this issue. Molotov had avoided it at Paris. In Moscow, when it no longer could be avoided, he rejected the proposal.

For six weeks, during protracted formal and informal sessions, the council dealt daily with these major questions:

How the economic unification of Germany could be achieved.

The character of a provisional government for Germany and the boundaries of the German state.

Whether the Soviet Union was to win its demands for reparations from current production to satisfy its claim for over-all reparations totaling ten billion dollars from Germany.

The extent to which Allied occupation forces in Germany could be reduced.

Which states would participate in a peace conference to draft the German peace treaty.

The definition of "German assets" in Austria, an important issue that would determine the amount of property in Eastern Austria that would remain in Soviet possession.

Yugoslavia's claim for a portion of Austrian territory in the province of Carinthia.

While there were agreements on many minor points discussed by the Foreign Ministers and their deputies, there was no substantive agreement on any of the major issues.

Indicative of the way things went was the dialogue on March 28—at the sixteenth meeting—between Mr. Bevin and M. Bidault:

"Where are we?" Mr. Bevin asked.

"God knows," M. Bidault replied.

"I didn't know He was a member of the Council of Foreign Ministers," Mr. Bevin rejoined.

And, on April 7, after the council had been in session for nearly a month, Mr. Bevin summed up its accomplishments thus: "There doesn't appear to be any agreement anywhere."

A few minutes later, when the Ministers were wrangling over

procedure and the question of which item was to precede another on the agenda for the following day, the disgusted British Foreign Secretary declared that, as nothing had been accomplished in four weeks, "I don't care what you take up tomorrow."

With the censorship bars down, and a considerable number of newspapermen on hand, the Foreign Ministers' conference was better reported than any other spot-news story during the period I was in Moscow. The American and other delegations regularly briefed their correspondents on developments at each meeting, with the exception of the rare closed or informal meetings on which only brief uninformative communiqués were issued.

There were dramatic incidents behind the scenes that highlighted far more clearly the clash of policies, the trends of thought and the growing disillusionment that marked what Foreign Secretary Bevin characterized as probably the most important meeting the Council of Foreign Ministers had held. One of these occurred at Spaso House during the formal dinner given by Secretary Marshall for the other conferees.

The conference that day had climaxed a series of discussions on the regime for the Saar, an area vital to the industry of France, since it is a major source of French coal supply. M. Bidault had proposed the detachment of the Saar from Germany and an economic and monetary union between France and the Saar as the best means of organizing for the future the relationship between the two areas. The United States and the United Kingdom, after considerable discussion and some modification, had come to support the French proposal. Molotov had played with it for days, like a cat with a mouse. No matter how he was pressed, he would never take a stand either for or against the French proposal. He obviously was trying to hold back his answer for use as a trading point to obtain French agreement for Soviet participation in the control of the Ruhr, the great industrial area of Germany. M. Bidault must have been greatly tempted, for the future of the Saar was a matter of genuine concern to every Frenchman. Finally, on April 10, M. Bidault pressed for a decision. Mr. Bevin and Secretary Marshall voted to accept the French proposals. Mr. Molotov countered by asking for a reply on the Soviet proposals on the Ruhr. M. Bidault said that he was ready to discuss the Ruhr but that the question of the Saar was now before the council and a decision had been asked for. Molotov replied coldly that he had no further remarks to make. This was a rejection of the French proposals, since in the absence of unanimity they went by default, and it was a bitter pill for the French delegation to swallow.

During the dinner that evening, M. Bidault ate nothing, and, although he joined in the general conversation with great courtesy and self-possession, it was obvious that he felt deeply the rebuff of the afternoon. When his time came to propose a toast, he did not, like the others, make the stereotyped remarks about friendship and the future, but, raising his glass, he said, crisply, that he drank "to those of us here who love freedom." As both Molotov and Vishinsky were well aware of the French statesman's opinion of the Soviet idea of freedom, their exclusion from this toast was clear and unmistakable.

We had minor daily comedies and tragedies within our own delegation. Its members were working sixteen and eighteen hours a day. They felt keenly the frustrations of the conference. They were tense, and during discussions and drafting meetings, feelings often ran high. I did what I could to pour oil on troubled waters, but it was Mrs. Smith who was most effective in smoothing down "ruffled feathers" and seeing that trays of hot lunch got to those who could not, or would not, take time away from their desks to come to the dining room to eat with their colleagues.

Not that agreements were easy, even on matters on which, in general terms, all Americans are in agreement. It took all of the senior advisers of the delegation about six hours, for example, to agree on the wording of our definition of the term "democracy."

One of our greatest sources of difficulty in dealing with the Soviet Union in the past has been that we naively assumed that the word "democracy" meant the same thing to the Politburo as it did to us. It does not. Lenin wrote much about democracy. In his *Collected Works* the statement appears that "democracy is a state which recognizes the subordination of the minority to the majority; that is, an organization for the systematic use of violence by one class against another, by one section of the population against another."

It was high time to pin down this basic and irreconcilable

difference between the Communist idea and our own, for the Kremlin's double talk about democracy and democratic governments in interpreting previous Big Three compacts had caused enough confusion, misery and suffering.

In the version that he himself revised, Secretary Marshall's statement to the conference on March 14 of what the American people understood democracy to be constituted what was probably the most forthright statement on the rights of man ever made in Russia.

The United States Government and its citizens, said the Secretary, understood the term "democracy" to specify certain inalienable rights that may not be given or taken away. These include "the right of every individual to develop his mind and soul in ways of his choice, free of fear or coercion—provided only that he does not interfere with the rights of others.

"To us," the Secretary said, "society is not democratic if men who respect the rights of their fellow men are not free to express their own beliefs and convictions without fear that they may be snatched away from their home and family. To us, a society is not free if law-abiding citizens live in fear of being denied the right to work or of being deprived of life, liberty and the pursuit of happiness."

I wondered, as I drove to the Kremlin with General Marshall and Mr. Bohlen on the night of April 15, whether Stalin had read the minutes of the meeting at which Secretary Marshall had given his definition of democracy. General Marshall purposely had deferred requesting an interview with Stalin until the pattern of the conference had been established. Since it was now clear that no amount of time and energy would be sufficient to give the conference a real basis for agreement, so far as the German problem was concerned, it seemed the time was appropriate for re-stating to Stalin the position of the United States—its willingness to cooperate and its determination not to be coerced.

Both Mr. Bevin and M. Bidault had already called upon Generalissimo Stalin, and Secretary Marshall's call could no longer be delayed without discourtesy.

The setting of the meeting was identical with that of my own first interview. Mr. Molotov and young Mr. Troyanovsky, the Foreign Office interpreter, were with Stalin when Bohlen and I followed General Marshall into the paneled conference room which adjoins Stalin's private office. Stalin greeted the Secretary in a friendly fashion, spoke to Bohlen and to me, and then took his usual seat at the end of the table, with Mr. Molotov on his right and Troyanovsky on his left. Bohlen, who is one of our outstanding Russian specialists and fluent in the language, interpreted for General Marshall, whose initial presentation was a quiet but forceful review of the difficulties which had beset us since the Potsdam Conference. Our present negotiations, said the Secretary, involved not only the security of Europe and the world, but the prosperity of all Europe. While our specific mission was to consider the terms of a treaty operating over a long term of years, we were faced with immediate issues which concerned in the most vital way the impoverished and suffering people of Europe.

Stalin listened impassively while the American Secretary of State reviewed the deterioration of relations between the East and West, and the tragic consequences which this seemed to portend to the entire world. From time to time, Stalin puffed at a long Russian cigarette, or "doodled" with a blue pencil on the notepaper before him. He did not comment, or interrupt, and only exchanged a quick, whispered word with Molotov when General Marshall referred to Soviet delay, or failure, to reply to our requests for a Lend-Lease settlement and similar outstanding questions of importance.

When Secretary Marshall concluded his remarks, Stalin began to speak in an equally quiet and friendly tone.

"It is wrong," he said, "to give so tragic an interpretation to our present disagreements."

He looked upon our differences like a quarrel within a family. With reference to the present conference, and the problem of Germany, the differences which had developed were "only the first skirmishes and brushes of reconnaissance forces" on this question. Differences had occurred in the past on other questions, he went on, and as a rule "when people had exhausted themselves in dispute, they recognized the necessity for compromise."

It was possible, he said, that no great success would be achieved at this session, but he thought that compromises were possible on all the main issues, including the demilitarization of Germany, its political structure, reparations and economic unity. It was necessary to have patience, and not to become pessimistic.

"With regard to Soviet delays in replying to your representations on various subjects," he continued, "I would remind Mr. Marshall that more than two years ago the Soviet Government made a request of the United States for a financial credit, and that to date no reply or acknowledgment has ever been received."

At this point, I thought it proper to pass to Mr. Molotov a note to remind him that when I came to Moscow I had brought the reply to this request. Mr. Molotov whispered this to Stalin, and received in return a distinct "family" look. The Generalissimo then corrected his statement accordingly, but remarked that even a year's delay in replying seemed to him to be somewhat excessive.

He certainly had a good point there. I doubt that he accepted the perfectly truthful if somewhat incredible explanation that the Soviet letter had, in some unaccountable way, become lost in Washington, which was the reason it had not been answered promptly.

When the Secretary rose to leave, I looked at my watch. The exchange of views had lasted eighty-eight minutes, and I felt that little had been accomplished. I had heard similar reassurances from Stalin before, and I had become skeptical. The Russian version of the old proverb goes, "What you do speaks so loudly that I can't hear what you say"—and the Russians were dramatizing it for us.

Certainly there was nothing in the conduct of the Soviet delegation during subsequent conference sessions which lent any substantiation to the Generalissimo's reassuring remarks.

On the important question of German economic unification, there had already been agreement in principle at the Potsdam meeting, but wide and critical differences developed when it came to the question of formulating the actual terms for producing this unity. The Soviet delegation, while paying lip service to the principle, steadily refused to provide any information regarding the availability of foodstuffs in the Soviet zone (which has long been the granary of Germany) or to give any real indication of the amount of reparations which had been taken out of the country. While bitterly attacking the economic unification of the British and American zones as a breach of the

Potsdam agreement and a step in the dismemberment of Germany, the Soviet authorities constantly refused any modification of the system under which the Soviet-occupied zone has been operated as a separate economic entity without regard to the economy of the other three zones. It was apparent that not even paper concessions would be made unless the Western states agreed to admit the Soviet Union to participation in the control of the Ruhr. That agreement, of course, would have put the Kremlin in position to strangle at will the economy of all Germany.

Molotov remained rigid in his opposition to any form of government for Germany except one that provided for strong and complete centralized control. This issue of the degree of centralization of the future German Government was of the greatest importance. An excessive concentration of power is particularly dangerous in a country like Germany, which has no strong traditions regarding the rights of the individual and of the community to control the exercise of governmental power. It is equally true that a tightly centralized government is too vulnerable to penetration, attack and capture by a ruthless, lawless, political minority group. The Western delegations favored a central government possessing carefully limited and defined powers, with the residue of authority left to the several states. France went much further than did Britain or America in her desire to limit the responsibilities of the central government, but all three were agreed in principle.

The establishment of a provisional German government was obviously an impossibility until the boundaries of the area that it would govern could be defined. Here again we ran into head-on disagreement. When the Soviet armies overran Eastern Germany, millions of Germans fled to the west of the Oder River, largely evacuating the area. The Russians moved Poles into the area. At the Potsdam Conference, President Truman accepted this only as a temporary situation, and it was there agreed that "the heads of government reaffirm their opinion that the final determination of the western frontier of Poland should await the peace settlement."

Mr. Molotov stubbornly disregarded this agreement, although he constantly reverted to the other agreements made at Potsdam, which he charged us with violating. He contended that a final agreement on the frontier between Germany and

Poland had been reached at Potsdam and that the statement I have quoted above merely meant that a formal confirmation of the frontier already agreed upon would be made at the peace settlement, after only technical discussions.

There was no fact, logic or reason to support this position—only the maddening Soviet formulas, "It is well known," or, "As it is generally known." I am sure that there is no statesman or diplomat who has dealt with the Russians who has not, at some time or another, sat in silent fury while a Soviet representative smugly produced one of these exasperating phrases to back up an absolutely false and untenable proposal. They were used at the Moscow Conference more extensively than ever before in my own experience, and I thought often of Benjamin Franklin's formula for a diplomat: "Sleepless tact, unmovable calmness, and a patience that no folly, no provocation, no blunders can shake."

Reparations from Germany's current production was another sticking point. With the bitter lesson of the Versailles Treaty of 1919 before them, the conferees at Potsdam had agreed upon the principle of getting reparations from capital assets; that is, by the actual transfer or removal of German industrial plants, machinery and physical assets to the Allied powers concerned. The Soviet Union had liked this idea at the time. It visualized a wonderful improvement in Soviet economy if fine, modern German industries were transplanted bodily to the Soviet Union.

At Moscow, the Soviet conferees flatly denied their agreement and demanded reparations from current German production. I knew why. The destructive and unskilled methods used by the Soviet Army in dismantling German industrial plants had been enormously wasteful, and it had proved difficult for the Russians to re-establish these plants in the Soviet Union.

Foreigners who traveled by rail from Berlin to Moscow reported that every railroad yard and siding was jammed with German machinery, much of it deteriorating in the rain and snow. The plan had proved a disappointment. Molotov's demand for ten billion dollars in reparations from current German production (he refused to give any information as to the value already taken out of Germany) meant that a very large portion of the daily production of almost all German factories would go for reparations payments to the Soviet Union for a long time. The United States was putting money into Germany in the expectation that the German economy would become self-supporting in three years. The Soviet demand would delay indefinitely the day when Germany would be self-supporting. Since her economy would collapse without United States aid in the meantime, the granting of the full Soviet claim for reparations would mean simply that the American taxpayers were paying for operating an industrial complex to manufacture products for the Soviet Union. We were willing to study the possibility of a limited amount of reparations from current production to compensate the Russians if they left in place industrial plants previously scheduled for removal to the Soviet Union. But Molotov wanted to eat his cake and have it too. For this reason, he made no response to our suggestion.

The debate over the American proposal for a progressive reduction in the number of occupation troops in Germany found the Soviet authorities attempting to confuse the issue by declaring that they needed for their zone 200,000 troops, but that the British and the Americans should have only 100,000 each, or a total of 200,000 between them, because they had unified their zones. Mr. Molotov proposed that the French should have 50,000 troops. To this proposal, Mr. Bevin replied that he had been instructed to agree to 145,000 for the British zone, the Soviet figure of 100,000 being a little too low. M. Bidault said the French Government could not agree to a figure below 70,000 for the French zone. Being unable to agree among themselves, the Foreign Ministers referred the issue to the Allied Control Council in Germany.

The Russians, it seemed clear from the outset, were determined to nullify the economic fusion of the British and the American occupied zones of Germany (which the French later were to join) and put the meeting of their full reparations demands, including payments from current production, as the price for economic and political unification of Germany as a whole. Although there were at that time differences between the French, the British and the Americans as to the best political and economic policies to be pursued in Germany, none of the three Western powers could accede to the Soviet demands.

The Soviet proposals, Secretary Marshall told the Council of Foreign Ministers on March 31, could be accomplished immediately only by reducing imports, which he said inevitably would reduce German per capita consumption to about 1,100 calories per day, "which is inadequate over any considerable period of time to sustain life.

"The people of Europe lack the elementary necessities of life," General Marshall continued. "This lack can be filled only by the production of goods of all kinds. A reasonable increase in the level of industry in Germany will help in time to produce more goods. With the four-power treaty which we have proposed guaranteeing the continued demilitarization of Germany, a reasonable increase in the level of industry should not endanger European security but should contribute materially to European recovery.

"The United States is opposed to policies which will continue Germany as a congested slum or an economic poorhouse in the center of Europe. At the same time, we recognize that Germany must pay reparations to the countries who suffered from its aggression. Within these limits, we want Germany to use its resources of skilled manpower, energy and industrial capacity to rebuild the network of trade on which European prosperity depends. Ultimately, it desires to see a peaceful Germany, with strong democratic roots, take its place in the European and world community of nations."

The Western representatives were not entirely surprised over difficulties they encountered in attempting to reach an agreement on Germany, but they had expected progress in formulating a treaty for Austria. Here, at first, things went well, and agreement was reached on all but a few points. But these few were basic and of fundamental importance. The Soviet Union made much of its support of the claims of Yugoslavia for reparations and for the cession of a part of Carinthia from Austria to Yugoslavia. But from remarks made by members of the Soviet delegation, and finally from a covert proposal made by Molotov during the final days of the conference, it was clear that the Soviet Union would abandon its advocacy of Yugoslav claims at once if the Kremlin's definition of what constituted "German assets" in Austria, to which Russia was entitled by prior agreement, was accepted by the Western Allies. Acceptance of the Soviet definition would have meant the removal from Austrian control of so large a portion of Austrian economy that the little nation's chances of surviving as an independent and self-supporting state would have been almost impossible. All efforts to find a compromise were unavailing. The Austrian delegation, headed by its strong, young Foreign Minister, Herr Gruber, though grievously disappointed, showed great courage and fortitude in the face of the Soviet pressures to which it was subjected.

The Austrians are weary and apprehensive. They have had several years of liberation from Nazi domination, and now their devout hope is to be liberated from their "liberators," but their leaders are wise enough to realize that the liberation must be complete or not at all.

I saw nothing in the Soviet position to warrant any change in this estimate. I recorded in my journal in 1946:

"The U.S.S.R. wants a treaty with Austria which will sanction Soviet interference in Austrian internal affairs at any time under the guise of preventing anti-Soviet or pan-German propaganda and through retention of Austrian property claimed by the Soviet Union as German assets."

The best summary of the conference was given by General Marshall in these words:

"Agreement was made impossible at Moscow because, in our view, the Soviet Union insisted upon proposals which would have established in Germany a centralized government, adapted to the seizure of absolute control of a country which would be doomed economically through inadequate area and excessive population, and would be mortgaged to turn over a large part of its production as reparations, principally to the Soviet Union. In another form the same mortgage upon Austria was claimed by the Soviet delegation.

"Such a plan, in the opinion of the United States delegation, not only involved indefinite American subsidy, but could result only in a deteriorating economic life in Germany and Europe and the inevitable emergence of dictatorship and strife."

The last act of the drama took place in the Kremlin, where, in the magnificent hall of Catherine the Great, Stalin gave his dinner for the chiefs of the four delegations and their principal assistants. The American guests were Secretary Marshall, Mr. Ben Cohen, then Counselor of the State Department, Mr. Bohlen and myself. We assembled in a large anteroom, heavy with red velvet hangings, where were gathered the senior officials of the Foreign Office, several of the Marshals of the Soviet Union and all the members of the Politburo, with the exception of Stalin and Molotov, who entered only after all the others were assembled. Although I had been in Moscow more than a year, this was the first time that I had seen at close range in one room the small group of men who rule the Soviet Union. The officers of the Ministries of Foreign Affairs and of the Armed Forces wore their full-dress uniforms and medals. The Politburo members generally were dressed in dark, double- or single-breasted civilian suits. Malenkov, however, had the old party-uniform tunic, with high, turned-down cloth collar. After a few minutes, Stalin and Molotov entered, the former dressed in his usual uniform—not the blue-green uniform worn for dress by Soviet general officers and Marshals, but the color similar to that our own Army calls "suntan." Molotov wore a dark blue civilian suit instead of the Foreign Office uniform, in which he rarely appeared. As they passed around the room, each greeted the guests individually. Stalin then entered the dining room and we followed.

I had heard of the fabulous Kremlin dinners, with endless toasts drunk in vodka or champagne. This was nothing of the kind. It was instead a well-appointed, well-served banquet, no more ostentatious than the average American formal dinner and much less so than others I have seen elsewhere in Europe. Molotov and Stalin faced each other across the center of the long table. Secretary Marshall was on Stalin's right, Mr. Bevin sat on his left, and M. Bidault was next to Mr. Molotov. I was interested to find that Mr. Zhdanov (now dead), whom I had never met before, was on my right. Opposite me sat Voznesensky, the youngest member of the Politburo, who since has been removed without explanation. I noted that Zhdanov ate nothing whatever except a plate of clear soup, and he explained his abstemiousness by saying that he was on a diet. He talked little, but we exchanged a few words through an interpreter and later a phrase or two in French. Voznesensky went out of his way to be pleasant, smiling and lifting his glass whenever he caught the eye of a foreign guest.

Only five toasts were proposed, one by Stalin to President Truman and Secretary Marshall, one by Mr. Molotov to his other conference colleagues and the usual replies by the three Western statesmen, who in one way or another expressed some disappointment at current progress but added their hope for the future. The atmosphere was serious and quiet, but not unfriendly, and the dinner was not prolonged—it hardly lasted an hour. Afterward, Stalin led us down a curving flight of stairs, carpeted in blue, to a moving picture theater, decorated in blue, with curtains and upholstered individual seats of the same color. The seats were grouped in pairs, and in front of each pair was a small table on which stood a box of chocolates, cigarettes, two tall glasses and a double magnum of champagne. My "personal host" was Mr. Mikoyan, the intelligent and worldly-wise little Armenian who at that time was both a member of the Politburo and the Minister of Foreign Trade. The picture was the recently produced Soviet color-film *The Stone Flower*, a European prize-winning production, of which Stalin obviously was proud. He had reason to be, I thought, for both the story—a Russian folk tale of the Ural Mountains—and the actors were good, and the scenic effects in color frequently were splendid.

We were home by midnight—probably a record for entertainment at the Kremlin. It would have been a pleasant evening, had it not been for the general feeling of gloomy frustration on the Western side of the house. Many present wondered, I am sure, if this would not be the last conference of Foreign Ministers. The alternatives of a divided Germany, or a Germany under the effective economic and political domination of the Soviet Union had become unmistakably clear. The Westerners all were facing the cold reality that if the latter alternative were to be prevented, their desire for an undivided Germany could no longer be made an excuse for inaction in Western Germany, which now must be effectively associated with the Western European powers through economic arrangement and perhaps ultimately through mutual political understanding.

In the Kremlin it must have been fully appreciated that, at long last, Soviet objectives in Germany were clearly understood by the Western powers and now were impossible of attainment by diplomatic maneuver. Thus the stage was set for the crisis in Berlin.

XI

BERLIN BLOCKADE

It is not for nothing that the proverb says, "An obliging bear is more dangerous than an enemy."

> —Stalin: Address to Central Committee of CP of S.U., on the Right Deviation, April, 1929

ALLIED relations deteriorated during the first half of 1948 over the festering problem of Germany, which had not yielded to solution at the Moscow and London meetings of the Council of Foreign Ministers.

The Soviet Government persistently refused to carry out the Potsdam commitment signed by Premier Stalin, Prime Minister Attlee and President Truman for economic unification of Germany. It demanded as the price of keeping its promise rich additional concessions, including fulfillment from current production of its demand for over-all reparations totaling ten billion dollars.

The governments of the United States, Great Britain and France, which had not always seen eye to eye on German policy, drew closer together in the face of Soviet recalcitrance based on an obvious "rule or ruin" program. Agreement had already been reached to fuse the Anglo-American occupation zones economically, and, in the spring, the French agreed to add their zone.

To the Men in the Kremlin, on whose horizon Germany historically had always loomed large, either as the greatest potential threat or most valuable potential associate of the Soviet Union, this was a direct challenge—and they set out by every diplomatic maneuver to defeat the Western program for Trizonia and to reduce the political popularity of Western methods and policies among the German people.

On June 24, 1948, despairing of achieving success by diplomatic methods, the Soviet Government attempted a solution by force—the imposition of a complete blockade on all land and water traffic from the Western zones into Berlin, a tiny international enclave completely surrounded by the Soviet zone. This was only the last (and most serious) of a series of restrictions and impediments successively applied from April, 1948, onwards. The Kremlin was willing to gamble on the hunger and privation of 2,250,000 Berliners to halt the Western program of economic and monetary reform, and perhaps force the Western powers out of Berlin itself.

Three hundred and twenty-one days later—on May 12, 1949—without achieving a single stated Soviet objective, the Russians ended the blockade and normal traffic flowed again to a city whose Western areas had been supplied entirely by air for nearly eleven months. Operation Vittles had seen the Americans and British mobilize their air forces for an airlift without parallel in world history—a combined operation that up to the day the blockade ended had moved a total of 1,592,787 tons of food, coal and other supplies to prevent starvation, disease and economic stagnation in Western Berlin.

For the time being, at least, the Soviet Government had lost a desperate effort to gain mastery of Germany, by diplomacy and by force. Of the two failures, inability to achieve its objectives by force had been the more spectacular, and the Kremlin doctrine of infallibility, on which the ruling oligarchy depends so much and which had been shaken by the successful defiance of Marshal Tito of Yugoslavia, received another rude shock.

What had happened that made the Soviet authorities take such a big gamble on Berlin? Why did they finally admit defeat under circumstances that left them no opportunity to save face? We could not believe that they were abandoning their long-term strategy of making all of Germany a part of the Soviet orbit, but what did this change of tactics portend for the future?

I had witnessed the early development of the Soviet program for Germany while the war was still being fought; while on occupation duty in defeated Germany after the war, and from the American Embassy in Moscow since early in 1946, with many trips to Berlin and conferences with General Lucius D.

Clay sandwiched into my stay in the Soviet capital. And now it fell to me to attempt through diplomatic channels a solution to the blockade of Berlin that would restore in full the rights we held by solemn international agreements as an equal occupational authority in the former German capital.

Historical retrospect is necessary to a full appreciation of the German question as we faced it in June of 1948. Lenin had taught that Germany was the European country best suited for the development of communism. He called it "the principal link in the chain of revolution," and Stalin and his colleagues held to this view even with the advent of nazism. Despite the nightmare of war, the dream of a happy union between Soviet resources and manpower and German technical skill and administrative ability has always hovered about the pillows of the Soviet leaders. But the war left the Soviet Union with a deep and dearly bought appreciation of the realities of German aggression, and strengthened the Communist view that Germany must be a satellite and not an equal partner. The devastation wreaked by the Wehrmacht on Soviet land from 1941 to 1945 made the Kremlin unwilling to accept the reconstruction of a strong and independent (and, therefore, possibly hostile) Germany.

It seems apparent now that the Kremlin expected the entry of Soviet forces into Germany in 1945 would be followed either by a Communist revolution or by a strong Leftist movement of the "Popular Front" type, which would have greatly facilitated attainment of Moscow's political objectives. This was not an unreasonable expectation, considering the strength shown by the German Communists in the last free election before Hitler. It must have been a bitter disappointment to the Soviet leaders when they were forced to the realization that they would not receive the support and the cooperation of the non-Communist majority of the German population. Moscow's immediate reaction was to begin the forcible reshaping of the Soviet zone in Germany on the totalitarian pattern developed in the Eastern European satellite states. The economy of Eastern Germany was to be reoriented to fit into the Eastern European economic system under the aegis of the Soviet Union, which would derive most of the benefits from this arrangement.

The Western powers were left with no alternative but to

undertake the integration of the economic and political life of Western Germany into that of Western Europe. This they were forced to do although they realized full well and publicly acknowledged the fact that a division of Germany was undesirable and was not and could not be a lasting solution of the problems of Europe.

As the occupation progressed with the line of demarcation of Eastern and Western Germany becoming more distinct and the Iron Curtain descending along the line of the Oder and Neisse rivers, the Allied outpost in Berlin, far to the eastward in the Soviet zone, became an obstacle, an annoyance and a challenge to the Kremlin.

To understand the problem of Berlin itself it is necessary to go back to the decision that was made at Casablanca in January, 1943, by President Roosevelt and Prime Minister Churchill— later accepted by Premier Stalin—to demand from Germany "unconditional surrender." That meant that the Nazi regime could be expected to fight on until utter extermination. Germany would, therefore, be left in chaos and confusion, physically destroyed, morally bankrupt, without government of any kind.

Accordingly, when Secretary Hull flew to Moscow the following October, it was there agreed that the Allies would establish a European Advisory Commission with headquarters in London to prepare the necessary background studies and make preliminary recommendations for meeting the problems the victorious Allies would face in a thoroughly defeated Germany.

By September, 1944, the European Advisory Commission had come to some tentative conclusions. It was decided to occupy Germany temporarily in view of the certainty that there would be no responsible regime in Germany when the Nazi armies collapsed and because we believed the German people would be so demoralized and face such severe physical handicaps that they could not undertake on their own the establishment of a democratic regime immediately. A period of occupation, it was stated, would help assure eradication of the Nazi influence from German life. The commission proposed that each of the victorious powers (the United States, the Soviet Union, Great Britain and, eventually, France) should assume responsibility for the administration of a particular zone in Germany and for a sector of Berlin.

The following February, President Roosevelt, Prime Minister Churchill and Premier Stalin met at Yalta. They approved the proposal to divide Germany into zones, pending the setting up of a permanent government, and agreed to establish an Allied Control Council, consisting of the four zone commanders, to deal with problems relating to Germany as a whole.

On May 8, 1945, the last of the German armed forces surrendered, and on June 5 the four Allies assumed administration of their respective zones. The area around Berlin necessarily was in the Russian zone. It was logical that the Russians should assume responsibility for the Eastern zone, and the capital is only a short distance from Germany's eastern boundary. The rights of the United States, Britain and France as occupying powers in Berlin derive from international agreements that established four-power control of Berlin on a basis of friendly cooperation. The right of free access to the city was carefully specified in a message sent by President Truman to Premier Stalin on June 14, 1945. In accordance with a general assurance given by Stalin two days later that all necessary measures would be taken in accordance with the plan agreed upon, the United States, whose armies had penetrated deep into the Soviet zone in Saxony and Thuringia, withdrew these advanced forces to its own area of occupation in Germany and took up its position in its own sector of Berlin.

We had a little preliminary taste of what the future might bring while this withdrawal was in progress. As advance elements of our Second Armored Division, veterans of the campaigns of Sicily and France, moved east toward Berlin, they were halted at the Mulde River on the border of the Soviet zone, by bridge guards. A Soviet officer informed Major General Floyd Parks, Commander of the U. S. Sector of Berlin, that Soviet troops must count every vehicle and every man before allowing the Americans to pass, in order to make certain that the actual number tallied with the figure previously furnished to the Soviet Military Command. Rain was falling in torrents. We wanted our troops in Berlin on the following day to prepare for the Fourth of July celebration, but protests were of no avail whatever.

In July, 1945, the Chiefs of State met at Potsdam and agreed
that, while there was to be no central German government for
the time being, the country would be treated as a single economic unit during occupation. Despite this compact, Soviet
authorities carried out a systematic and drastic looting of the
Eastern zone. They failed, moreover, to deliver materials to the
Western zones as had been promised.

The Allied Control Council could not, or some of its members would not, agree on a procedure to administer Germany as
an economic whole. As a result, there was little sharing of
resources and no common foreign trade, banking, mail, telegraph communications or railroad policies. The volume of
trade between the two zones dropped to a low level. The
Western zones felt this most heavily, and the Anglo-American
subsidy to maintain a standard of living above a "starvation
and disease" level increased to a half billion dollars a year. In
retaliation, the United States stopped delivery of reparations
from its zone to the Soviet Union. Now both sides were unhappy, and the whole question was referred to the Council of
Foreign Ministers at its meeting in Paris, which continued from
April to July, 1946.

At this meeting, the Soviet Union insisted upon four-power
control of the Ruhr and demanded establishment of a strongly
centralized German government. The Western Allies favored a
federal type of state. On this issue, the Soviet leaders were following a classic Marxist doctrine, one enunciated in 1850, when
Karl Marx, speaking of the future organization of the German
state, said:

"The *democrats* will either work directly for a federative
republic or at least, if they cannot avoid the republic one and
indivisible, will strive to cripple the central government by
giving the greatest possible autonomy and independence to the
municipalities and provinces. The *workers* must strive against
this plan; not only for a German republic one and indivisible,
but after it for a most decided centralization of power in the
hands of the state (i.e., the central) government. They must
not let themselves be rushed by democratic talk about freedom
of municipalities, self-government, etc. In a country like Germany—it is not to be tolerated under any circumstances that
every village, every town, every province should put a new

obstacle in the path of revolutionary activity, which *can ema-nate in full strength only from the center."*

Americans will do well to remember these hundred-year-old words, for they are one of the keys to current Communist tactics.

As both sides stood pat on policies that apparently were irreconcilable, the United States Government announced in July, 1946, that it was willing to administer its zone in conjunction with any other occupying power or powers as an economic unit. The British Government announced its willingness to join its zone economically with the American zone in January, 1947, and Bizonia came into existence.

Subsequent conferences of the Foreign Ministers in Moscow and London made the basic issues clearer. The Soviet Union wanted a strong central government that would lend itself more easily to Communist infiltration and seizure. The Soviet Union also prevented economic unification apparently in the hope that chaos and misery would produce among the Germans a spirit of hopelessness that would induce them to accept Communist blandishments. In addition, Soviet authorities insisted upon collecting their full claim of ten billion dollars in reparations from Germany, because this would give the U.S.S.R. powerful economic and political controls over Germany.

The governments of the United States and Great Britain believed that the German people should be allowed to decide what form of government they desired and that this decision should be made under conditions of normal existence; in other words, after economic unification had been achieved. The United States and Great Britain also wanted to defer decision on the final amount of reparations to be collected until it was possible to determine what level of industry was to be established in Germany. They argued for a reparations total that could be paid from the German economy, and sought to avoid establishment of a reparations burden so harsh that, since the German economy could not satisfy it, it would in the final analysis have to be paid by American contributions to Germany.

The Soviet Union opposed currency reform because the lack of a sound currency was contributing in large measure to the economic stagnation of Western Germany. The old currency was so worthless that cigarettes had replaced the mark as a measure of value in many areas. For this reason, on June 18, 1948, a new currency was introduced in the Western zones. Following the introduction of the new currency, although many economic stresses remained, factory production increased, goods reappeared in the stores, workers returned to their jobs, agricultural products flowed in from the country, and the general economy was greatly improved.

On June 22, at the request of the three Western powers, a quadripartite meeting of financial and economic advisers took place in Berlin to discuss the problem of currency for Berlin. The Soviet representatives insisted that there could be no currency for Berlin that differed from the currency of the surrounding Soviet zone. They could not agree, they said, to quadripartite control of the currency for Berlin. The meeting ended without agreement, but, as soon as it was over, Soviet authorities issued orders for currency reform in the Soviet zone and *all* of Berlin. On the following day, the Western Allies announced introduction into the Western sectors of Berlin of the new Deutsche mark of the Western zones.

On June 24, 1948, the U.S.S.R., alleging "technical difficulties," halted all rail, road and barge traffic from the Western zones into Berlin. The Western powers countered with the airlift.

Hope for a solution of the impasse obviously lay in the field of diplomacy, and on July 6 the three Western powers delivered almost identical notes to the Soviet Ambassadors in Washington, London and Paris. The notes emphasized that the Western Allies were occupying their sectors of Berlin as a matter of right, arising out of the defeat and surrender of Germany and confirmed by formal agreement. This, of course, was true, regardless of the Communist allegation that the Western authorities were, in effect, guests in a city that formed part of the Soviet zone.

The notes reiterated that the three Western powers would not be induced by threats, pressures or other actions to abandon their rights. They demanded for this reason, and for the sake of the people of Berlin, that the blockade be lifted. They reaffirmed that the Western nations were willing, as always, to seek a solution to the extremely serious international situation which had developed in Berlin by negotiation or by the other methods provided in Article 33 of the Charter of the United Nations. But—and this was an important clause—the three Western nations strongly emphasized that they would not negotiate the Berlin issue or any other German question under duress.

In reply, the Soviet Ambassadors in the three Western capitals delivered on July 14 a note from the Soviet Government that claimed that the difficulties in supplying the population of Berlin in the Western sectors were created by the acts of the governments of the United States, Great Britain and France. The major complaint was the introduction of a new currency into the Western zones and separate currency in the Western sectors of Berlin. The Soviet note went on to assert that Berlin was in the center of the Soviet zone and was part of that zone. It claimed that the Soviet high command had been compelled to take urgent measures to protect the interest of the German population and also the economy of the Soviet zone and the area of greater Berlin. With regard to the expressed readiness of the Western governments to discuss the Berlin situation, the Soviet Government declared that while it did not object to conversations it could not connect the beginning of these conversations with the fulfillment of any preliminary conditions. Four-power conferences, said the Kremlin, could have effect only in the event that they were not limited to the question of the government of Berlin, since this question could not possibly be separated from the general and more important question of four-power control of Germany as a whole.

While the Soviet note was unsatisfactory in itself, it did not entirely close the door on the Berlin question. The Western powers, conscious of the increasingly critical nature of the issue posed in Berlin, believed that a more direct and informal approach might uncover some path to a peaceful solution of this situation, which was so charged with explosive elements.

With this in view, I was instructed to consult with my British and French colleagues in Moscow and to make an effort with them to confer with Generalissimo Stalin himself. My mission was to attempt to clarify the situation, looking toward direct negotiations in the search for a progressive solution of our outstanding differences regarding Berlin and Germany as a whole.

The new French Ambassador in Moscow, M. Yves Chataigneau, had been on post a relatively short time, but he had already become a valued friend in whose judgment I had great
confidence. Ambassador Chataigneau knew the United States,
and during the first World War, as a lieutenant, had served with
distinction as liaison officer with the American forces. His
liaison duties had not prevented him from getting into the thick
of the fighting as often as possible, and as a result he wears the
American Distinguished Service Cross, a decoration that is not
given lightly.

The British Ambassador, Sir Maurice Peterson, was absent
on account of illness, and because of the important nature of
the discussions that were contemplated, the Foreign Office sent
to Moscow Frank Roberts, an old Moscow hand who was at that
time serving as the private secretary to Foreign Secretary Bevin.
Mr. Roberts had been Minister-Counselor at the British Embassy when I arrived. He is one of the best of the younger
British career diplomats in a service the ordinary standards of
which are very high.

So far as I was concerned, I could not have asked for two abler
or more capable associates for a delicate diplomatic negotiation.
During the discussions that followed, we had frequent and
lengthy meetings, at which the most complete frankness and
understanding prevailed. When I think of this association, I
am again convinced that dealing with countries whose ideals
and objectives are similar to our own is a relatively simple matter when honesty and frankness prevail and when the individuals concerned understand and have confidence in each
other.

Our first step was to telephone for an appointment with Mr.
Molotov. Mr. Erfeev, Molotov's principal secretary, replied to
this request with the statement that Mr. Molotov was on a
vacation. He suggested that, as Mr. Vishinsky was also absent at
the Danubian conference in Belgrade, I should talk with Deputy Foreign Minister Zorin, then the junior of the Deputy
Ministers of Foreign Affairs. I pointed out to Mr. Erfeev that
the matter on which we asked to see Mr. Molotov was of great
importance and I asked if the Foreign Minister might be available within a few days. Mr. Erfeev said that he would make
inquiry and would let me know. Later in the day he telephoned

to say that since Mr. Molotov's vacation had only just begun he would not be available and that it would be necessary for us to see Mr. Zorin. Our guess was that Mr. Molotov was no farther away than his *dacha* in the country, a few minutes drive from Moscow. We believed that the Foreign Office simply wished to see, in advance of a high-level conference, exactly what it was that we intended to propose. We probably were right, because Mr. Molotov received us one day after our first talk with Mr. Zorin.

We called on Mr. Zorin early in the evening of July 30, and each of us presented him with identical memoranda, which pointed out that in the opinion of our governments the best way to a solution of existing difficulties lay in direct approach. We requested that arrangements be made for an interview between Generalissimo Stalin and Mr. Molotov on the one hand and the French Ambassador, the special envoy of the United Kingdom and myself, on the other, "in order to discuss the situation in Berlin and its wide implications."

Mr. Zorin was cool and uncompromising. He said that Mr. Molotov's absence on vacation made such a meeting impossible at this time. There was no indication in my memorandum, he continued, that the position of the United States had changed on any subjects that would make profitable a discussion with Generalissimo Stalin and Mr. Molotov. He added, however, that he would transmit the request to his government for consideration.

My purpose was to obtain a conference with Stalin, and I knew I would have to run the gantlet, not only of Zorin, but also of Molotov. I replied, therefore, that this preliminary presentation purposely had been made brief, since the general position of the United States had been made clear, but that it would be redefined and amplified during the proposed discussions.

Mr. Zorin stated that he could say only that the position of the Soviet Government also had been clearly defined in its note of July 14, but that he would, as he had said previously, present our request to his government.

This left us somewhat in the dark, but we felt quite certain that Mr. Molotov would take in hand a matter as important as this. So it proved, for on the following day we were informed that separate appointments with Molotov had been made for us that evening.

I found Mr. Molotov in his office at the Foreign Ministry, and he came to the point at once by asking what kind of discussion and negotiations the Western governments had in mind both for the present and for the future. I had no intention of using up my ammunition on Mr. Molotov alone, so I answered that my memorandum had been intentionally brief and lacking in detail, since it was the purpose of the proposed conversations to develop the necessary details.

Mr. Molotov re-emphasized the point in the Soviet note that conversations regarding Berlin were of no useful purpose except within the framework of conversations regarding all of Germany. He continued to probe for some statement of our views on the latter question, and I continued to reply that while the formal position of the respective governments had been set forth in formal notes, the formal written word was very rigid, and much more might be accomplished by informal exploration.

Finally Mr. Molotov said that he would report to his government and that "he hoped Generalissimo Stalin would agree to meet the representatives of the three governments."

Mr. Roberts, M. Chataigneau and I met late that night to compare notes. There was no longer any doubt in our minds that Stalin would meet with us. We had to decide how we should proceed in presenting our case to him. We all felt that there should be one spokesman for our side of the discussion, and because I was the senior of the three from point of service in Moscow, the duty (and responsibility) fell to me. We agreed also that we should compare and coordinate our respective reports to our governments, so that London, Paris and Washington all would get the same general picture. We also would compare and coordinate the instructions we received.

We knew, of course, that there would be difficulties. The time difference between Moscow and our several capitals was one source. I think we also were conscious of the fact that back in the Foreign Offices at home there were a lot of very able young experts who would feel quite sure (possibly with some reason) that they could conduct the negotiations far better than we could. For this reason we agreed that we would have to be tactful but firm with our own Foreign Offices in order to maintain some freedom of maneuver. Most important of all was the necessity to safeguard carefully the position of our military commanders in Germany, who did not operate directly under Foreign Office or State Department instructions. I had, from the time I arrived in Moscow, been in close touch both officially and personally with General Clay and Ambassador Murphy in Berlin.

We had our first meeting on the Berlin blockade question with Stalin at 9 P.M. on August 2, 1948. He seemed affable from the beginning, and I must say that to me his good humor was certainly justified from his point of view. By blockading all our communications with Berlin, except by air, it looked at that time as if he had confronted us with the flat alternative of getting out of Berlin in ignominious defeat or of staying on under sufferance and abandoning our announced plan of setting up a separate government for Western Germany.

I must say also that at the time the situation did not look too hopeful to me, either. We had done some remarkable things in the way of supply during the war, but I had serious doubts whether we could feed and supply a huge city by air for a prolonged period, especially during the winter months, when flying conditions in Eastern Germany were notoriously uncertain. Nor was I by any means sure that the morale of the German people would stand the strain. I knew, however, that General Clay was confident and determined. He had told me that he was sure that he could, if necessary, build up the airlift to ten thousand tons a day, and I felt certain that, if it lay within the scope of human capability to supply Berlin and defeat the blockade, he would do it. In the realm of supply and logistics, General Clay's ability approaches sheer genius, and he had some of the best airmen in the American and British forces supporting him. So far, also, the morale of the Berlin Germans in the blockaded sectors had remained high. They had rejected flatly all blandishments from the Soviet side of the line, and almost every day they held mass meetings, cheered the airlift and defied communism.

Thus we also held a few good cards when we faced Stalin and Molotov across the conference table in the Kremlin. We believed that we might draw even better ones, as this "poker game" progressed.

Speaking for the three Western governments, and addressing Stalin, I made this statement of our position:

"It is not our purpose at this time to rebut in detail the charges contained in the Soviet note. It is highly important, however, to make completely clear certain fundamental points in the position of the United States, the United Kingdom and France and to clarify the position of the Soviet Union which in certain respects is obscure. The three governments must re-emphasize their right to be in Berlin to be unquestionable and absolute. They do not intend to be coerced by any means whatsoever into abandoning this right.

"Action taken by the Soviets in interfering with rights in connection with occupation, derived through the defeat and surrender of Germany and through international agreement and usage, by interrupting communications between Berlin and the Western zones, thus interfering with duties of Allied Military Forces of Occupation, is viewed with extreme seriousness by the governments of the United States, the United Kingdom and France. It is incumbent on them to take such measures as are necessary to assure the supply of their forces and discharge of their occupational duties. The United States, the United Kingdom and France do not wish the situation to deteriorate further and assume that the Soviet Government shares this desire. The three governments have in mind restrictive measures which have been placed by Soviet authorities on communication between the Western zones of Germany and Western sectors of Berlin. It was the feeling of our governments that if these measures arose from technical difficulties, such difficulties can be easily remedied. The three governments renew their offer of assistance to this end. If in any way related to the currency problem, such measures are obviously uncalled-for, since this problem could have been, and can now be, adjusted by representatives of the four powers in Berlin. If, on the other hand, these measures are designed to bring about negotiations among the four occupying powers, they are equally unnecessary, since the governments of the United Kingdom, the United States and France have never at any time declined to meet representatives of the Soviet Union to discuss questions relating to Germany. However, if the purpose of these measures is to attempt to compel the three governments to abandon their rights as occupying powers in Berlin, the Soviet Government will understand from what has been stated previously that such an attempt could not be allowed to succeed.

"In spite of recent occurrences, the three powers are unwilling to believe that this last reason is the real one. Rather they assume that the Soviet Government shares their view that it is in the interest of all four occupying powers, of the German people and of the world in general to prevent any further deterioration of the position and to find a way by mutual agreement to bring to an end the extremely dangerous situation that has developed in Berlin.

"The Soviet Government will, however, appreciate that the three governments are unable to negotiate in the situation which the Soviet Government has taken the initiative in creating. Free negotiations can only take place in an atmosphere relieved of pressure. This is the issue. Present restrictions upon communications between Berlin and the Western zones offend against this principle. When this issue is resolved, such difficulties as stand in the way of resumption of conversations on the lines set out above should be removed."

Stalin announced emphatically that it was not the purpose of the Soviet Government to force the Western governments from Berlin.

"After all," he said, "we are still Allies."

But he added in no uncertain terms that the Western powers no longer had a juridical right to occupy Berlin, implying that we had forfeited this right by the decision to set up a Western German government at Frankfurt and by introducing the new Western currency in Berlin. He developed the argument that the communications restrictions in Berlin were a measure of self-defense by the Soviet Government because of the actions of the Western powers to which he referred.

We explained that, contrary to his apparent understanding, it never had been contemplated that the government at Frankfurt would be a central German government. The agency to be set up now would in no way hamper eventual understanding on a central government for united Germany.

The remainder of the meeting, which lasted for more than

two hours, was consumed by the discussion that developed from these points. We seemed to be in agreement, or approaching agreement, on several moot questions, and the atmosphere, I thought, remained friendly. Stalin and Molotov, who was with him, raised frequent technical questions regarding currency. We replied that these were issues with which we were not competent to deal but which could be settled by technical experts. We reiterated that the Western powers were in Berlin as equals and as a matter of right. We declared that the blockade measures were uncalled-for if they were in any way related to the currency problem, since this could be adjusted by representatives of the four powers in Berlin.

Finally, when we seemed to have progressed as far as possible, and I myself was beginning to be at a loss for new avenues of approach to the same old question, Stalin threw himself back in his chair, lighted a cigarette and, smiling as he looked directly at me, asked:

"Would you like to settle the matter tonight?"

I replied of course that there was nothing I would like better.

"Very well," Stalin said, "I can meet you on this proposal. There should be a simultaneous introduction in Berlin of the Soviet zone Deutsche mark in place of the Western B mark, together with the removal of all transport restrictions. Second, while the Soviet Government will no longer ask as a condition the deferment of the implementation of the London decisions for setting up a Western government in Germany, this should be recorded as the insistent wish of the Soviet Government."

This proposal seemed promising to me. I had been accustomed for years to mapping specific programs of action within broad general decisions of principle. Stalin's proposition seemed to me to be a decision in principle, within which we could work with Mr. Molotov and his assistants in framing a directive to the Allied representatives in Berlin, under which they in turn could settle all details.

I accepted Generalissimo Stalin's statement in this light. I told him of my own approval and that the three of us would present his proposals to our respective governments for action.

Later, in my office at Mokhovaya, I compared impressions with Ambassador Chataigneau and Mr. Roberts. We felt decidedly encouraged. It seemed to us that the atmosphere of the discussion and Stalin's proposal were such that a settlement of the Berlin crisis could be effected immediately. The Soviet authorities, it appeared, were prepared to remove all transport restrictions between Berlin and the Western zones. Resumption of negotiations on Berlin and a meeting of the Foreign Ministers to consider other outstanding foreign problems affecting Germany might clear the air a good deal further. While Stalin wished it recorded as the insistent desire of his government that the establishment of a Western German government should be suspended until the four powers met and tried to reach an agreement concerning Germany, he had not made this a condition of settlement of the immediate crisis.

Our reports that night to our governments reflected this encouragement and raised hopes that were later to be shattered.

In this atmosphere of optimism, we approached the task of working out general details with Molotov and arranging the technical questions that would accompany substitution of the Soviet zone mark for the Western B mark in Berlin. Our problem was to write a formal agreement with the Soviet representative, which would lead to a lifting of the blockade.

While Stalin had given assent to general principles, Molotov proved again to be a stubborn, intransigent and difficult bargainer in matters of detail. Time after time, it seemed to us that he reneged on statements that Stalin had made. For instance, contrary to our understanding of Stalin's statement, Molotov wanted to make the postponement of the establishment of a Western German government a condition of lifting the blockade, and on several occasions he endeavored to put this condition into the formal agreement.

Stalin had spoken of lifting "all transport restrictions," and we had understood this to mean a complete lifting of the blockade as soon as Soviet currency had been substituted for the Western currency in Berlin. Molotov, however, would agree only to lifting those transportation restrictions that had been imposed "after the announcement of currency reform in the Western zones," that is, after June 18. In brief, we understood that Molotov would continue in force all those restrictions introduced by Soviet authorities on our traffic between March 30 and imposition of the total blockade. Moreover, his attitude challenged our juridical right to be in Berlin at all—and to us this was the basic and vital issue of the blockade. Molotov made it clear that from his point of view the position of the Western governments in Berlin would have to rest entirely on whatever new agreement might be reached as a result of our discussions.

The question of currency control was the greatest ostensible stumbling block. We insisted and tried to make Mr. Molotov understand that there must be genuine four-power control over the issue and control of Soviet marks circulating throughout Berlin. We were sure that if provisions for four-power control were not made absolutely certain we would simply be transferring our difficulties from one field to another; that is, we would be giving the Soviet Union the power to strangle us by currency restrictions, just as they now seemed to have the power to starve us by a traffic blockade.

It became increasingly apparent that if Molotov's attitude meant anything more than playing for time for the blockade to do its worst, it meant that the Kremlin was bent on controlling the life of Berlin whether the Western occupation troops remained there or not. If the Soviet Union kept up the traffic control measures imposed before June 18, they could control all Western Allied traffic to and from the city. If, in exchange for lifting the blockade, their central bank in their zone were given complete control of all Berlin currency, they could disrupt the economic life of the Western sectors at any time they chose. Moreover, we could not escape the fact that the Kremlin was always in a position to reimpose a blockade whenever it suited the Soviet purposes to pretend that the new agreement was being violated. If we could be forced to delay our plans for establishing a Western German government, the Soviet Government and the cause of world communism would have won an enormous political and propaganda victory, for which the partial lifting of the blockade would be a cheap price to pay. We were not prepared to accept this dubious bargain.

During our talks with Molotov, when technical questions arose, our position consistently was that these could be settled only in Berlin by our representatives on the spot. Molotov, as consistently, rejected this theory. He wanted everything settled in Moscow on his own grounds.

Gradually we reached the position of stalemate that one so often encounters in dealing with the Soviet Union, whose repre-

sentatives understand Fabian tactics so well. The only possible
way out seemed to lie in another talk with Stalin. This we
asked for and it was arranged.

In preparation for this meeting, the three Western governments had agreed upon a new plan to put before the Generalissimo. This draft embodied the points discussed in our first
meeting with him but took into account also the issues
subsequently raised by Molotov during our four long and laborious meetings. In so far as these issues could be harmonized
with the rights and duties of the Western occupation forces in
Berlin, our proposal took the form of a directive to our military
governments in Berlin, requiring them to work out the detailed
arrangements for implementing the principles with respect to
currency and transport restrictions as formulated in Moscow.
It also contained a proposed communiqué to be issued by the
Moscow conferees on behalf of the four governments, finalizing
the arrangements worked out by the military governors, and
putting them into effect.

We met with Stalin for the second time on August 23. He
was still jovial, and after greeting us in a friendly fashion, said
quickly, "Gentlemen, I have a new plan."

I remarked that Stalin's reputation as a strategist certainly
had been justified, because he had anticipated us, but that we
too had a new plan.

"Good," Stalin rejoined, "we can compare them."

We proceeded to a paragraph-by-paragraph comparison, and
I was pleased to see that the two drafts were close to each other
in many respects.

But because Molotov's position on a number of important
points had been so much at variance with statements Stalin had
made to us at our previous meeting, I tried to get definite and
specific answers to two vital questions:

1. Was Stalin willing to lift the blockade completely or was
he only willing to lift those restrictions that had been imposed
after the middle of June, thus leaving the blockade partly in
effect?

2. How did Stalin propose to have the four powers control
the money to be circulated in Berlin?

In reply to the first question, Molotov answered quickly that the Soviet Government would lift only the restrictions imposed after June 18. We replied immediately that this would be completely unacceptable to the Western governments. Stalin then suggested that it might be better to say "the restrictions lately imposed would be lifted." He made it clear that it was his intention that all restrictions of any consequence would be lifted.

This was most important, because very serious restrictions had been imposed by the Soviet authorities before the middle of June. They had required every passenger and every piece of baggage entering Berlin to be inspected. Every bargeload of freight entering Berlin by water had to be licensed. The automobile highway to Berlin, which we had used since our occupation, had been cut off, on the pretext of "bridge repairs." But Stalin's assurance covered these things, we thought, and we went on to the second question—that of currency.

Stalin said that the same kind of currency would circulate in Berlin as in the Soviet zone of Eastern Germany. The Soviet zone bank that printed and issued money would have to control its use in Berlin and in the Soviet zone alike. But, he said, "if the question was asked whether it did so without being controlled itself, the answer was 'no.'" Such control, he added, would be provided by a financial commission under the four commanders in Berlin, and by the four commanders themselves, who would work out the arrangements connected with the exchange of one currency for the other and with the control of the issuance of the currency and who would supervise in general what the bank was doing.

This sounded very good indeed, coming from the "Boss," but before we had time to become too elated, Stalin gave us a dash of cold water by insisting that something be said in the agreement about the plan to establish a Western German government. I reminded him that he had not made suspension of these plans a condition of the agreement. He persisted, however, that some mention of this question be made and suggested the following paragraph be included in a four-power communiqué:

"The question of the London decision was also discussed, including the formation of a Western German government.

The discussion took place in an atmosphere of mutual understanding."

Taken by themselves, these words would seem harmless enough to the average Western reader—indeed, they might seem desirable, as indicating a friendly understanding. But in this context, they were dynamite. The people of Germany and all Western Europeans knew very well that it would have been impossible for us to have discussed this question in an "atmosphere of mutual understanding" unless we had secretly accepted the Soviet condition and had agreed to abandon the Western German government idea in exchange for some blockade concessions—an action we could have taken only with a figurative pistol pointed at our heads. The effect on the people of Western Germany would have been enormous.

I had learned previously from reliable sources that Soviet diplomats in satellite countries had predicted confidentially the imminent announcement of a great political-diplomatic victory. This was to be it. The point of the hook was cleverly covered, but the barb was there nonetheless.

I said that I would inform my government of Stalin's desire, but that I did not anticipate that the United States could accede to any such wording unless the proposed paragraph also contained the definite statement that "no agreement was reached on this subject."

For all practical purposes, I believe the conference really ended at this moment. Initially, the Soviet Government had expected that we might be willing to surrender our plans for Western Germany in exchange for a complete lifting of the blockade, which might be only temporary, and a currency plan that would leave us with the shadow but not the substance of control. After our first two meetings, Molotov had realized that this was impossible. He then tried for a lesser, but still important, objective—a partial lifting of the blockade in exchange for a currency system that still would give the Soviet administration a stranglehold on Berlin's finances and a harmless-appearing statement on Western Germany that, in the light of previous events, could mean to the German people only that we had sold out for a precarious stay of execution in Berlin.

The West German representatives were about to meet at Bonn to begin the drafting of a West German constitution.

Stalin was determined, if possible, to delay these plans. If he could do so, the confidence of the Germans in the West would be shattered. The Western Allies themselves had not come to agreement on the West German state without difficulty. France had never been enthusiastic about the idea and had wanted a much looser federation. It had required a good deal of courage for the French Government to meet its Allies on a solution that aroused much criticism from both the extreme Right and extreme Left. Such an agreement, if abandoned now, might not be possible again for a long time.

Now the three governments set out to see how far they could go to satisfy Stalin without compromising their basic decision. They were unanimous in the conviction that Stalin's proposed statement about the discussion of plans for a Western German government would be misunderstood and, therefore, could not be accepted. They were willing to announce publicly that they still desired a four-power agreement on establishment of a central government for all of Germany and that they would make a sincere endeavor to find out whether there was any real prospect of such agreement. They would affirm that the London decisions did not preclude such an agreement. Further than this they would not go.

Soviet disappointment was reflected by Mr. Molotov's attitude at our next meeting. Before he had been restrained and courteous, but now he became truculent. His pleasant manner disappeared, and we wrangled over each word and every sentence in our proposed directive to the military commanders in Berlin. Nevertheless, it now was the objective of my associates and myself to produce this directive, even though it left much to be desired definitively, because it was only by applying the acid test of a conference in Berlin that the sincerity or insincerity of Soviet intentions could be determined. Finally, on August 27, we reached agreement on the wording of this directive, and it was transmitted to the four military governors in Berlin. Very briefly, it required them, within a week, to find practical ways of doing two things at the same time: lifting the blockade and introducing Soviet currency into Berlin under effective, four-power supervision.

I thought it was ominous that Molotov, without argument, reversed completely his former position that details about the currency should be settled and agreed to in Moscow before they were referred to the military governors in Berlin. It was even more disquieting when he rejected a draft communiqué to the press, which we thought was already agreed upon, unless we were willing to insert a final paragraph concerning the London decisions and the West German Government.

During our final session, Mr. Roberts, on instructions from his government, called Mr. Molotov's attention to the increasingly turbulent situation in Berlin, where the Communists, in a rising crescendo of disturbances, had seized the Berlin City Hall in the Soviet sector and driven out the non-Communist City Council on the very day our directive was agreed upon. In courteous, diplomatic language, Roberts suggested that instructions be transmitted to the Soviet military governor to do his utmost to preserve a calm atmosphere for the Berlin negotiations. Molotov snapped back that Marshal Sokolovsky had adequate instructions and did not need any further orders.

Subsequent reports of the first two sessions among the military men in Berlin more than justified our apprehensions. The Soviet military governor refused to accept both the meaning of the directive and the clear understanding we had reached with Stalin.

At our last meeting with Stalin, we had agreed to meet again on the date fixed for the military governors to conclude their discussions. But before this day came I heard that Stalin had left Moscow on vacation, and I knew beyond question that the Politburo intended the session in Berlin to end in disagreement. But I still was astonished at the open hostility and indifference displayed by the Soviet commander, who not only disregarded the terms of the joint directive but even insisted on new traffic restrictions.

I was not, however, surprised at the final result. Molotov had tried to make a trade and failed. Stalin, confident of the effectiveness of the blockade, had given us a chance to delay our plans for a Western German government, without loss of prestige. When we refused, he lost interest in discussions that would produce nothing of benefit to the Soviet Union. From the Kremlin's point of view, it remained only to conclude the incident in such a way as to get the greatest amount of propaganda for itself and to place the maximum blame on the West.

Neither Stalin nor Molotov believed that the airlift could supply Berlin. They must have felt sure that cold and hunger, and the depressingly short, gloomy days of the Berlin winter, would destroy the morale of the Berlin population and create such a completely unmanageable situation that the Western Allies would have to capitulate and evacuate the city.

From the Soviet view, there was nothing to gain from an agreement that did not postpone the German constitutional convention. It is characteristic of Kremlin tactics that this—the main issue—was never approached directly or made an outright condition for the lifting of the blockade. Instead, the question of currency, actually unimportant as subsequent events have proved, was treated as the main issue. We all realized this in Moscow, and during our discussions with Stalin and Molotov, I felt quite sure that we could have produced an agreement in fifteen minutes at any time by an offer to abandon the London decisions. This, of course, was impossible from our side.

But the Kremlin made the same mistake the Germans made in the past—they underestimated their opponents. I don't wonder at this, because I had my own doubts. Certainly I had far greater knowledge of our capabilities for action than did Mr. Molotov and his associates.

When Molotov handed us his final note, reversing every important assurance Stalin had given, and officially demanding control of air as well as land traffic into Berlin, I was less interested in it than I was in how the entire matter would be presented to the Soviet people. All during our conversations, Soviet censorship had maintained a blackout at home, although the Western press was full of speculation and rumor. When the release finally was given, the Soviet propaganda machine went into high gear. One of the real masterpieces was an article in the *Literary Gazette* by D. Melnikov, entitled "Who Created the Berlin Crisis?" This article is worth reading by Americans as an example of what the Soviet people are told and what the majority of them believe, and I have included it with no deletions except a few quotations from other newspapers. Mr. Melnikov wrote:

The so-called "Berlin crisis" is a typical example of the way in which "international incidents" are manufactured by the contemporary diplomatic operators, the masters of provocation. The history of this "crisis," concocted on orders from Washington by the representatives of the Western powers, is very instructive.

The beginning of the "Berlin crisis" and its whole course are a chain of continual provocations. It was a provocation first of all when the Western powers introduced their separate currency, the so-called "B" mark, in the Western sectors of Berlin. As is known, Berlin is located in the center of the Soviet occupation zone. The circulation of a second currency in Berlin creates a threat to the economic life both of Berlin itself and of the whole Soviet zone. Economic sabotage, disorganization of finances and inflation—this is what the Western powers counted on and such would have been the inevitable consequences for the Soviet zone of the introduction of a second currency in Berlin, had not the Soviet command taken swift and decisive counter-measures.

The answering measures of the Soviet Government were thus called forth by the moves made by the Western powers. Had there been no separate currency reform, there would have been no "Berlin crisis." Grievously mistaken they were who thought that the Soviet command would react indifferently to an attempt to destroy the economy of the Soviet zone.

Simultaneously dispelled were the expectations that the Western powers would succeed, despite the separate policy, in strengthening their economic positions in Berlin. The "air-bridge" proved incapable of coping with the problem of the supply of the population of the Western sectors and, on the contrary, turned into an enormous burden upon the population of Berlin. The Berlin population, including the inhabitants of the Western sectors, is being supplied not by American and British planes, but by the Soviet occupation authorities. Over nine hundred tons of food daily are delivered to the Western sectors of Berlin from the Soviet sectors.

The Western powers, having gone bankrupt with the "air-bridge," have also proved unable to consolidate the "B" mark in their sectors. The "B" mark has turned into a unit of exchange solely in intercourse between the population of the Western sectors and the representatives of the occupation powers, and also in the black market deals which, as is known, are the source of tremendous profit for the officials of the occupation administration of the Western countries. To purchase the goods and food, which are mainly available in the Soviet sector, Soviet zone money is needed. This is why even the Berlin Magistrat, which consists in the majority of hirelings of Britain and the U.S.A., proved obliged to adopt a decision to pay seventy-five per cent of the wages of its employees in Soviet sector currency, and only twenty-five per cent in "B" marks.

The bankruptcy of the policy of the Western powers in Berlin obliged them to address a proposal to the Soviet Government at the end of July to open negotiations on the Berlin question.

The published documents, and primarily the Soviet Government's note of October 3 on the Berlin question, have revealed the picture of these negotiations, now broken off through the fault of the Western powers. Having begun the negotiations, the representatives of the Western powers tried at the same time to continue their old policy of utilizing the "Berlin operations base" to dislocate the economic life of the Soviet zone and bring pressure upon the Soviet occupation authorities.

The Western powers insisted above all on the maintenance of the "airbridge" uncontrolled. It must be said that from the very outset this notorious "bridge" pursued definite, military-strategic ends: it was a pretext for organizing a network of air bases on the territory of Western Germany, on the borders of the Soviet occupation zone. Furthermore, it furnishes the Western powers with the opportunity to import war materials into Berlin without control, to export raw materials and industrial equipment and also to continue the currency machinations aimed at disrupting the economic life of the Soviet zone. It is for this reason that the Western powers cling so feverishly to the retention of absence of control over the "airbridge," cloaking their real aims with the hubbub about a "blockade."

The Western powers also propose to broaden the functions of the quadrilateral finance commission, establishment of which is provided for by the directive to the commanders-in-chief agreed in Moscow on August 30. Contrary to this directive, they insist upon the extension of the control functions of the finance commission to the emission of currency. It is easy to understand that by this means the Western powers are endeavoring to seize control over the economic life of the Soviet zone, for the economic situation of any country or part of a country depends upon, in considerable degree, the quantity of money in circulation.

The illegitimate demands of the Western powers advanced during the negotiations on the Berlin question completely expose their expansionist policy in Berlin. It is no accident that the representatives of the Western countries were so embarrassed by the publication of information on the course of these negotiations.

Now the details of the negotiations have been published—and the confusion exists. The confusion was experienced by those who desired to utilize the negotiations to mask their real aims in Berlin, who desired to shift the blame for the fruitlessness of the negotiations onto the Soviet Union.

If the Western powers had really desired to reach an agreement on the Berlin question, they would not have assigned the conduct of negotiations in Moscow to people of secondary importance such as Mr. Bevin's Private Secretary Roberts, who himself had to admit in embarrassment that in the future he would be replaced by a "more responsible person." If they had sought a real settlement of this question, they would have made use of those organs which were especially established for such a settlement—the Council of Foreign Ministers and the Control Council in Berlin.

Nothing has so exposed the lack of desire of the Western countries to reach an agreement on the Berlin question as their submission of this problem to the Security Council for discussion.

Why did the representatives of the U.S.A., Britain and France impose upon the Security Council a discussion of this question, clearly violating article 107 of the UN Charter, which plainly asserts that responsibility for affairs in the territories of enemy countries over which the Allied states exercise control is borne by these states? It is not difficult to give the answer. They pursued a double aim—one end, a political one, was to drag out the solution of the Berlin question and at the same time to endeavor to remove from themselves the blame for the protraction of this solution; the second end is a propagandistic one, that of diverting by means of the hubbub of the Berlin question the attention of the public both from the essence of the whole German problem in general and from the Soviet proposals for a reduction of armaments and the prohibition of the use of atomic energy for military purposes, which have deeply stirred world public opinion and have attracted the sympathies of fresh millions of simple people toward the Soviet Union.

The Western countries began their original game in the Berlin question with a provocation, and wish to end it with a new provocation. But Soviet diplomacy has upset all the cal-

Scene from the play *The Court of Honor.*

A conference at Spaso House. Left to Right: General Mark
Clark, Ambassador Smith, Secretary of State Marshall, Benjamin
V. Cohen, General Lucius Clay.

State box at the Bolshoi Theater, Moscow.

culations of the American, British and French reactionaries. Baring before the whole world the true motives of the actions of the Western countries and substantiating with irrefutable arguments the position of the Soviet Union, the chief of the Soviet delegation at the UN General Assembly, A. Y. Vishinsky, declared that the Soviet delegation will not participate in a discussion of the Berlin question in substance in the Security Council. The delegation of the Ukrainian S.S.R. associated itself with the delegation of the Soviet Union. After A. Y. Vishinsky's statement, the meeting hall of the Security Council emptied—no one had any desire to hear out the empty and already wearisome speeches of Jessup, Cadogan and others like them.

Mr. Melnikov's premature estimate of the ineffectiveness of the airlift is simply a reflection of the views of his government.

When, in December, 1948, at their city elections, the people of Berlin repudiated the Communist Party, the Kremlin certainly knew that their offensive in Berlin had failed. Our "counter-blockade," preventing shipments from Western Germany to Eastern Germany, was hurting the economy of the Soviet zone and, indirectly, that of the Soviet Union, more than the direct blockade of Berlin was hurting its people or us.

It remained for the Kremlin only to pick the best tactical moment to reopen the discussions, and those results are too recent to require repetition.

The blockade was lifted; but we did not give up our plans for a Western German government or abandon the currency reform. The attempt to "starve out" Berlin gained the Russians nothing. Indeed, they lost a great deal.

This does not mean that Berlin is a settled question. Germany has become the pivot of power in Europe, and Berlin is in many respects the heart of the German problem. The real nature of the Soviet advance in Europe is cloaked under the Stalinist doctrine of the "unequal development of socialism"— that is, that the extension of Communist power depends on the gradual and uneven breakdown of "bourgeois democracy" in countries situated on the perimeter of the Soviet Union.

Thus foreign Communists can render active support to these expansionist plans while at the same time taking what is ostensibly a nationalist position. An example is the statement of Jacques Duclos, the French Communist leader, on the eve of the Polish elections on January 19, 1947, that "Frenchmen can sleep more tranquilly over the thought that Silesia is no longer in the hands of the Germans."

The Soviet Union has moved steadily and rapidly to establish a Communist society in the Soviet zone of Germany. Already the mass organizations for charity, youth, women, culture and labor are essentially part of the Communist-dominated state. The trade unions are rapidly losing their functions of representing the workers' interests and becoming instruments of political control on behalf of the Communist Party.

On July 14, 1948, Marshal Sokolovsky announced the appointment of Dr. Kurt Fischer as President of the German Administration of the Interior, which to the Communists is the key governmental post because the man at the head of the Interior Ministry bosses the police, including the secret political police. Dr. Fischer is an Old Bolshevik with a long record of Comintern activities and missions, particularly in the Far East, and his first important public statement in Berlin was significant.

"Capital, supported by the military government of the Western powers, is making all preparations for a civil war against the Socialist democracy of the Eastern zone," he said. "The prerequisite for a successful battle against the enemies of the working class is a strong government. The police, as the armed section of the government, is the most important group. A compromise between East and West is merely an illusion and will always lead to the capitalist camp; thus no administrative employee may show any deviation from Eastern orientation. The most important task, therefore, is to set up a unified, well-organized, well-armed, well-disciplined, and powerful police. In order to achieve iron discipline, we may have to accept the necessity of permitting such things as standing at attention, drills, decorations, insignia of rank and maybe even the epaulettes of general officers. It is but a side issue that the black, red and gold flag, with the police star superimposed, will fly over the Interior Administration Building. The outside form is not important. It is the inner content that counts. The purpose is determined by the party. Therefore, it is absolutely necessary that the party's purpose be carried out with iron discipline. It is only in this manner that the police, as the armed section of the government, can fulfill its function."

General Walter Schreiber, who was chief medical officer of the military organized police in the Soviet zone, and who deserted that post to the Western zone, is reported to have said that all German prisoners of war in Russia were given the standard "Antifa training" (literally translated, that would mean anti-Fascist training, but it would be more accurate to call it a Communist orientation course). Selected pupils were sent to one of two major Antifa schools for advanced training. If they qualified, they were returned to their homes in the Soviet zone of Germany, where they were expected to spread the Communist gospel and to act as contacts and missionaries for the local Communist parties. A number of those who qualified, including several generals, have been assigned to the newly organized Soviet zone police force. Schreiber was one of these. In September, 1948, Fischer told this group:

"The Soviet zone police force will be equipped with good weapons, such as were in use by the former German Army. The police force will also have tanks, armored cars and light and heavy artillery. In the course of this rearmament we have already encountered difficulties with police personnel. In one place, they refused to load heavy machine guns which were to be transported from one depot to another. They reminded us of the fact that Germany was not permitted to rearm. In order to make the moving of weapons possible, it became necessary for higher agencies to intervene and enlighten the men."

In training the general officers selected for this new police force, which is to be armed with tanks, armored cars, light and heavy artillery, and presumably with airplanes (because at least two former Luftwaffe generals have been selected for the duty) the Soviet authorities have developed a course of Communist instruction designed to convince those who have accepted Communist doctrine and who will see in communism the one and only chance of a speedy resurrection of a Nationalist Germany. Thus, for Eastern Germans, the goal of nationalism is based on communism.

It is possible that the Soviet Union will seek to avoid the necessity of deciding ultimately between Poland and Germany on the Oder-Neisse line by endeavoring to weld Poland, Czechoslovakia and Eastern Germany into a tight economic unit, which would be oriented toward a little Ruhr in the Silesian basin.

In view of the Soviet line of action, the importance of integrating the economy of Western Germany into that of Western Europe can hardly be overestimated. Western Germany would not, of course, be given any priority by us over Western European countries that have suffered at German hands. On the contrary, the Western German economy will be rehabilitated within the framework of the program for general European economic recovery. Certainly the Western European Union will have a place for Germany when it has been reshaped politically along democratic lines. Restrictions on German control of the Ruhr, which necessarily would result from an international agreement covering the control of these resources so vital to the economy of Western Europe, would be much more acceptable to the Germans if that plan envisaged a contribution on their part to a larger Western European Union in the same way as other Western European countries also would be making substantial contributions of one kind or another toward this goal.

In the final analysis, the solution of the German problem, at least in so far as Western Germany is concerned, will depend inevitably on the Westward economic and political orientation of the Germans, as fostered by the common policies of Western occupying powers, and on integration of Western Germany into the Western European community. A development along these lines seems to offer the best guarantee of future security.

XII

RELIGION IN RUSSIA

The directions of the XIIIth Assembly of the Communist Party
should be remembered: "Anti-religious propaganda in the country
should be exclusively the materialistic explanation of natural events,
with which the peasants come in contact. The explanation of
the origin of hail, rain, thunder, droughts, of the appearance of pests,
of the nature of the soil, the action of manures, etc., is the best form
of anti-religious propaganda." . . . Special attention must be given
to the matter of instruction in atheism in Soviet schools. Organs of
popular education, together with Party and Komsomol organizations
must supply teachers with the necessary information for the struggle
against prejudices and superstitions, arising amongst school children,
and see to it that in the course of teaching of school subjects general
observations and conclusions should be made, assisting the formation
of a materialistic, scientific outlook.

—*Party Organization* No. 13-14, July, 1945

G REAT issues of religious freedom still are unresolved in
the Soviet Union, but seen at first hand the staying power
of the Russian "believer," after thirty years of anti-religious
propaganda and persecution, is impressive proof that the state
as of this date still has not succeeded in establishing absolute
moral dominion over the masses of people outside the Communist Party.

"Religion is the opium of the people," wrote Lenin. "Religion is a kind of spiritual vodka in which the slaves of capital
drown their human shape and their claims to any decent human
life."

The new revolutionary state accepted his judgment on religion as on other questions, and, for a score of years, a militant
"League of the Godless" assumed the leadership in a campaign
to suppress and wipe out the church—partly by propaganda,
persecution of the clergy and discrimination against church
members, and partly by dynamiting many of its finest cathe-
drals, converting others into museums for anti-religious displays,
and still others into garages and storehouses, while training

schools for the clergy were closed. Until the war, religion was to some extent being driven underground and increasingly being practiced clandestinely; signs of anti-religious activity were everywhere visible.

My first Easter in the Soviet capital convinced me, in dramatic fashion, that the crusade against religion had been one of Lenin's less successful efforts. The Easter celebration is the greatest of all religious festivals of the Russian Orthodox Church, and, a few weeks before the date, I had been formally invited, together with other members of the diplomatic corps, by the Metropolitan of Moscow, second only to the Patriarch as the ranking ecclesiastic authority in the Soviet Union, to attend the midnight services at the great and beautiful Moscow Cathedral. We were warned to come an hour early, in order to avoid the last-minute crowd and in order to meet the Metropolitan and the officiating clergy before the services began.

The night was a series of surprises. The first took place early in the evening, during a reception at one of the other embassies, when, in conversation with a high-ranking Soviet official, I remarked that I was going later to attend the midnight service at the Cathedral and that I looked forward with pleasure to the opportunity to hear the magnificent choral singing.

"How I wish I could go!" he responded spontaneously. Realizing quickly what he had said, he then glanced rather furtively about to see if any of his Soviet colleagues were within hearing distance.

Since he was a confirmed Communist, I must assume that his interest was primarily in the spectacle and in the singing, both so dear to Russian hearts, but the spontaneity and sincerity of his desire to attend surprised me more than a little.

Later, as our car approached the Cathedral, we were again astonished. The great square was a solid mass of people—thousands and thousands of them. In their effort to get as near as possible to the Cathedral, entry into the building itself being by this time out of the question, they were packed together as tight as human beings can get and still be able to breathe.

The best efforts of the police had been ineffective in maintaining an open path, and it took about twenty-five soldiers and militiamen, in a wedge formation, to force a way for us to the Cathedral doors. The crowd was quiet and orderly, but the feeling of its great mass pressing against the thin line of our escort was almost frightening, and indeed Mrs. Smith and Miss Ruth Briggs, my secretary, were twice almost carried off their feet.

The interior of the vast building was a solid mass of humanity, packed together even closer, if possible, than the crowd outside. The congregation seemed to represent every stratum of Soviet society, with the important exceptions of the political and military. Men and women, divided about equally, had been in the church since early afternoon in order to hold their places. The heat of their packed bodies and the warm moisture of their breath rising in the cold air of the unheated building were condensing on the high vaulted ceiling, and tiny drops of water dripped from the arches.

Two large choirs of mixed male and female voices sang without organ or other accompaniment the full-volumed, magnificent chants of the Orthodox Church as they can be rendered only by Russians.

The music, the grandeur of the ancient Cathedral, the splendid and colorful vestments of the officiating priests and deacons, and the solemn reverence of the congregation combined to create an atmosphere of Byzantine splendor which could hardly be equalled anywhere else in the world.

When the lighted tapers, symbolical of the Resurrection, were passed out to the congregation, the body of the church became a sea of tiny lights, one in the hands of each man, woman and child. Impressive though the beauty was, I could not help thinking what would happen if someone, fainting, should drop his candle and ignite the draperies or the pine boughs with which the Cathedral was decorated. I was somewhat relieved when the solemn moment arrived when the Metropolitan, having made his symbolic search for the body of the crucified Christ, discovered that the Saviour had risen, announced the glad tidings as the candles were extinguished, and pronounced his blessing upon the congregation and the assembled multitude outside in the square, who were still packed as tightly together when we left as they had been when we arrived.

To understand fully its significance you must remember that this startling demonstration of the depth of religious feeling that still, in spite of Communist opposition, animates the masses of Russia, took place in Moscow, almost under the shadow of the Kremlin walls. For thirty years, every means of influencing and directing public sentiment has been monopolized by the Communist Party. Press, radio, the privilege of public meetings, facilities for public announcement and public transportation, the complete control of education—all have belonged exclusively to the party and to the state. The church was made to work within the confines of the few run-down edifices left to it when the anti-religious crusade began to diminish, and even within these narrow limits it labored under every disadvantage which the state could enforce. It has not been able to announce its services publicly. It has not been able to transport its congregations to its services, or to bring the services to scattered congregations. It has been unable to influence the youth of the country, and it has not been permitted to reply to the violent attacks by the party and the state against its moral authority. It has had to suffer in silence the conversion of hundreds of churches into anti-religious museums.

Nevertheless, when it becomes known by word of mouth that an important religious event is to take place, people crowd the churches and even whole city districts surrounding them in an atmosphere of intense religious devotion. The Communist Party can call out its members and all other Soviet citizens for mass demonstrations at any time, in any number. They will appear without question, will carry whatever banners are put in their hands, and will comply with any orders that are given them. They will even enjoy the event with the characteristic Russian enthusiasm for pageantry in any form.

But what I saw in the Cathedral square went far deeper than the usual Moscow demonstration. The party, I felt certain, could not produce among the Soviet masses even a shadow of the genuine emotion which was stamped on the faces of the thousands of worshippers that Easter night in Moscow.

It was a convincing proof of the fact that while the Communist Party has been successful in retaining that which is Caesar's, its direct efforts to capture also that which is God's has been quietly but decisively rejected by the masses of the older Russian people.

This may have little visible practical significance at the present time, but it is an indication that certain sources of emotional enthusiasm have been lost to state control, and, therefore, it is indicative of a possible danger with which the state must reckon. As long as the church is kept within harmless channels, and as long as no outside force is permitted to touch these particular springs of human nature and human action, there is little danger. But if they were ever to be grasped and activated by outside influence, the threat to the regime might be incalculable.

Signs of an easing attitude toward the Eastern Orthodox and Armenian Churches began to appear in 1941, after the Nazi invasion of the Soviet Union, when it became vital for the government to utilize every possible stimulus to intensify the loyalty of the embattled population and, at the same time, increase good will among peoples of the West toward the Soviet Union. In 1942, the Orthodox Patriarchate of Moscow was given governmental permission and cooperation for the publication of a book, *The Truth About Religion*, which pledged loyalty to the Soviet cause and denied persecution of the church faithful. In October, 1943, a council for Russian Orthodox affairs was established to supervise church affairs, and the Patriarchate was given greatly increased freedom of activity. In January, 1945, amid a blaze of publicity and propaganda by Soviet agencies, the Metropolitan Alexii of Leningrad was elevated to the Patriarchate. Since that time, there has been a gradual, but strictly controlled, religious revival in the Soviet Union.

But, though the reasons why the action was taken were obvious to outsiders, the shift in the emphasis of the party line from one of severe reprisals against the church to a more moderate attitude of religious tolerance for *non-party members* came as something of a surprise to the party, and required explanation despite the Soviet constitutional guarantee of religious freedom, which had been more honored in the breach than in the observance since its promulgation in 1936. Victor Kravchenko, a former official of the Soviet purchasing mission in the United States who refused to return to Russia during the war, tells the story of one such explanation in his book, *I Chose Freedom*. An official of the Council of People's Commissars, Misonov, justified the change in policy with this statement:

"Our new religious policy will be valuable in meeting the

anti-Soviet propaganda of the Roman Catholics, Lutherans and other religious groups. . . .

"We have the chance to draw the Orthodox Church in other countries closer to Russia and make Moscow the 'Third Rome'. . . .

"Don't worry about the new generation being spoiled by religious superstition. . . . It's clear to everyone that a young man with religious inclinations can't possibly make a career. The Komsomols, you may be sure, will be a stronger force than the priests."

It is clear now, of course, that whatever may have been the hopes of churchgoers at the news from Moscow during the war, the Soviet regime has given little more than lip service to its new pledge insofar as real freedom of religion is concerned. The state has evidenced more liberality toward the Russian Orthodox Church, which has proved to be as staunch in its support of the present Moscow rulers as of the Czarist regime, than it has toward the other religious denominations which look elsewhere than to the Kremlin for leadership. New policy and post-war developments seem to have stirred some of the anti-Semitism always latent in the Soviet Union. There is not, of course, any direct persecution or officially acknowledged discrimination, but there is an active propaganda campaign against Zionism and "cosmopolitanism," which causes uneasiness to the majority of Soviet Jews, with the exception of a few highly placed individuals, such as Kaganovich, a member of the Politburo, and Ilya Ehrenburg, the skilled Soviet writer and propagandist.

And, despite all announcements to the contrary, the opportunity for religion to develop in the Soviet Union is handicapped severely by the lack of facilities.

Moscow, as a result of population gains during and since the war, is now estimated to be a city of between 4,000,000 and 7,000,000 persons, spread over twenty-seven and a half square miles. For this great number of people in such a large area, there were, as of June, 1948, about thirty churches operating, an average of one church for every 130,000 persons if one accepts the lowest population estimates. These included twenty-five Russian Orthodox churches, one Old Believers' Cathedral, one Jewish synagogue (for an estimated 300,000 Jews in Moscow), one Evangelical Lutheran-Baptist church (the result of a recent merger), and a single Roman Catholic chapel.

By comparison, New York City, with a population of about 8,000,000, has at present a total of 2,052 Protestant and Roman Catholic churches alone—or an average of one church for every 4,000 persons, not counting the places of worship maintained by other religions.

Since the granting of true religious freedom was demonstrably not the cause of the Kremlin's shift in policy toward religion in the war years, it is worth while evaluating this move by the standards set up by Mr. Misonov:

It would be valuable for disarming the criticism and opposition of foreign religious bodies: In this respect, the new policy has already been a successful one. It promises to be even more so as the Russian Church emerges from its isolation and reestablishes its relations with world religious organizations. In this connection, a recent Geneva dispatch reports: "Signs of a rapprochement between the Russian Orthodox Church under the Moscow Patriarch and the Protestant and other Orthodox churches of the world, through the World Council of Churches, continue to increase. . . . Religious News Service is able to state authoritatively that a basis for cooperation of the Russian Church with the World Council is being sought."

It would attract support for the Soviet All-Slav policy: Religious penetration was one of the most effective elements of the Pan-Slavism of Czarist Russia. After the Soviet Revolution, however, religious opposition was second only to fear of communism in creating and maintaining the long estrangement between the Eastern European and Russian Slavs. The removal of that opposition and the restoration of fraternal ecclesiastical relations would be a factor of primary importance in solidifying Soviet control and influence in Eastern and Central Europe and the Middle East. The Moscow Patriarch has already undertaken a vigorous offensive, and can report success in gaining control or hegemony over the Slavic Orthodox churches in the Baltic states, Poland, Czechoslovakia, Rumania and Bulgaria, and over some Russian émigré churches in France, Germany, Manchuria, Korea and Japan. Avoiding the historic complexities of international ecclesiastical politics—more devious even than secular politics—and at the risk of over-simplification, it still is apparent that Moscow's only serious competition comes from the Oecumenical Patriarch at Istanbul. But the Istanbul Patriarchate gradually has lost all temporal support and protection except that of weak and bankrupt Greece and cannot continue to offer serious resistance indefinitely if it is not strengthened. Even the historic and holy Orthodox Patriarchates of Jerusalem, Antioch and Alexandria need support and might be unable long to withstand the persuasions of the Russian Church. If they were to fall, Lenin would surely turn in his tomb—for Stalin would have succeeded the Czar as the "protector" of the Christians of the East, and Moscow could indeed claim to have achieved its ancient ambition to become a "Third Rome."

The new tolerance for the Orthodox Church can be seen, therefore, as severely limited and primarily designed to serve as an instrumentality of an expansive Soviet foreign policy. I would not have the temerity to estimate the extent, if any, that the Kremlin may be able to impose its will upon the Moscow Patriarchate. But I noted with grave misgivings a three-page article by Arch-Priest Aleksander Smirnov, under the title "Demoniacal Spirit of New Aggressor Threatening the People's Peace," published in December, 1947, in the *Journal* of the Moscow Patriarchate. This article, dedicated to Christmas, was a violent attack upon the United States and "the Anglo-Saxon warmongers" in terms identical with those employed in *Pravda* and the other standard Communist Party organs. So far as I know, this was the first time that the Russian Church officially had printed and circulated an article wholly devoted to the Soviet Union's anti-Western foreign policy. Others appeared subsequently.

In announcing its new tolerance toward religion the Soviet Government promptly took other actions lest the domestic revival attain too much momentum. Satisfied apparently that anti-religious propaganda and persecution could not work among the older people, the new campaign was directed particularly to the young, especially among the Komsomols, to whom Stalin was quoted in 1947 as expounding the Leninist-Stalinist policy on religion in the following words:

The party cannot be neutral regarding religion and it conducts anti-religious propaganda against all religious prejudices because it stands for science, and religious prejudices are opposed to science since any religion is contrary to science. . . . There are cases in which some of the members of the party occasionally hinder the thorough development of anti-religious propaganda. If such members of the party are expelled this is very good, since there is no room in the ranks of the party for such "Communists."

It goes without saying that only that Komsomol can correctly clarify the harm in superstition and religious prejudices who is free of them himself. A young man cannot be a Komsomol unless he is free of religious convictions.

That such measures were successful was testified to by the Patriarch Alexii, who, in a Moscow sermon in 1947, complained that "under unfavorable conditions, many of us are ashamed to worship God openly because of fear of being subjected to unpleasantness and ridicule." While the Patriarch did not describe the nature of the unpleasantness to which churchgoers were subjected, he did say that the majority of Russian Orthodox churchgoers were women and children.

Some members of the Russian clergy apparently took the grant of religious freedom literally, seeking to enlist new church members among the youth—party members or not. That, at any rate, seemed the conclusion to be drawn from an angry outburst in a 1947 issue of the magazine *Young Bolshevik,* which printed the following "Letter to the Editor" from Fedor Garkovenko, identified as a Komsomol member:

Dear Editor:
A few days ago a priest called at our house and began to talk about religion. He talked of how religion cleanses a man's conscience and sets him at peace. According to him, it appears that anyone can believe in God—party member and non-party member, learned and unlearned, the ordinary worker and the Stakhanovite, and so on.

When he suggested that I should enter on the path of religion, I said that faith in God was not compatible with my convictions, that I was a Komsomol member. He replied that the church forgives sins and error.

After the conversation I still held by my convictions, but there may be people who as a result of such "visits" will go to church, will be made captive by religious delusions. So I am writing to ask you to publish an article which will demonstrate the incompatibility of religion and science.

The Editor's reply, which I briefed in my notes, showed clearly how little the Soviet attitude toward religion had changed since Lenin described it as the "opium of the people," despite the window-dressing of a war-inspired tolerance which, it now appears, was intended only to serve the interest of the state.

". . . The guiding force of the Soviet people is the Communist Party of Bolsheviks, which builds its activity on scientific foundations and implants in people a wholesome outlook, incompatible with any superstition, with any reaction, with any defense of bourgeois oppression," wrote the Editor of *Young Bolshevik,* quoting from Lenin.

Following the theory of Marxism-Leninism, the party leads the people to the complete victory of communism in our country. The success of our party in solving all the problems connected with building up of a Communist society is to be explained by the fact that its actions are based, not on blind guessing, not on fancies about an unknown future, but on a deep, scientific understanding of the laws of social life, on a certainty which is founded on scientific fact that we shall reach our goal. . . .

The whole system of social life in our country furthers the development and confirmation of the scientific outlook and the liberation of people's minds from religious beliefs. The reason for this is that millions of Soviet people who but a short time ago were believers have rejected their prejudices, while the younger generation, brought up with the scientific outlook, is in the main free from religious fallacies.

Nevertheless, there are not a few members of Soviet society who still believe, who have not yet parted with their religious convictions. This is quite understandable. The recent past of our country is one of a bourgeois, landowner system: Soviet society has not been able to rid itself all at once of the "birthmarks" of capitalism. Only as it gradually develops from socialism to communism will it outlive the relics of the past.

This has direct bearing on the question of overcoming religion. . . . Religion in our country now is a relic of the social life of the past, and survives in the minds of some of our people by the power of tradition. Like other relics of the past, religious beliefs may, under certain conditions, come to life again. Those, for example, who have no firm outlook, who are weak-spirited, when they come up against the hardships of life sometimes seek illusory "consolations" in religion. The strengthening and development of a Socialist society, its progress towards communism, the cultural growth of the people and their education in the Communist spirit, will help to free all Soviet people, once and for all, from anti-scientific religious convictions.

Scientific-educational propaganda is an important means of overcoming religious survivals. It must, above all, provide the materialistic explanation of the phenomena of nature and society, must elucidate the achievements of science and techniques. There should be lectures and talks and reading aloud from popularly written pamphlets and articles on the formation of the universe, the origin of the Sun and of the Earth . . . the causes of illness and how to fight it . . . and so on.

Komsomol organizations must patiently explain to young people the incompatibility of the scientific and the religious outlook. It is their duty to show the young the superiority of the scientific outlook over the religious, of knowledge over blind faith.

That is why religion cannot be a private affair of a member of the Communist Party, of a Komsomol member; Komsomol organizations must allow their members no deviations from the theses of the Communist Party on questions of religion.

The Soviet Constitution recognizes freedom of religious practices and freedom of anti-religious propaganda for all citizens. It would be a mistake to persecute a believer for his prejudices —they are not his fault, but his misfortune. He must be helped to free himself of them by patient scientific-educational work.

The overwhelming majority of the young Soviet generation has been brought up with a scientific outlook incompatible with any faith in supernatural powers, with any superstitions. The task of the Komsomol lies in active opposition to the influence of any other ideology on the young, including religious ideology; in bringing them up stouthearted, believing in the cause of Lenin-Stalin, worthy to carry on and complete the building of communism in our country.

Strong as this may seem to you and me, it didn't please the Men in the Kremlin, and the official Komsomol newspaper,

Komsomolskaya Pravda, appeared a few weeks later with an editorial sharply attacking the editorial staff of *Young Bolshevik* for having published "a politically harmful and theoretically illiterate" article on the attitude a Komsomol should adopt toward religion. *Komsomolskaya Pravda* asserted that *Young Bolshevik* had clumsily criticized and cast doubts upon the completely correct attitude of Komsomols who "consider it impossible and inadmissible for a Komsomol to believe in God and to observe religious rituals." Educational methods were not the way to eliminate religious beliefs, said *Komsomolskaya Pravda,* which reiterated the need for categoric prohibitions against ecclesiastical practices.

"Such a presentation of the matter is nothing other than an attempt to prove the possibility of the reconciliation of materialism with Popishness and idealism," the official newspaper said. "Such a position signifies a departure from Marxism."

The one church, other than the Russian Orthodox, which benefited, at least in part, from the Kremlin shift on religion was the Apostolic Church of Armenia, one of the oldest religious bodies in Christendom and the principal custodian of Armenian nationalism.

In June, 1945, a congress of delegates from Armenian communities all over the world was held at the religious capital of Echmiadzin for the purpose of electing a new Catholicos, the pontiff of the Armenian Church. After disposing of its ecclesiastical business, however, the congress turned to political matters, vigorously affirming the Armenian claim to certain Turkish territory in a petition to Stalin, which said in part:

"We hope that the statemanship and political wisdom of the U.S.S.R. will find both the means and the way to redress the injustice to which our people was subjected during the last World War."

It could hardly have been by coincidence that this petition was released just as Soviet demands for territorial adjustment were being presented to the Turkish Foreign Minister, and helped to stir public pressure on the issue. Rather it appears to be another demonstration of the Politburo's use of the church as an instrument of foreign policy.

In the Moslem world, the religious power potential of the

Soviet Union has been little exploited thus far although some pilgrimages to Mecca have been permitted. The Caucasian, Ural and Central Asiatic areas of the Soviet Union contain a population of many millions who have been raised in and who adhere to the Mohammedan religion. This vast reservoir so far has been tapped only to provide prospective diplomats and Communist agents for training at the Moscow University of the Peoples of the East, that remarkable institution described by Stalin as having one foot on Soviet ground and the other foot on the soil of colonial and vassal lands where the people have still to win their independence by clearing out the "imperialists."

The Kremlin has been disappointed by the scanty success of its efforts to penetrate the Moslem world of the Middle East by political methods, and its program for the future may well include intensified efforts via the channel of religious penetration.

But two religions—the Jewish and the Roman Catholic— did not gain even temporary benefits from the wartime policy of greater religious tolerance; in fact, on balance, it is probably safe to say that attacks upon them have been stepped up rather than relaxed in recent years.

Since my return to the United States, I have often been asked about the extent of anti-Semitism in the Soviet Union and how much this campaign draws inspiration from the Communist Party. It should be made clear again, even at the risk of repetition, that while there is anti-Semitism among the Soviet peoples, this feeling must not be thought of as in any way comparable with that which existed in pre-war Germany. The record of the Soviet Government in suppressing the historic anti-Semitism of the Russian people was a very good one for nearly thirty years, and we in the Embassy were reluctant for a long time to accept the recent manifestations in the Moscow press and elsewhere as evidence of a clearly anti-Jewish line.

The campaign began on ideological lines with a slashing attack on January 28, 1949, in *Pravda* upon "cosmopolitanism," which was associated with international Jewry, with Zionism, with Pan-Americanism, and with Catholicism, all of whose followers were said to be "cosmopolites actively serving the interests of imperialist reaction." To this term the Soviet propagandists added the frequent use of such expressions as "people without kith or kin," "passportless wanderers" and "people without tribe." The first assault was upon certain Jewish theater critics, but it rapidly was extended to the fields of literature, music, the cinema, philosophy, natural science, atomic energy, and even sports and the circus. In late February, at a plenum of Ukrainian writers, a resolution was passed condemning "serious manifestations of Jewish bourgeois nationalism, especially in the periodical, *Der Stern,* publication of which we had to discontinue." Even before this, the Moscow authorities had closed down the Jewish publishing house and halted publication of the newspaper, *Einikait.* Fuel was added to the campaign on March 14 by a particularly vicious article published in the *Vechernaya Moskva,* which clearly labelled the victims of its attack as Jews by publishing in brackets the Jewish names they had before they adopted Russian pseudonyms. This was the most violent of a series of articles which had appeared in the Soviet press after *Pravda's* January salvo, and when the American correspondents in Moscow offered for transmission abroad stories which merely quoted the article, they were censored in toto without explanation.

About this time one of the most distinguished Soviet news writers, Ilya Ehrenburg (himself a Jew), published an article which laid down the principle that the solution of the Jewish question lay in the achievement of socialism in the countries where Jews resided, rather than in the establishment of a Jewish state in Israel.

The current offensive, which transcends similar campaigns which have taken place in the Soviet Union, has deep roots in Russian chauvinism, with its traditional anti-Semitism as well as anti-foreignism. But it involves much wider considerations. The establishment of the State of Israel has revived the attraction of Zionism for Jews in the Soviet Union, and the Kremlin undoubtedly considers it necessary to warn them periodically that only unbounded devotion to the Soviet State can bring them acceptance and salvation.

During an official reception shortly before I left Moscow, I was talking to the Israeli Minister, Mrs. Golda Myerson, when she mentioned the bitterness of some of Ehrenburg's articles

and remarked that she would like to meet him, since she believed she could convince him that he was mistaken in his
hostility to Israel. I had seen Mr. Ehrenburg only a few minutes before, so I asked one of my diplomatic officers to find
him and bring him to meet the Minister.

In a few minutes Ehrenburg came up, and after some conversation through an interpreter, Mrs. Myerson asked him if
he spoke English.

Ehrenburg, who speaks excellent French, looked at her for a
moment and then replied in Russian: "I do not speak English,
and I have no regard for a Russian-born Jew who *does* speak
English."

The Minister, who was born in Russia, but who had lived
much of her life in the United States, was, of course, deeply
hurt and offended, but Ehrenburg's rude and brutal behavior
taught her a lesson she never would have believed or accepted
from another source.

Soviet law specifically prohibits any racial discrimination or
anti-Semitism. A few Jews, such as Kaganovich and Ehrenburg,
hold high positions in the Soviet Union, and are always
pointed to by the Kremlin to refute any implication of anti-
Semitism. But during the past decade, it seems that Jews have
systematically been removed from influential positions in the
Soviet Government and the diplomatic and armed services.
Reliable reports attribute these removals to Soviet suspicion of
Jews as persons who have a tradition of international culture
and ties abroad, and who cannot be relied upon to conform to
the increasingly tight ideological straitjacket demanded by the
party under post-war conditions. From the Foreign Office
alone, while I was in Moscow, Litvinov, Lozovsky, Maisky and
less important but almost equally able Jewish officials were relieved or relegated to retirement or to positions of less importance.

During my stay in the Soviet Union, the only reported violence against Jews was in the Ukraine, where latent anti-Semitism had been inflamed by the racial theories of the Germans
during the war. This, however, was the work of anti-Soviet
Ukrainian nationalists, and the government acted promptly,
employing stern measures in an effort to suppress these illegal
acts. However, many Jews were killed in the Ukraine in small-

scale "pogroms," and others felt unsafe in leaving their homes at night. There were reports, which I consider reliable, that this campaign became so widespread that the government has not been able to suppress it completely, and, as a result, many Ukrainian Jews migrated to the Asiatic Autonomous Jewish Oblast of Birobijan, which was founded in 1924 and which for a time held the attention of World Jewry, attracting some immigrants and, during the nineteen twenties and early nineteen thirties, a fair amount of foreign financial aid. A more recently reported transfer of Jews from the western area of the Soviet Union to Birobijan would appear to have been carried out by the government for its own purposes.

The Birobijan experiment was of great interest to the American Embassy and we made repeated requests to the Soviet authorities that an officer be permitted to stop off and visit the area in the course of trips between Moscow and Vladivostok. But permission to visit this area was always refused, and we could only assume that the authorities did not want us to confirm at first hand the stories we had heard of the relatively poor condition of the settlement and the low standard of living prevailing there. The effort to build this up as a prospective Jewish national home apparently had failed, and the government seemed to take little interest in the project, except as a haven for some of the Jews of the Ukraine.

There was, while I was in Moscow, only one "foreign" church, the small Roman Catholic Church of St. Louis of France, which had been erected before the Revolution by the French colony of Moscow and to which an American priest, the Reverend Leopold Braun, was first assigned as a result of an agreement between President Roosevelt and Maxim M. Litvinov, the then Soviet Foreign Minister, when the United States granted diplomatic recognition to the U.S.S.R. in 1933.

In the course of the negotiations, the President expressed his "deep concern" that Americans who would reside temporarily in the Soviet Union "should enjoy in all respects the same freedom of conscience and religious liberty." Mr. Roosevelt made it clear that the United States Government expected its nationals to be able "to conduct without annoyance or molestation of any kind" all kinds of religious services in English in churches, houses or other appropriate buildings "which they will be given the right and opportunity to lease, erect or maintain in convenient situations." Such churches, the President specified, would be under the direction of clergymen, priests, rabbis and other ecclesiastical functionaries "who are nationals of the United States of America" who would be protected "from all disability or persecution and will not be denied entry into the territory of the Soviet Union because of their ecclesiastical status."

In his reply, M. Litvinov assured the President that in the Soviet Union "every person may profess any religion or none." He categorically denied there would be any impediments placed in the way of religious freedom for Americans or other persons. He assured the President that Soviet law clearly provided the right to rent or erect churches and said his government was willing to make a consular convention with the United States specifying such rights. As far as the admission of clergymen, priests and rabbis was concerned, M. Litvinov declared that while the Soviet Government reserved to itself "the right of refusing visits to Americans desiring to enter the U.S.S.R. on personal grounds" it did *not* intend "to base such refusals on the fact of such persons having an ecclesiastical status."

Father Braun served his Moscow parish under great handicaps for eleven years, climaxed by the long, hard and trying war period, and finally came home to the United States for a rest at the end of 1945 on the airplane that brought Secretary of State James F. Byrnes home from the second Moscow Conference of Foreign Ministers. Father Braun was replaced by another American, the Reverend George Antonio Laberge, who spoke both French and Russian fluently, as had Father Braun.

Just before I left Moscow, there began an incident involving control of this "foreign church" which is typical both of the devious methods of the Soviet authorities and the importance which they attach to the necessity of isolating the Soviet public from all foreign contacts. Partly because Father Laberge could preach in Russian as well as in French and English, the Russian congregation of this church was large. Immediately after the war, the continuing increase in church attendance caused the assignment to Moscow of a French priest, Father Thomas, who could assist Father Laberge in handling services for the French-speaking parishioners. On the occasions when I attended this church, Russians crowded the building, even filling the aisleways.

After three years in Moscow, Father Laberge was ready for home leave in the United States, and he therefore asked the Soviet authorities to grant him visas authorizing him to leave the Soviet Union and specifying that he had permission to return to Moscow after his visit to America. He made it clear that he would not leave his post unless his re-entry visa was granted in advance. After some considerable delay, Father Laberge was given both visas and left for home, turning over his duties to Father Thomas.

But then the Russians put into operation their plan for gaining control of this "foreign church" in the heart of Moscow. Almost as soon as Father Laberge reached the United States he was notified that his re-entry visa was cancelled. No explanation was given for this action. At that time we hoped that an entry visa for a replacement would be issued promptly. That left only Father Thomas to administer to the entire Roman Catholic community of Moscow.

The next act, which occurred after my return to the United States, but which has been reported to me by my associates in the Moscow Embassy, brought the Soviet Government directly into the direction of this Catholic church. Two Russian women, accompanied by a representative of the Council for Religious Affairs (which had been established in June, 1944 to regulate non-Orthodox religions), called upon Father Thomas, declaring on behalf of the Soviet congregation that they desired the services of a pastor who could speak their language and that they had petitioned the Council for Religious Affairs to provide a Russian-speaking priest. They had a petition bearing the signatures of many Soviet members of the congregation, and, in their names, they demanded that Father Thomas turn over the keys to the church. The government official supported this demand, declaring that failure to comply would result in "unpleasant consequences."

Father Thomas, he said, would be permitted to officiate at one service a day, for the foreigners, but Soviet citizens would attend other services at which a Russian-speaking priest would officiate.

The keys of the church were turned over—Father Thomas being admitted for one Mass each day. No other clergyman appeared for a long time. Finally, a priest called upon Father Thomas and announced that he had been assigned to the parish by the Archbishop of Riga (whose ecclesiastical authority, incidentally, does not extend to Moscow). When Father Thomas asked for his credentials, the new priest stated that they had been deposited with the Council for Religious Affairs, which had provided him with its certificate of authority. This he displayed—and Father Thomas had no choice but to accept it, invalid though it was from the ecclesiastic point of view.

By this tortuous process, the Soviet members of the one Moscow Catholic congregation were isolated from foreign contact— the real purpose of the complicated maneuver involving Father Laberge and his cancelled visa. As this was written, no other American priest had been granted a visa to replace him, despite the Litvinov agreement with President Roosevelt in 1933.

The Kremlin stands guard over the souls of its human charges with a watchful and jealous eye, and the latter accept this with all the outward signs of agreeable acquiescence. Ordered to admire, they applaud cheerfully and enthusiastically. Ordered to abhor or hate, they respectfully strike an attitude of indignation. The Russian people have dissembled for so many years that, as one of my officers said, "They have dignified the quality almost into a national virtue." By this means alone they have challenged, and challenged successfully, the power of the Kremlin to control their spiritual lives.

And the persistence of an independent spiritual life is at once one of the important and one of the mysterious things that has transpired in the Soviet state. It is important because it may one day determine the strength and the character of the Soviet national effort, and its influence on the world. It is mysterious because it is impelled by forces and governed by laws of its own, which not even the Kremlin understands.

XIII

CULTURE AND THE PURGE

I know but one book on Russia, of foreign origin, that is admissible into the Empire; nor do I know a single one of domestic production, from which a stranger can derive any certain information touching the revenue, the expenditures, the strength of the army and navy, or any other matter having a political bearing. Whether all this is wise or unwise, belongs properly to Russian statesmanship to determine. It presents however to the American mind the most unpalatable part of Russian tyranny.

—Excerpt from a dispatch of the American Minister to Russia, Neill S. Brown, dated St. Petersburg, January 27, 1853

E to nye kulturno is a phrase one hears often in Moscow, especially among earnest young Communists. Literally, the Russian phrase means "that isn't cultured," and it has a variety of applications to describe widely varying acts and objects. It is equally applicable when reference is made to the rude behavior of an uneducated person or to the poor quality of a toothbrush. This is a valid form of self-criticism, reflecting a genuine desire for self-improvement and a craving for culture which has become almost a national obsession with the Soviet people.

From the very beginnings of the Soviet state, the Communist leadership recognized the equal need for a cultural revolution to accompany an industrial revolution, thus raising both the mental and economic standards of the people.

Once, in analyzing the weaknesses which had caused the downfall of Czarist Russia, Stalin listed "backwardness" in five major fields of endeavor, and, of these, the cultural deficiency was mentioned only after military weakness but ahead of political, industrial and agricultural shortcomings.

"We are fifty or a hundred years behind the advanced countries," Stalin had said. "We must make good this lag in ten years. Either we do it or they crush us."

Hurry, hurry, hurry!—this was Stalin's exhortation to the Soviet people whether they were building a steel mill, composing a symphony, harvesting a wheat crop, writing a book, constructing a hydro-electric dam, performing in a drama or drilling an oil well. The military, cultural, political, industrial and agricultural revolutions, which were to make the Soviet Union impregnable to attack, were to be carried through in feverish haste.

Looked at from the broadest point of view, the results after thirty years of speed-up effort, interrupted by four terrible years of war, were by no means unimpressive.

On the positive side, Soviet culture has made certain remarkable advances. Illiteracy is being eradicated, the enrollment in schools and universities has multiplied, access to literature has been made easier, and a state-supported program has brought the theater, the ballet and the opera ever closer to increasing numbers of people although the subsidies were cut off recently. In 1914, enrollment in the primary schools numbered only 8,000,000, but by 1938 it was 31,500,000, according to the 1946 *Statistical Yearbook,* which gave university enrollment in 1913 as 112,000 compared to 620,000 in 1939. The same source said that pre-revolutionary public libraries in Russia had only 640 books per 10,000 residents, while in 1938 there were 8,610 books for each 10,000 persons.

The Soviet Government has retained and encouraged the beautiful and the aesthetic in the arts, and many of the standards established by the Soviet authorities in the opera, ballet and non-propaganda radio programs are generally higher than our own public demands. The ballets of Moscow and Leningrad are the best in the world, and the legitimate theater is very good indeed when it is not being used primarily for propaganda purposes.

The state sees to it that musicians can compose and play, writers can write, and artists can paint in comfortable circumstances, because the government is well aware that the task of raising the cultural level of the Soviet peoples to that of most of their European neighbors is still far from complete.

On the positive side, there has been this vast extension of the outward signs of a cultured nation. The negative aspects of the situation are less obvious but more significant. In the first place, everything has been done with such speed that much of the accomplishment is superficial. In the second place, because it has been done under the direction and for the benefit of the ruling Communist Party, the result is a standardized, mass-produced article.

For the masses, this is a "Blue Plate Special" and they are expected to accept it as such without cavil and complaint; but the cultural gourmet will find a limited menu from which to select his dinner.

At the much publicized "World Congress of Intellectuals," held at Wroclaw, Poland (formerly Breslau, Germany), in August, 1948, the Soviet writer, Illya Ehrenburg, made the remarkable statement that "Russian culture is beyond the intellectual comprehension of Western Europe." He added that bourgeois culture no longer existed, having been supplanted by "bourgeois barbarianism, with its automobiles and Frigidaires."

But if Mr. Ehrenburg were an inquiring and open-minded reporter, he would be asking himself why the West could not comprehend the Soviet brand of culture as it exists today, since he is well aware that the West understood and deeply appreciated cultural giants of Russia of other days—Tolstoy, Dostoyevsky, Chekhov, Gorki, Turgeniev, and Pushkin among the writers; and Tschaikovsky and Rimski-Korsakov among the composers, for example.

In my opinion, Mr. Ehrenburg overstated the case for Soviet culture and underestimated Western capabilities for cultural understanding.

At the time I read his indictment, one of the current Moscow jokes was of the Soviet citizen who, after a cautious glance over his shoulder, whispered to a foreign friend:

"Being in the Soviet Union is like being in an airplane. We have beautiful, broad horizons, our stomachs feel empty, and we can't get out."

Culturally, there have been beautiful, broad horizons in the Soviet Union. If they are becoming less and less broad, a great deal of the beauty remains, and the restricted view is not the fault of Russian intellectuals, but of the Communist Party.

It is worth while to recall history before attempting to evaluate the Soviet cultural pattern today.

It is often not fully realized that the Russian people have an almost completely different cultural background from that of the Western world. They were cut off and isolated from the developments which grew out of the fifteenth and sixteenth century movements of the Renaissance and Reformation, and of the full effect of the French Revolution. In fact, it was not until the nineteenth century that members of the Russian intelligentsia began to impress themselves on the sophisticated West.

This delayed full-flowering of Russian culture happened to coincide with another awakening—the result of the American and French Revolutions—which showed itself in the frustrated attempts of self-expression, nationalism and liberalism of the revolutions of 1848 and their subsequent developments. The extreme repressive measures taken by Czar Alexander II after his liberation of the serfs in 1861, and those of his son, Czar Alexander III, after his father's assassination in 1861, aroused among this newly awakened intelligentsia, particularly the students of the day, a fervent desire to free the Russian people from the autocratic Czarist yoke.

The revolutionary movement which culminated in the overthrow of the Romanov dynasty was fostered primarily by the intellectuals of the period, who, through their greater knowledge of the outside world and general enlightenment, were in a position to make comparisons and see more clearly the shortcomings of the pitiful reforms granted by the last of the Romanovs.

Although Stalin cannot be classified as one of the prerevolutionary intellectuals, as were Lenin and many of his close supporters, it is obvious that he fully appreciates the dangers which uncontrolled erudition would represent to an authoritarian state.

During the first decade after the Revolution, the new Soviet intelligentsia had a comparatively free rein. But shortly after Stalin eliminated his rival, Trotsky, he began to harness the arts to the party chariot.

As early as 1929, Soviet musicians were told to "fight the influence of decadent bourgeois music among young musicians, impress the necessity of absorbing the best, the healthiest and ideologically acceptable elements of the musical legacy of the past, and prepare the ground for the formation of new proletarian music."

These dictates obviously were not fully effective in forcing Soviet music, science and art to conform to the party line, for the pressures were kept up for the next fifteen years. It culminated finally in the all-out campaign against the Leningrad Literary Group, initiated in August, 1946, by the Politburo under the leadership of the late Andrei A. Zhdanov, whom many regarded as Stalin's "heir apparent." This blast turned out to be only the opening gun and was followed by attacks upon Soviet musicians, philosophers, scientists, architects, statisticians, physicists, actors, playwrights, critics, etc. The pattern was always the same—they were accused of being apolitical, non-Communist, formalistic, and of looking too often to Western culture for their inspiration. The campaign has progressed with increasing intensity during the last three years.

Why such a herculean effort to curb intellectual thought and cut off all cultural pursuits from the outside world? Will this not stifle development? Is not such a policy short-sighted, particularly at a time when the Soviet Union has grown greatly in stature and prestige? These were questions the Westerners in Moscow asked. The Kremlin, it was plain, had answered the inquiries negatively.

For obvious reasons during the war, the Soviet leaders had been obliged to relax many of their ideological controls. It was inexpedient, for the time being, continually to attack the West and its accomplishments. Much greater latitude was permitted, and those who had suffered under the stifling party controls of the thirties may have begun to believe that a new era of relative intellectual freedom had arrived. Very soon after the war it became apparent that this was not the case. The Government began an all-out effort to rekindle the fires of Stalinist ideology and to enforce blind acceptance of the promised glories of the regime.

Stalin and the other members of the Politburo knew all too well the tremendous influence wielded by the nineteenth century intellectuals in the successful effort to utilize the discontent of the masses in the overthrow of the Czarist regime. They knew that a totalitarian secret police state built on unfulfilled promises could not, for instance, tolerate the satire of the popu-

lar writer, Zoshchenko, who was one of the principal targets of
Zhdanov's blast against the Leningrad Literary Group. Zoshchenko had dared to write a satire, based on the life of an ape,
and because of this Zhdanov criticized him as an "anti-social"
writer who had satirically depicted an ape as the supreme judge
of Soviet social order. Through the lips of Zoshchenko's ape
came the impression that in the Soviet Union "it is better to
live in a zoo than outside" and that "one breathes easier in a
cage than among the Soviet people," Zhdanov said.

Such heretical thinking had to be stopped. And if the ideological machine were to be put back on the party main line, the
intellectuals must cooperate loyally and obediently.

In the second place, since the theoretical basis of Soviet ideology is founded on the "scientific" theory of dialectical and
historical materialism, all developments, facts and theories must
be brought into conformity with this fundamental "truth."
According to this "scientific" discovery of Marx, all progress is
brought about by opposing forces—a struggle between the old
and the new, between that which is dying away and that which
is being born in a transformation of quantitative and qualita-
tive changes. Since this theory is immutable, all proven scientific laws, ideas and concepts which do not fit the theory must
be changed or brought into line or the whole foundation of the
Soviet regime will crumble. There can, according to this theory,
be no lasting good or scientific future for capitalism; it has the
seeds of its own destruction within itself. Since Stalinism is the
ultimate in human development, it can have no inner conflicts,
and, therefore, no matter what progressive developments may
take place in the outside world, they are bound to fail in the
end and the Stalinist utopia will envelop the world.

Adherence to this rigid theory accounts for the now famous
biological controversy which raged last year in the Soviet
Union. No matter how many scientists, including many of the
most prominent Soviet biologists, accepted as proven the fundamental truth of the Mendelian theory of inherited characteristics, the Kremlin has ruled that it cannot be true. If, contrary
to the claims of Soviet biologist Lysenko, man cannot inherit
acquired characteristics, then one of the fundamental props of
Soviet ideology falls to the ground. If the Soviet state, by environment and outside pressure cannot cause fundamental

changes in man's character—in other words, in human nature—
the future of the whole Soviet system is questionable.

Soviet intellectuals must refrain, therefore, from exposing
the shortcomings of the Soviet regime. They must cooperate
to the fullest extent in reselling the ideology and glories of the
regime to the masses, even if they have to create new "proven"
scientific theories in order to do so.

If the Kremlin had been willing to put it in a nutshell, it
would have said: Reality must be twisted to fit the ideology;
black must be made white; the gods must be served.

The new party line on satire, for instance, was succinctly
stated in the Soviet newspaper, *Literary Gazette,* on December
11, 1948, when it demanded that Soviet motion picture comedies must satirize "everything that does not fit into a Soviet
conception of morality and the Soviet way of life."

The question that naturally comes to mind is: "Why were
the Soviet authorities so apprehensive about the loyalty of the
masses, particularly after the conclusion of a successful war?"

The simplest and best answer is the war itself. Until the
Soviet Army advanced into Central Europe and the Balkans in
1944, the masses of the Russian people had been for all intents
and purposes hermetically sealed from all knowledge of and
contact with the outside world. Soviet propaganda had painted
a picture of abject misery as the normal condition of life of the
peasants and workers in the capitalist world, and contrasted
this with the better life of the Soviet people under their great
leader, Stalin.

The authorities were well aware that their propaganda might
boomerang to plague them as soon as the Soviet troops found
out for themselves that Stalin's slogan about the glories of the
Soviet Union, "Life is better, life is happier," applied to the
outside world, not to Mother Russia.

Shortly after the Soviet Army entered Rumania, two well-
publicized dispatches from a Soviet correspondent in Bucharest
cautioned Soviet troops serving outside the U.S.S.R. as follows:

"We will have to pass through many foreign countries. A
lot of tawdry brilliance will blind your eyes, Red Army men.
Do not believe these deceitful phantoms of pseudo-civiliza-
tion."

He also warned them not to be taken in by the pretty, "standard-looking" women, with their painted faces, short skirts, and open-toed and open-heeled shoes.

But these dispatches and others couldn't convince the comrades that all this gold did not glitter. Posters were put up warning the people at home: "Do not believe all returned soldiers." The posters went on to explain that, after all the blood and hardship that the troops had undergone, their judgments were lopsided, that they were nervous and dazed, and that some even would try to claim that the cities and villages of capitalistic countries provide everyone with a mansion filled with luxuries.

By August, 1945, the problem had reached such alarming proportions that the late Mikhail Kalinin, the nominal Chief of State of the U.S.S.R., found it necessary to address a large group of political agitators who were about to stump the country, admonishing them to explain away the alleged attainments of foreign culture. This is a part of what he said:

"There was talk here about people coming back from Germany who have seen 'cultures' of German villages which made a certain impression on them. Our agitators must uncrown this German culture. . . . There are people both in towns and villages who hardly ever read and are really very little developed, who yearn to dress more fashionably, to wear hats, even smoking jackets, and use toilet water. They want to seem to be educated people. But by themselves and from inside themselves they are not cultured. Such seems to me to be the culture of the German burgher or rich farmer. This is pure external culture, an empty one, not grasping the depths of the human soul. . . . All this may create an impression on inexperienced people with no aesthetic taste. In general, the German standardized way of life cannot blind a reasonable person. . . ."

Apart from the awakening to the realities of life abroad, which was bound to have serious repercussions among those who saw the outside world, the Soviet authorities during the war also had deliberately given the impression that a new era of ease and comfort would come with peace.

Thus Stalin's announcement in February, 1946, of at least three more five-year plans, primarily devoted to the production of capital instead of consumer goods, came as a shock to the tired and disillusioned Soviet peoples.

All these considerations, together with fear of the possible disruptive force of a free intellectual movement, prompted the decision to launch the all-out campaign which began in 1946 to recall Communist ideology and to build up the ego of the Soviet people. It is this latter objective which provides the explanation of the long list of invention "firsts" which have flooded the press of the world during the past three years. Russians are now declared to have "invented" everything important from the steam engine to penicillin, including the radio, airplane, submarine, Diesel engine, telegraph, jet propulsion, long-range rockets, atomic energy and the caterpillar tractor.

When it was announced in the Soviet press a few years ago that a Russian had perfected the caterpillar tractor in the eighteen thirties, but that no one outside knew about it because it was not sent to a famous agricultural fair in Vienna, a foreigner in Moscow remarked that the only reason that they could not get the machine to Vienna, of course, was that the Russians had not yet invented the railroad.

As the Zhdanov ideological campaign progressed, its magnitude became more and more apparent. On the twenty-ninth anniversary of the Revolution, Zhdanov, in the principal speech of the day, stated:

"The *Central Committee of the party* has recently revealed a lack of ideology and an apolitical bent in literature and art. There were still survivals of capitalism in the people's consciousness which had to be overcome, and the recent decision of the Central Committee on questions of ideological work had this aim."

A year later the battle obviously still had not been won, and Molotov, in his thirtieth anniversary speech, took up the same line.

"Not all of us," he said, "have yet rid ourselves of obsequious worship of the West, of capitalist culture. It was not for nothing that the ruling classes of old Russia were often in a state of such profound spiritual dependence on the capitalistically more highly developed countries of Europe. This facilitated the cultivation among certain circles of the old intelligentsia

Ambassador and Mrs. Smith pictured on the veranda at Spaso House.

Easter Eve in Moscow. The most solemn moment of the midnight service: the Metropolitan turns to the congregation and pronounces the words, "Christ is risen!"

of a slavish inferiority complex and spiritual dependence on the bourgeois countries of Europe."

He added the somewhat ominous warning: "Unless one rids oneself of these shameful survivals, one cannot be a real Soviet citizen."

This statement gives confirmation of the Kremlin's fear of a free-thinking intelligentsia, the existence of a train of Soviet thought about the glories of capitalism, as well as the tacit admission that there were many in the Soviet Union who would like to have an interchange of ideas with the West.

These statements of Molotov and Zhdanov, and many others since 1946, are the best answers to those sincere persons and groups throughout the non-Soviet world who believe that we can crack the Iron Curtain and bring about better understanding by a free exchange of ideas.

It is certainly reasonable to expect that if student and professor exchange arrangements could be effected, if other cultural exchanges were possible, if there were no censorship in the Soviet Union, and if Soviet and foreign citizens were permitted freely to live and circulate in each other's country, the present tension between the East and West would be greatly diminished. I had strong hopes for this myself.

During my tour in Moscow I made a special effort to effect such exchanges. On many occasions and on the highest official level, I took up specific as well as general proposals for student or professor exchanges, reciprocal visits of Soviet and American cultural groups, and other proposals of this nature. None of these efforts was successful. Often I did not receive any reply at all; if my note was answered, the Soviet statement was evasive.

There is very little likelihood that any such efforts will be successful in the foreseeable future, for there is complete and forceful evidence that Soviet participation in international culture or scientific efforts is impossible under Soviet policy. One such piece of evidence was an article by the Minister of Higher Education of the Soviet Union, Sergei Kaftanov, entitled "Science Called upon to Serve the People," published in the March 3, 1948, issue of *Pravda*. Kaftanov, as spokesman of Soviet policy, condemned world scientific organizations as foreign politi-

cal schemes designed to serve the interests of the "imperialists."
His words were:

"Behind the pompous, demagogic phrases of reactionary
foreign politicians, particularly American and British, about
world science and about the establishment of a world organization for scientific research, is concealed the desire to subordinate the development and achievements of world science to
imperialist interests."

He then warns Soviet scientists that "the oblivion of a certain
part of the scientific intelligentsia to the very important principle of the Communist Party nature of science results in
deference to bourgeois science, to the acceptance of the idea,
foreign to Soviet society and the Soviet man, that science is a
non-party and supra-class matter, and even results sometimes
in the commission of anti-state and anti-patriotic deeds."

The Minister concluded his article with a covert threat to
those Soviet scientists who, "engaging themselves in pseudo-
scientific problems, are trying to find refuge in their labora-
tories from the burning issues of Socialist construction."

I had a unique personal experience which illustrated the
jealousy with which the Soviet Union guards the accomplishments of its scientists and the extent to which it eschews collaboration with the West, even in those fields which have no
military or industrial implication, but which, on the contrary,
would only be for the benefit of mankind. This came about
because, in my ignorance and impatience with official inertia,
I had the temerity to make direct approach, and it resulted, I
fear, in causing trouble to two very remarkable people.

The work of the Russian Doctors Nina Kluyeva and Gregory
Roskin, directed toward the development of a serum which
would destroy the giant cells of cancer, began to be known at
about the same time that experiments of Professor Bogomolets,
in attempting to prolong life through the use of bone marrow
serum, were attracting world-wide attention. Doctors Kluyeva
and Roskin were much more reserved than was Doctor Bogomolets, who hid neither his light nor his theories under a
bushel, but the news of K-R cancer serum had leaked out.

The Embassy had received letters from all over the United
States from victims of cancer or from those who loved them

who, having given up hope, were now grasping at the straw provided by this rumor of a new cure. As the number of these appeals increased, and our formal inquiries for information produced little result, I decided to ask myself, and to ask direct from the source, in the belief that science and human suffering knew no international boundaries. Accordingly, by telephone, I asked and obtained an appointment with the President of the Medical Academy, who proved to be a distinguished old doctor, over seventy, who obviously thought of medicine and science as something quite distinct from politics or foreign policy. He told me what he knew about K-R serum, which he described as still very much in the experimental stage, but about which he felt, as he described it, that the researchers had something of great importance "just at the tips of their fingers —just at the tips of their fingers."

I was impressed by this, for he had not shown the same enthusiasm about the Bogomolets serum, and, indeed, in a very amusing way, remarked that he had rejected Bogomolets' repeated offers of treatment because "my observation is that while Bogomolets helps some people, his serum kills about as many as it helps, and at my age I prefer to adhere to the more conservative treatment for my ailment." (He had stomach ulcers.)

At the conclusion of our talk, he suggested that I see the scientists themselves, in their Moscow laboratory, and when I eagerly assented he telephoned them then and there and made an appointment for the following afternoon.

I was sarcastic with my own people for their previous nonproductive efforts, but it turned out that I was a bit premature. The following morning a phone call from the Ministry of Health indicated that I had violated protocol by not obtaining permission of the Minister, who desired to see me prior to my interview with Doctors Kluyeva and Roskin. I went to the Ministry, accompanied by an interpreter, and was courteously received by the Minister and several assistants.

The Minister obviously was neither a doctor nor a scientist, but an official of the Communist Party. He gave me, from notes, an account, part of which I knew was not very accurate, of the K-R serum development. He confirmed my appointment with its discoverers, and said that I would be accompanied by his representative, an English-speaking doctor who had acted as liaison officer with our Red Cross and whom I already knew by reputation. I went with him to the research institute, where I found the Institute Director in his office, together with Doctors Kluyeva and Roskin. These three were pure scientists—and "K" and "R" turned out to be wife and husband, charming, modest, and obviously devoted to each other and to their work. They told me their story.

Dr. Roskin, the husband, while working on a different project, had noticed that the trypanosome of Chagas disease, in its fatal course, seemed to attack first by preference the cells of the mammary glands of both animals and humans. Later, at his microscope examining some slides of cancerous tissue, he was struck with the resemblance between these cells and the so-called giant cells of cancer. This led to a prolonged series of experiments, on which his wife worked with him, during which they established to their satisfaction that the trypanosome would by preference attack and destroy cancer cells before going on to attack and destroy the normal cells of the victim with fatal results. They then developed an attenuated serum which destroyed the cancer cells but did not kill the mice on which the experiments were made. After countless experiments on mice, the researchers arrived at the point where they felt that the serum might be used on a human being—but there was no assurance that even in its attenuated form the usually fatal Chagas disease would not kill the patient. At this point, the pretty Doctor Kluyeva proudly told me, to her husband's obvious embarrassment, how he secretly had taken the first injection of the serum to be given to a human being, and had told her about it only after he felt sure that the period of danger was past. Since then, they said, they had used the serum in Moscow on a number of cases of cancer, previously considered incurable. In the first of these, a case of throat cancer, they described the results as "miraculous." They claimed equally favorable results in several other cases, where the cancerous lesions were on the surface. In cases of internal cancer with large affected areas, the serum, they said, did indeed destroy the cancer cells, but this very destruction left a large ulcerated area which, if not susceptible to surgery, might itself be fatal. The serum, they said, was stable only for a very short time—a matter of a few days, and therefore it could not be shipped. Thus far the amount they had been able to produce was very small, for they had been successful only with mice, of which they were using thousands.

I assured them, as I could with complete safety, that the United States Government would lend them every possible assistance, including, if needed, a special refrigerated airplane for the transportation of a sample of the serum to America when the experiment had reached the stage where this could be done. On their part, they assured me that a part of the first stable product would go to the United States. They added that Dr. Vassili V. Parin, Secretary General of the Academy of Medical Sciences of the Soviet Union, was soon to head a group of Soviet medical men to the United States on an official mission and would give a full report to the doctors of America. At the same time they offered me all of the data they had so far compiled and published. They kept their word. The publications were delivered the following day, and, in due course, Dr. Parin gave his report at a press conference in the Office of the Surgeon General in Washington.

The aftermath of this incident is not so well known outside of Russia.

Dr. Parin, on his return, was tried and sentenced for prematurely revealing the secrets of Soviet science. Doctors Kluyeva and Roskin, although not punished, are said to have received strong admonition. The Minister of Health, himself, was relieved some weeks later. What, if any, connection there was between his removal and the incident I have described, it is impossible to say—but current Moscow sources, often surprisingly accurate, had it that he was reproached for knowing less than the American Ambassador of the accomplishments of Soviet science.

However, if the Soviet scientist seems regimented, his mental horizon still is less restricted than is that of the Soviet writer, who is controlled completely.

This control is exercised primarily by an organization called Glavlit (The Main Administration for Affairs of Literature and Publishing Houses). Glavlit was established in its present form in 1931 by a decree which states:

1. For the exercise of all forms of political-ideological, military and economic control over production of the press, manuscripts, photographs, pictures and so forth, which are intended for publication or dissemination and also over radio broadcasts, lectures and exhibits, a Main Administration for Affairs of Literature and Publishing Houses (Glavlit) is established as part of the People's Commissariat of Education of the R.S.F.S.R.

2. For the accomplishment of the tasks entrusted to it, Glavlit is authorized to forbid the publication, promulgation and dissemination of works which:

a. Contain agitation and propaganda against the Soviet authority and the dictatorship of the proletariat;

b. Divulge state secrets;

c. Arouse nationalistic and religious fanaticism;

d. Bear a pornographic character.

Glavlit is further charged with:

The issuance of permission for the establishment of publishing houses and periodicals, the closing of publishing houses and publications, the prohibition and authorization of importations from abroad and the exportation abroad of literature, pictures and so forth in accordance with regulations in effect . . . The prosecution of persons violating the demands of Glavlit, its organs and authorized representatives . . .

With this type of rigid internal control of the printed or spoken word, it is not surprising that the authoritative magazine, *Party Life,* in May, 1947, stated: "A leading article [editorial] by definition of the Central Committee of the Party, 'must give direction and guidance, must lay down the basic line of conduct. Leading articles and such articles are not mere talk or discourses, but rather political decrees, directives.' "

Soviet intellectuals are constantly being reminded that they may not think independently but must follow the party line. The important party magazine, *Bolshevik,* in its May, 1948, number, says: "An unfailing condition for the artist in Socialist realism is the party tendency of his works. . . . In their work, Soviet writers are guided by the policy of the Bolshevik Party and the Soviet state."

In order better to get the "word" to the people and utilize, for party purposes, the harnessed talents of the intellectuals, there was organized in July, 1947, "The All-Union Society for the Dissemination of Political and Scientific Knowledge." This organization, according to one of its directors, must: "(a) assist the growth of Socialist consciousness in the masses, (b) explain the external and internal policy of the Soviet Government to the masses, (c) inculcate a feeling of national pride, (d) popularize the attainments of science and technology, (e) combat all anti-scientific views and remnants of alien ideology."

From this description, it is clear that this organization has been mainly responsible for whipping up patriotism, ideology, getting the "facts" on all the great Russian "inventions," and for squaring the scientific circle; in other words, making sure that if scientific facts do not conform to the basic ideology, the facts must be changed.

Under the guiding hand of Glavlit and the secret police, intellectuals in all fields are sent about the country to accomplish the objective of the organization.

How have the intellectuals been brought back into line and how effective has the campaign been?

In a totalitarian secret police state, it is not difficult to bring people to heel. The only question is, how much does it cost in human values and in other intangible factors, and what will be the long range effects?

The "purge" of the intellectuals does not resemble in any way the bloody political purge of 1935 to 1938. It seems reasonable that the Politburo, remembering the disruption of the economy and administration caused by the earlier purge, would be very reluctant to stage another. The cost would be too high. And so the Kremlin apparently decided that a "horrible example purge," affecting a limited number of prominent individuals, coupled with an all-out ideological and publicity campaign, would be less harmful to the regime and, in all probability, would accomplish the desired results.

The method used was a highly organized campaign of criticism directed against individuals who had produced works or made statements which do not now conform to the party line. It made no difference if these writers and composers formerly had been praised to high heaven, honored officially and by the public, or were winners of the coveted Stalin Prize for their previous works. They were publicly chastised and humiliated.

The party line had changed; therefore, facts, ideas and concepts must be changed to conform.

The music purge attacked such well known composers as Shostakovich and Prokofiev, both several times winners of Stalin Prizes, whose compositions had been acclaimed at home and abroad. They, with the other composers under attack, were accused of following "bourgeois ideology fed by the influence of contemporary Western European and American music," of not making "use of the wealth of popular melodies, songs and refrains in which the creative work of the people of the U.S.S.R. is so rich," of "adhering to a formalist and anti-popular trend" and of having "anti-democratic tendencies in music." The composers, as well as all artists, were admonished by *Pravda* in January, 1948, "to play an outstanding part in Communist education; the party places before them the task of carrying Communist ideology to the masses."

There was amusement as well as tragedy involved. During the winter of 1947-1948, there opened in Moscow an opera, *Velikaya Druzhba, (The Great Friendship)* by the composer Muradeli, based on a political theme, with contemporary characters. I was told by an eyewitness that several major party leaders were completely overcome with mirth at the idea of Malenkov singing a political harangue, which was entirely too much for their Russian sense of humor. Later, they remembered that the audiences which would see this opera also had a Russian sense of humor, and the matter became serious at once. Called to task, the composer replied that he could only write as he had been taught. He had studied at the Moscow Conservatory, and mentioned Prokofiev as one of his teachers.

Muradeli's opera, which must, I think, be regarded merely as a straw that broke the camel's back, was first mentioned in the Soviet press at the beginning of 1947, when it was referred to as being written with a view to presentation under the title of "Commissar Extraordinary." The title was subsequently changed to *The Great Friendship* and the première was eventually given in the Bolshoi Theater during the celebrations of the thirtieth anniversary of the Revolution. Press criticism subsequently was scanty and restrained, but not unfriendly until the opera was condemned by the Central Committee of the Communist Party.

The long preamble of the resolution leading up to the positive decisions taken by the Central Committee began by describing Muradeli's opera as "a vicious, anti-artistic production," both as regards its musical form and its subject matter. The music was called "unexpressive" and "inharmonious." It was said to lack memorable melodies, to be devoid of folk-tunes, and, in its pursuit of "originality," to have neglected the rich classical tradition of Russian opera, the popular nature of which had made it loved by and accessible to the broad masses of the people. Historically, the opera was also at fault. The reason for these failings on Muradeli's part was "the faulty, formalistic path, fatal to the work of a Soviet composer," on which he has set forth, it added.

The resolution then went on to relate the findings of a conference of workers in the musical field summoned to discuss the question by the Central Committee of the party, and over which Zhdanov presided. This meeting had agreed that Muradeli's failure was not an isolated example but that it was symptomatic of "the unhappy state of contemporary Soviet music" and the spread of "a formalistic trend" among Soviet composers. Despite warnings by the Central Committee, Soviet musicians had failed to remedy their defects. Notable offenders were D. Shostakovich, S. Prokofiev, A. Khachaturian, V. Shebalin, G. Popov and N. Miaskovsky, whose music is characterized by the rejection of the principles of classical music, both Western and Russian, by dissonance, and by a predilection for "confusing and neuropathic combinations which turn music into cacophony and a chaotic accumulation of sounds." Such musical workers, the resolution continued, cherish the theory that if their innovations are incomprehensible to the people it is because the people are not yet mature enough to understand them. This anti-popular theory is doing great harm to Soviet musical culture and, in particular, is having a disastrous effect on the training and education of young composers in the conservatories, where the formalistic trend is dominant.

The musical critics fared no better than the composers. The former were charged in the resolution with championing this "degenerate, formalistic music," making themselves the "mouthpieces" of certain so-called "progressive" composers and, instead of criticizing on the basis of objective principles, "humoring and showing subservience to this or that musical leader" for reasons of personal friendship.

"All this," the resolution continued, "means that, among a section of Soviet composers, survivals of bourgeois ideology, fed by the influence of contemporary decadent Western European and American music, have not yet been overcome."

At the session where the matter was discussed, Prokofiev, I was told, kept his back turned while Shvernik and Zhdanov talked, and when reprimanded for his inattention said bitterly: "Oh, I know it already," adding in a loud aside to Shostakovich, "What do Ministers know of music? That is the business of composers." If true, Prokofiev's moment of independence was brief. As is usually the case, Prokofiev, Shostakovich and the others confessed their errors in order to save their skins. As of December, 1948, however, the "reformation" of Prokofiev was said to be proceeding slowly.

Shostakovich's confession read in part: "I know that the party is right, that the party wishes me well, and that I must search for and find creative paths which lead me to Soviet realistic popular art."

In other words, the composers were told that they must create music of a simple stereotyped style to which the people can beat time and hum as they struggle to meet the ever higher production quotas, all for the glorification of the five-year plan.

The same type of abject confessions has been the usual routine whether the "culprits" were previously honored philosophers, authors, directors, critics, economists or scientists.

The orchestration and players are different for each performance, but the conductor and tune are the same: fight the West, stamp out foreign influences, cease being "objective," re-study Marxism-Leninism, stop collecting facts, work to whip up militant party spirit.

Eugene Varga, the renowned Marxian economist, was humiliated several times (although he still is a member of the Academy of Science) because he gave too realistic an appraisal of developments abroad, based on facts which often conflicted with the need to support Communist morale, inside and outside the Soviet Union. He had asserted that the state could play a decisive role over the economy in a capitalist state. As the party doctrinaires saw it, he should have stated categorically that the state is under the complete control of the financiers—Wall Street. He also, of course, made the other mistake of predicting a serious depression in the United States in 1948, and then he made the heretical statement that an inter-imperialist war was not inevitable, as Lenin and Stalin had asserted.

Perhaps the most humiliating and revealing confession was that made by the Mendelian biologist, Zhebrak. In his written recantation, he states: "As long as both trends in Soviet genetics were recognized by our party and the disputes between these trends were regarded as creative discussions on theoretical questions of contemporary science, helping to find the truth, I persistently defended my views which in individual questions differed from the views of Academician Lysenko. But now that it has become plain to me that the basic theses of the Michurin [Lysenko] trend in Soviet genetics are approved by the Central Committee, CPSU(b), as a member of the party, I do not consider that I can adhere to the positions which have been acknowledged false by the Central Committee of the party."

Not only do the speeches of the "prosecutors" and the detailed confessions appear in the press, but almost all other writers and commentators—big and small—take their cue from the official denunciation and write long articles condemning the scapegoats, who often have been their close friends.

These castigations followed a pattern so closely that one almost knew what the next line would be without turning a page. One day we had a very funny example of summation in our official family. John Emmerson, one of our Chancery officers, has a devoted young son, Donald, then aged seven years. Donald wanted very much to please his father and, after infinite labor, wrote for his pleasure and presented to him the following poem:

THE MONKEY WRENCH

By Donald Kenneth Emmerson

I speak in German,
    I speak in French,
But to tell you the truth
    I'm just a monkey wrench.

I live in China,
   My cat's named Dinah,
But to tell you the truth,
   I'm just a monkey wrench.

All I have for lunch
   Is a bottle of punch,
But to tell you the truth
   I'm just a monkey wrench.

I sleep at night
   If the moon is bright,
But to tell you the truth
   I'm just a monkey wrench.

A copy of young Donald's masterpiece came into the hands of Bob Magidoff, the clever American radio commentator who could no longer speak over the Moscow Radio for foreign transmission, but had instead to send his dispatches by cable. Bob immediately saw in the poem an opportunity for a facetious review in the best style of the *Literary Gazette* in these words:

The Spiritual Tragedy

OF

DONALD KENNETH EMMERSON

AUTHOR OF

"The Monkey Wrench"

The American poet, Donald Kenneth Emmerson, is a typical product of his age—the age of the decline of monopolistic capital in the United States, that last obstacle in humanity's march toward its crowning achievement: world Communism.

Just as a droplet of water reflects the entire sun, so does Emmerson's poem, "The Monkey Wrench," reflect the depraved psychology of the poet and his Muse.

It is the psychology of an Imperialist. Influenced by the Marshall Plan which is seeking to catch in its net all of suffering, post-war Europe, the poet roams the world. "I speak German, I speak French," he says significantly, and "I live in China."

Here is cosmopolitanism. Here is the psychology of a reactionary race-hater. Emmerson has been insolent enough to rhyme his cat "Dinah" with "China," thus hinting that the free, democratic, liberated regions of China are akin to the treacherous lowly cat. No Chinese Communist, heir to humanism as he is, would ever think of naming his cat Erica, to rhyme with America! . . .

The eminent Soviet critic, Vladimir Yermilov, editor-in-chief of the *Literary Gazette*, has recently written with penetrating, dialectical materialism: "Bourgeois literature strives to corrupt the souls of men, crush their will to fight. A bitter, irreconcilable struggle for the souls of men is raging between progressive and reactionary literature. The progressive camp is, of course, led by our Soviet literature."

What role does Emmerson's creative work play in this struggle? To whose camp does he belong?

The irrevocable and implacable answer our conscience dictates is: he belongs to the camp doomed by the evolution of social forces, the reactionary camp led by predatory U.S. Imperialism.

One must admit that the poem, "The Monkey Wrench," reveals talent and maturity, but it is the maturity of overripe American Capitalism.

Yes, there is no future for the forceful but mutilated genius of the American poet. He is immoral and addicted to drink. He himself has confessed:

> "All I have for lunch
> Is a bottle of punch."

His nights are tortured and sleepless:

> "I sleep at night
> If the moon is bright."

But we all know that the moon is never bright in the dismal world of Capitalism on its downgrade.

But this physical disintegration is sheer joy compared to the spiritual purgatory in which this representative American poet lives.

His spiritual world is full of all the unspeakable horrors that ever harassed his intellectual predecessor, the Russian writer Dostoyevsky. The words Comrade Yermilov said about Dostoyevsky, in accordance with Marxism-Leninism, fully apply to Emmerson's poetry:

> "He wasted the entire power of his enormous talent to prove the weakness, insignificance and vulgarity of human nature."

But, being a Russian, even Dostoyevsky had a soul. The American poet does not possess a soul. All he has is a monkey wrench, that vulgar symbol of America's Machinistic civilization.

We have had enough of the poet and his degenerate art. Let us leave him to his sick, aging, decaying Capitalist world, and join the free, joyous masses celebrating the Stalinist Constitution at the Park of Culture and Rest.

While done in fun, Magidoff's "review" nevertheless conveyed with complete accuracy and full flavor the Soviet form of literary criticism of Western authors, and of their own Soviet contemporaries who happen to come under the cloud of Kremlin displeasure.

The full-fledged effort to batten down the ideological hatches is undoubtedly having its effect on the thinking of the people. Sometimes, however, such efforts backfire in a big way. An example was the movie version of *The Russian Question,* the extremely anti-American play by Konstantin Simonov, which depicts the trials, tribulations and frustrations of an honest American reporter who tries to write objective stories about the achievements of the Soviet Union.

The play had been fairly effective in depicting cold-blooded capitalism at its Marxian worst, and a great deal of effort was made to produce a screen version to carry the word to the villages. The authorities allowed it to run in Moscow for less than two weeks. The newsreel shots of New York skyscrapers, traffic-laden streets, and of New York's worst slums, all roused nothing but admiration in the audiences. Pictures of clotheslines suspended between slum buildings produced gasps and exclamations of "How many clothes they have!" And apparently the well-appointed sets of the interiors of the five-room California-type, Westchester bungalow of the frustrated reporter caused even deeper envy.

One could not help but wonder whether the frustrated Soviet producer might not be getting in a few private licks at the authorities.

Some must be very tempted to do so. Unquestionably, Soviet writers and lecturers have a much greater knowledge of the realities of Soviet foreign and domestic policy than their public utterances indicate. Their performances in the press and on the lecture platform are typical of the role played in Soviet society by those whom the Kremlin calls the "new Soviet intelligentsia" and whom our Counselor in Moscow, Foy Kohler, described as "intellectual tailors, well paid by the state to hack up the tapestry of Western civilization to clothe the nakedness of Soviet totalitarianism."

XIV

WAR OR PEACE?

A strange superstition prevails among the Russians, that they are predestined to conquer the world, and the prayers of the priests in the church are mingled with requests to hasten and consummate this "divine mission," while appeals to the soldiery founded on this idea of fatality and its glorious rewards are seldom made in vain. To a feeling of this sort has been attributed that remarkable patience and endurance which distinguish the Russian soldier in the midst of the greatest privations.

—Excerpt from a dispatch of the American
Minister to Russia, Neill S. Brown, dated
St. Petersburg, January 28, 1852

JUST before leaving Moscow during the latter part of 1948, a year of disturbing events and increasing tensions, I took a quiet and informal poll of the most experienced and best informed foreign representatives in Moscow on the probabilities of future peace or war between the Soviet orbit and the West. I was particularly interested in the views of the Ambassadors and Ministers representing the Soviet satellite nations, and as a direct approach to them on such a vital subject would have been difficult, I obtained their views through an intermediary, a "neutral" chief of mission.

While the opinions of Westerners varied, those of the Communist satellite diplomats were practically unanimous. They all expressed the opinion that it was impossible for the two systems to live together in peace and that a clash was inevitable. They foresaw two possible exceptions. One was that the capitalist United States, as the result of the long predicted economic collapse or for other reasons, would give in and withdraw from Europe, allowing the Soviet Union a free hand. The other was the possibility of a change in the Stalinist interpretation of irreconcilable hostility between the capitalist and Communist systems which they felt would be accompanied by a change in the foreign policy of the Soviet Union. None of the satellite representatives attached much importance·to the second alternative. Their estimates of the possible time factor differed considerably. Some said war would come "when the Soviet Union is prepared." Others estimated that hostilities might be expected in five, ten or fifteen years. The latter, I thought, obviously were thinking of the present series of five-year plans as a gauge of Soviet industrial preparedness.

The more moderate thinkers did not consider that war necessarily would occur in the near future, and one or two thought in terms of twenty-five or fifty years, or even longer.

All gave the impression of believing that the initiative would rest with the Soviet Union, thus paying an unintentional tribute to the basically pacific policy of the United States and the other Western democracies.

This unanimity of opinion among the Communists was not unexpected, as it was a reflection of the current party line, but it should be nonetheless alarming to our part of the world, which longs and plans for peace, to realize that the rulers of a large segment of the human family actually seem to believe profoundly in the inevitability of conflict.

At present, beyond question, there appears to exist a war psychosis among Soviet leaders. The constant and violent charges with which they assail the West are simply a manifestation of the Communist characteristic of loudly accusing others of the acts which they themselves are committing, or intend to commit.

Some time ago the famous English psychoanalyst, Dr. Ernest Jones, writing in *The New Statesman and Nation*, presented in the following words an excellent analysis of this apparent psychosis:

> The U.S.S.R. (i.e., their rulers) apparently apprehend the existence of danger in the outer world. They observe that many people in the Western world disapprove of both their internal and external political actions and furthermore distrust their intentions. This would in itself justify a degree of concern, and possibly some heart-searching. But there is a wide gap between knowing oneself to be disliked and believing that one's life is in danger. The frequent references in leading articles to Russia's "natural anxiety," must, therefore, be said to raise a very debatable point. I venture the opinion that no one

in the Western world, except perhaps a Communist, considers that either America or Britain is likely to attack the U.S.S.R.: geographical, military, political, economic and above all moral considerations render such a contingency extremely remote. Yet all the evidence . . . points to the conclusion that the U.S.S.R. (again, their rulers) feel this contingency to be very probable. If we, who ought to know something about the likelihood of our intentions, are convinced they are mistaken, then we are bound to conclude that the greater part of their apprehension arises from internal sources—to put it plainly, from unavowed or half-avowed aggressive tendencies of their own which they "project" on to the Western world. . . .

All this does not, of course, mean that the U.S.S.R. desires war or intends to bring it about. In all probability they would be well content with what has recently been termed the "fruits of war," with obtaining, free of opposition, all they may want. But it is a dangerous game to postulate the absence of all opposition, or to defy it. It is what the Germans did. Apart from a few irresponsibles who longed for the excitement of war, most Germans, including the Nazis, would have been quite content to absorb peacefully first Poland, then the Ukraine, then the rest of Europe and Russia, and finally the U.S.A. . . . One further point, the main one: It is of the very nature of aggression derived from internal sources (with the dependent anxiety) not to be influenced, i.e., appeased, by either concessions or successes in the outer world. Its intrinsic insatiability forbids this; *vide* Hitler. Only definite opposition can break in on the world of fantasy and restore that of reality. Whether it be more advantageous to make this inevitable stand at a time when war-weary people might prefer sanity to bellicosity or to wait until the nations are refreshed and re-equipped is a question for statesmen to decide.

At the time I saw Dr. Jones's interesting analysis, I was reading a remarkable document—the book written in 1839 by the French observer, De Custine, which I have quoted in previous chapters. One paragraph of De Custine's book strikes the modern reader with terrific impact. It says:

An immense, inordinate ambition, the kind of ambition which can take root only in the soul of an oppressed people and be nourished only on the misery of an entire country, is now astir in the hearts of the Russians. This essentially aggressive nation lives in a state of submissiveness so degrading

that it seems to be expiating in advance at home its expectation of tyranny abroad over other men. The glory and the
booty to which it looks forward turn its thoughts away from
the shame to which it is being subjected; and in the hope of
washing himself clean of his impious sacrifice of public and
personal liberty, this kneeling slave fills his dreams with visions
of world domination.

There is a direct analogy between the analysis of the political
philosopher of 1839 and the modern psychoanalyst. For us, the
vital question is: Are the Russians driven inexorably by their
ancient heritage and their modern anxieties toward the abyss
of war and conquest, or as others believe, is the Kremlin's "war
scare" campaign only feigned for reasons of politics, both
internal and external?

Three years of living with this problem brought us in Moscow to the conclusions that:

Soviet policy has always been directed toward the ultimate
goal of world revolution and Communist world domination.
This is still the policy of the Kremlin, and will continue to be,
so far as can be foreseen in the future.

The Soviet Union is not likely to resort to deliberate military aggression in the immediate future if the Atlantic Pact
nations do not waver in the positive application of their program. The U.S.S.R. leadership is not likely to gamble without
favorable odds. The Soviet Union's present line of internal
and external policies seems to be based on the expectation of
peace for several years.

The Kremlin is confident that the Soviet Union is safe from
attack, and has recently adopted several lines of action which
actually weaken the Soviet Union for the time being in order
ultimately to be stronger for the inevitable conflict in which
the Soviet leaders continue to believe.

The fear of imminent war has been deliberately fostered for
the past three years by the Soviet Government and its propaganda agencies in order to impede the economic recovery of
the West, to spur the Soviet people to greater industrial effort,
and to hide present Soviet weaknesses.

The resurrection of the Comintern in its new "Cominform"
cloak, the aggressive attitude of the Soviet delegations at international conferences, and the violent anti-Western propa-

ganda campaign in the Soviet orbit all confirm that, despite soothing statements to the contrary, the Kremlin has not given up its basic aim, the defeat of capitalism and the conquest of as much of the world as possible.

The fulminations of Soviet statemen and the Soviet press against imperialism, aggression, warmongering, interference in internal affairs and alleged attempts to gain world domination so accurately reflect Soviet practices, policies and aims that one sometimes wonders why they insist on constantly calling attention to the fact.

There have been many fluctuations in Soviet tactics during the past twenty years, but the more one studies Soviet statements and policies the more one realizes how fundamental and deep-seated are the basic tenets of Leninism-Stalinism and how antagonistic they are to the aims, desires and hopes of Western democracy. Despite many window-dressing declarations to the contrary, a review of the statements of party leaders and spokesmen at party gatherings during the past twenty years reveals the consistency of Soviet thought—fundamental hostility to Western democracy, capitalism, liberalism, social-democracy, and all other groups and elements not completely subservient to the Kremlin. The never-changing objective was outlined by Stalin in his speech on the tenth anniversary of the Revolution in 1927, when he said that the Soviet Union must be made "the prototype of the future amalgamation of the toilers of all countries in a single world economy."

Speaking to a visiting American labor delegation in 1927, Stalin also said:

". . . in the future progress of development in international revolution, two world centers will be formed: the Socialist center, attracting to itself all the countries gravitating toward socialism, and the capitalist center, attracting to itself all the countries gravitating toward capitalism. The struggle between these two centers for the conquest of world economy will decide the fate of capitalism and communism throughout the whole world. . . ."

I have often pondered Stalin's 1927 prediction, and always the question arose in my mind whether Stalin was indeed able to penetrate the future through the Marxian dialectic; or whether and to what extent he was the prisoner of a slavish

and unquestioning devotion to Communist ideological concepts. I have come to the conclusion that the second alternative
is in fact correct: that Stalin and his regime are driven inexorably by the necessity of the maintenance of power and of the
fulfillment of Communist ambitions deliberately to say and
do the things which would bring about in fact the world situation envisaged by Communist dogma.

At the end of the second World War, the Soviet Government
stood at a crossroads. The Soviet Union had gained not only
awed respect as a national power, but also legitimacy and ac-
ceptability. A great reservoir of good will for Russia existed
among practically all the peoples of the world. The Soviet
Union might well have lived in peaceful possession of her wartime conquests and gains, much of which she owed to her
grateful and trusting Allies. Had she chosen to play the international game cooperatively, these gains today would be little
less than those she now possesses and they would have been
securely held in a relatively calm and peaceful world.

Instead, the Soviet Government deliberately chose the opposite course—the course of doubly insuring and heavily exploit-
ing its gains, of rejecting and antagonizing its wartime Allies,
of preparing the Soviet peoples for future conflict, and of re-
doubling efforts to increase the scientific and industrial war
potential of the U.S.S.R.

When I left the Soviet Union, wartime cooperation with the
capitalistic world was being portrayed by Soviet propaganda as
an unholy alliance, and the successful outcome of the war as
attributable solely to the might of the Soviet armed forces,
both in the European and Pacific theaters. In fact, reading the
Soviet press in 1949, one might well gain the impression that
the United States, Britain and France had been allied, not with
the Soviet Union, but with Hitler.

The Kremlin's concept of the division of the world into two
great warring camps not only justifies, but absolutely requires,
the tightest possible organization and control of their own
camp.

I believe two factors impressed me more than any others as
having fundamental influence on the organization of the Soviet Union itself, of the Soviet satellite areas, and of world

communism as a tool of the Kremlin. The first is that all the organizational concepts are *Russian*. It is essential to bear constantly in mind that Marx and Engels were historical analysts preoccupied almost exclusively with the question of when and how to make a revolution. They gave very little thought to what would happen if and when that revolution should take place and be successful. In all the millions of pages he wrote during his lifetime, Marx just once mentioned the phrase "dictatorship of the proletariat." The Russian revolutionaries adopted it for their ideological propaganda; but they have effectively proved in practice, as any reasonable man could discover by a bit of historical research and a few minutes of thought, that a dictatorship by definition is unlikely to be more than one man and has never been known to encompass more than a limited oligarchy. Consequently, the organizational basis of so-called Marxian communism is purely Russian and was developed by Lenin and Stalin on the basis of age-old Czarist Russian traditions of despotic power and absolute control. It would be a great mistake to fail to appreciate this, or to be misled into thinking that any system of government could conceivably issue from the dark depths of Russian despotic history that could really understand the hopes and aspirations of the Western states, whose concept of government has issued from the great progressive and liberal traditions that have marked the steady rise of Western civilization.

It is very necessary to keep in mind when considering Soviet objectives and intentions that for all practical purposes communism today is *Great Russianism*.

The second factor is the complete control of policy that is exercised by the Bolshevik Party. The government, the various economic administrations and the innumerable social organizations are operational or service organs. They have little to do with the determination of real policy.

Throughout her history Russia has been a backward, poor and ill-developed country. She has repeatedly paid for this backwardness in the suffering she has endured at the hands of foreign invaders. The political effect of this background on the thinking of the present rulers of the Soviet Union has been profound.

Some excerpts from a speech made by Stalin on the forced

pace of industrial development in the first five-year plan give
a deeper insight into the background that has motivated his
actions than anything else I have read. On this occasion, ten
years before the Germans attacked the Soviet Union, Stalin
said:

> At times people ask whether we could not slacken the pace
> and slow down. To slacken the pace means to lag behind,
> and those who lag behind get defeated. The history of the
> Russia of olden days was that she was always getting defeated
> for her backwardness. The Khans of Mongolia defeated her.
> The squires of Poland and Lithuania defeated her. The capi-
> talists of France and England defeated her. The Barons of
> Japan defeated her. Everybody defeated her—for her back-
> wardness. For her military backwardness, for her cultural back-
> wardness, for the backwardness of her state administration, for
> her industrial backwardness, for her agricultural backwardness.
> They defeated her because it gave them plunder, and because
> they could get away with it unpunished. Such is the law of the
> exploiters—to beat those who are backward and weak. Such is
> the jungle law of capitalism. If you are backward, if you are
> weak, that means you are wrong, that means you can be de-
> feated and enslaved. Do you want our Socialist fatherland to
> be defeated and to lose its independence? If you don't, you
> must liquidate its backwardness in the shortest possible space
> of time. There is no other way out. We have either to catch
> up with the capitalist countries or die. We are fifty or one
> hundred years behind their leading countries. We must catch
> up within ten years. Either we do it or we shall be destroyed.

Russian poverty has persisted to the present day. To understand the policy of the Soviet Government, one must bear in
mind that its struggle to put itself on a footing of economic
equality with the Western world has been desperate in the
fullest sense of the word. In this desperate struggle, the driving force has been the fear of defeat in war.

Hence the importance of the corollary question of security.
In the past, Russia has suffered severely from the lack of natural defense frontiers to protect her from the incursions of
hostile people upon her borders. These borders have changed
with the ebb and flow of Russian success in war and, since
defense in depth has been Russia's easiest method of wearing
out her foreign invaders, she has had a tendency to push out

her frontiers as far as possible whenever she has been in a position to do so.

Many years ago, Lord Palmerston described the impelling effect of this urge for geographical security that has been a constant factor throughout Russian history. He put it this way:

"It has always been the policy and practice of the Russian Government to expand its frontiers as rapidly as the apathy or timidity of neighboring states would permit, but usually to halt and frequently to recoil when confronted by determined opposition; then to await the next favorable opportunity to spring upon its intended victim."

Now a new and quite different problem has been added by the Communist Party's preoccupation with its own security. Its members form a minority group, numbering not more than one-thirtieth of the population. To retain power, the Communists resort to means as ruthless as those by which they acquired it, and they carry with them always the sense of insecurity which haunts those who have usurped power and who retain it by force. As keen students of history, they have always been on the watch for counter-revolution. To protect themselves, they have established a massive police system, and even though the position of the party has grown enormously stronger as the result of victory in war, it cannot yet feel completely secure, nor can it relax its precautions. Their lives depend upon retaining office. They have used terrorist methods and imposed great privation upon the mass of people of the Soviet Union. They are aware of a widespread discontent with the hardships of life.

But the chief causes of the party's obsession with security have been directly or indirectly connected with the fear of war —foreign or civil. In the first place, there was the fear that Russia would inevitably be defeated if she were involved in a major war before she had built up her strength. She had no margin of safety. She was vulnerable, and the party knew it. In the second place, there was the fear that if the outside world knew too much about Russia's weakness and her ultimate objective, an effort might be made to crush the Soviet system before it was too late. Thirdly, there was the conviction that the capitalist world was implacably hostile to the Soviet Union.

Lenin's theory that it is impossible for communism and capitalism to exist side by side for any length of time in the same world—that sooner or later one or the other must go down, and that before that end supervenes the most frightful collisions will occur between the two systems—still is the cardinal principle of Soviet political doctrine.

The conviction of capitalist hostility is based, in part, on past experience. The leaders of the party remember the German war of 1914, followed by the peace of Brest-Litovsk, the Allied intervention, the Polish attempts to seize the Western Ukraine, and the Japanese attempts to probe the Far Eastern frontiers of the Soviet Union.

Then they saw and remembered paragraphs in *Mein Kampf* about the transformation of vast areas of Russia into a German colony, and finally they have never forgotten Munich, which they interpreted as an attempt by the Western democracies to turn the German drive eastward against Russia. These lessons, derived from their own experience, reinforce their preconceived theory—the belief that the Soviet Union and the capitalist world will inevitably clash.

This conviction is a part of the ideology with which the Soviet Union's foreign policy is inextricably woven, and which must be understood before any study of its foreign relations can be made.

Stalin's book, *Problems of Leninism,* repeatedly emphasizes that, although Soviet socialism can and must be established in the Soviet Union, its security cannot be guaranteed in view of the hostility of capitalist environment unless socialism also is established in a number of other countries. Security and expansion are inseparably linked. But, according to Stalin's interpretation of history, no form of social organization has ever been known to give way peaceably to another. Hence, Soviet leaders expect that the spread of Soviet socialism eventually will be met by capitalistic force of arms.

Obviously, then, according to this ideology, the Soviet Union must increase its armed forces and its war potential in order to be prepared for this struggle. Pending the outbreak of hostilities, no opportunity must be lost to strengthen and consolidate the Soviet position. During this period, peaceful relations are to be maintained, although the fundamental doctrine of class struggle precludes the possibility of actual friendship.

In this struggle, it is assumed by the Men in the Kremlin, that the natural allies of the Soviet Union will be the working class all over the world, and especially the inhabitants of colonial and dependent countries. One of the aims of Soviet policy is to win these classes to the Soviet cause. And however long the period of conflict may be, Communist ideology teaches that inevitably the Soviet variety of socialism will emerge victorious. It asserts that in the constant flux of events outlived forms of social organization go downhill and new ones rise to the top. It concludes from this that the Soviet Union must ally itself with the rising forces of the future, however weak they may be at the present time, and that it must undermine the powers of the present day, which, in spite of their apparent strength and stability, are in the process of disappearing from the political scene.

This doctrine gives to believers in communism a confidence that any reverses they may experience are no more than temporary. Their immediate aim is to establish communism in a number of countries outside the Soviet Union, in the interest of Socialist security, but their long-term aim is to work for the disintegration of capitalism elsewhere and to hasten its disappearance from the face of the earth.

If one considers the number of countries along the borders of the Soviet Union in which communism has been established since 1939, it becomes immediately apparent that Communist doctrine is not a matter of words only. Like *Mein Kampf*, Stalin's writings deserve to be taken at their face value.

Viewed in this light, Soviet Communist expansion, which is so agitating and disturbing the world today, appears as a revival, a continuation of Great Russian expansion, which loomed so threateningly during the last century and recurringly for centuries before that, with this one important difference. The policies of the Soviet Union are now directed and implemented by the intelligent, disciplined, dedicated leaders of the party, with an ability and efficiency that were completely unknown to the corrupt and venal Czarist regimes which preceded them.

The stamp of Great Russia is to be found everywhere. About

two-thirds of the area and population of the Soviet Union is, in fact, Great Russian and is more or less included within the borders of the great state known as the R.S.F.S.R. This is the homeland of the real Russians. These are the people whom Stalin toasted "first of all" at the great Kremlin victory banquet on May 25, 1945, when he referred to them as "the most out-standing of all the nationalities forming part of the Soviet Union."

Soviet policy is thus the offspring of a marriage between Great Russian imperialism and Communist ideology.

In Communist eyes, the second World War was the first of the great clashes with the capitalist world that Lenin had pre-dicted. It brought the Soviet Union four years of desperate struggle for survival, and it ended in a victory that left the Soviet state as one of the two giant powers in the post-war world. Soviet policy since the war has developed against the background of these two facts and of its racial and political heritage.

The one really fundamental issue that divides the Soviet Union from the Western democracies is that—while each wants one world—each camp wants an entirely different kind of world. The Soviet Union is striving to attain a totalitarian Stalinist type of world subject to its control. We want the world or-ganized along the lines of Western democracy, in which the individual is accorded certain inalienable basic rights.

This is true despite any tactical maneuvers or strategic re-treats that may at first glance give the impression that the Soviet leaders have renounced their long-standing belief: the inevitability of a conflict between socialism and capitalism. The Western mind, which is trained in the school of live and let live, too often believes that Soviet gestures represent sub-stance, when in reality such Soviet gestures usually have proven to be merely smoke screens.

For years these Soviet tactics have been successful primarily because we want to forget unpleasant events and cherish the hope that "things somehow will get better." The blackout of information regarding the actual situation in the Soviet Union, coupled with its intensive propaganda campaign, which is de-signed to confuse issues by half-truths, outright falsehoods and double-talk about such things as Soviet "democracy," has effectively hidden the realities of the Soviet system from the outside world.

Most people outside the Soviet Union either have forgotten or never heard Lenin's own description of the tactics Communists would have to use to triumph in the future. But in his collected works, one finds these frank declarations:

"We have to use any ruse, dodge, trick, cunning, unlawful methods, concealment, veiling of the truth. . . . As long as capitalism and socialism exist, we cannot live in peace; in the end one or the other will triumph—its funeral dirge will be sung over the Soviet Republic or over world capitalism . . . but until this takes place the principal role is to dodge and maneuver."

The history of the twenty-nine years of Soviet maneuvers in the international and domestic field is replete with concrete examples of these tactics: the Rapallo Treaty with Germany in 1922, Lenin's New Economic Policy of 1921, the Popular Front tactics directed against Hitler in the middle thirties, the Soviet-German pact of 1939 and the Soviet-Japanese non-aggression pact of 1941. There are many others.

For anyone who wishes to, it is not difficult to understand the aims and policies of the Soviet leaders. They are consistent and are constantly announced and published. The ruses, the dodges and the tricks do not, in general, show a consistent pattern. But their basic policies do.

The most fundamental and far-reaching policy is the repeatedly announced conviction of the basic antagonism between the Soviet system and "capitalism." Until recently, "capitalist encirclement," which was a basic tenet of Lenin, had been the rallying cry of Stalinism. Now it is unworthy of the Soviet giant. Stalin has said that it is no longer possible, and it has been replaced by the Stalinist concept of the development of "two world centers." In other words, the picture of a world divided into two camps that Stalin in 1927 drew for the future, he today considers to have become a reality.

Actually, there is no blinding ourselves to the fact that since the war the two hostile centers predicted by Lenin and Stalin have come into being. The fact that this has resulted from a deliberate choice made by the Soviet leaders at the end of the war can only mean that the Kremlin has chosen to launch what Stalin described as the struggle between these two centers that is to decide the fate of capitalism throughout the whole world.

Given the background, training and creed of Soviet leaders, it is quite natural to understand why it would be difficult, if not impossible, for them to adopt any other basic policy. Their entire lives have been conditioned to the "fundamental truth" of the antagonism between the two systems. They have no other yardstick with which to measure. They have neither lived outside Russia nor under any other system than one of oppression. The tremendous sacrifices they have caused the Soviet people to undergo for more than thirty years have been premised on this belief. It would be most unrealistic to expect human beings with such training and background to change their longstanding fundamental beliefs unless circumstances forced them to do so.

Does the fact that the struggle has been joined by the deliberate choice of the Kremlin necessarily mean that the achievement of world communism is to be sought in the near future and primarily through the use of Soviet armed strength?

This is the question that many of my diplomatic colleagues in Moscow answered affirmatively. It is possible to make a very good case in support of this point of view.

The strenuous efforts of the Soviet Union since the end of hostilities to restore its war potential is apparent to all. As recently as September 17, 1949, the Senate Foreign Relations and Armed Services Committees released a formal report which included the statement that the Soviet Union still has more than five million men under arms and is constantly increasing its military strength. It has increased its visible military budget for 1949 by nineteen per cent over that of 1948, and it is impossible to estimate the size of the concealed items of a military nature, hidden within the budget under other classifications. Certainly the men actually under arms are backed by a reserve about twice as numerous.

The only Soviet troops I have seen in real strength are those of the Moscow garrison of 150,000 men. Granted that they are the showpiece of the Soviet Army, as Moscow is the show window of the nation, they are sufficiently impressive to create the belief that inferior units could still be very good troops indeed. Their uniforms and equipment and the precision of their movements can hardly be equalled and certainly not surpassed anywhere else in the world. And it is an interesting comparison that as we have more and more discarded the outward signs of military discipline, the Soviet Union, having initially abolished all such "bourgeois" trapping as salutes, insignia of rank, gold braid and "brass," has, as the result of its extended war experience, gone to the other extreme.

The Soviet Army is now more "military" by far than we have even been. The Germans considered the Soviet tanks the best in the world—even including their own—and our own artillerymen paid tribute to the excellence of the Russian artillery materiel and technique of fire. French air officers who served with the Normandy Squadron in Russia, and who served with us after the liberation of their own country, classed the YAK fighter as the best short-range interceptor pursuit plane in use during the war. The Russians pioneered in the field of airborne operations and military rockets. From the statements of Stalin and others, it is apparent that the continuing production and development of military weapons are given a very high priority, and that they far exceed in quantity normal replacement requirements.

Soviet naval strength is not vast by our standards, but it is concentrated on submarines and motor torpedo boats of the latest and most effective German types. Strangely enough, there has never even been a gesture in the direction of a general demobilization of Soviet Navy personnel. On the contrary, exhortations are continually made to direct all efforts toward the building of a Soviet Navy "commensurate with the leading international position of the Soviet Union." Part of this is national pride, but most of it is indicative of serious intention to make the Soviet fleet, whatever its composition, a formidable fighting force.

The Soviet Navy at the present time is estimated to number somewhat less than half a million men. It is deficient in seagoing experience and lacking in training, but intensive efforts are being made to improve it in these respects. Naval morale is high.

Russia always has keenly felt the lack of allweather ports and naval bases, and those she has acquired in former German territory and by treaty with Finland are undoubtedly being developed.

Her surface fleet is weak, unbalanced and largely obsolete, except for the modern units obtained in the form of reparations and war prizes. But these have not added materially to Soviet naval strength. Russia has enormous natural resources to support a great shipbuilding program, however, and when her industrial potential is adequately developed, she may, if she wishes, develop a powerful Navy and merchant fleet. This will take time—a good many years, in fact.

Russians always have distinguished themselves for daring and imagination in the field of airplane design, and it is safe to assume that there are those in the Soviet Union not less talented than the aviation engineers of Russian birth who have distinguished themselves in our own country. Lately, they have concentrated on the development of jet aircraft, all types of which have appeared in the aviation day parades in Moscow, including four-motor jet bombers. I saw three of these parades. In the first there were a few—a very few—jet planes, one large four-engine bomber, obviously a copy of our B-29, and a large number of smaller, obsolescent types. In the second, there were a large variety of different types of jet planes, many of them apparently experimental types. Last year there were a large number of jets, but of only two or three different types, which suggested the probability that quantity production of selected models had begun.

There is no question of the courage, skill and daring of Soviet fighter pilots. The Soviet Air Force, however, has so far had comparatively little experience with long range aircraft and their employment against strategic objectives.

There is a very strong civil air fleet—the importance of which cannot be overestimated in this country of poor communications. I flew several times in Soviet aircraft, and the American Embassy plane was always required to carry a Soviet navigator and radio operator when coming in from Berlin and returning to its base there (it was not permitted to remain in the Soviet Union except for servicing). My impression was that most Soviet pilots fly "contact," and that they are likely to get lost when they cannot see the ground. Blind landing equipment, and that for the ground control of landing aircraft, are very scarce. In fact, during the war, the Soviet Union took a cold-bloodedly practical view of special equipment. Even now few of the older planes are provided with de-icing equipment. One of our senior air officers operating from the Poltava Air Base when American bombers used this Ukrainian airfield as a base for "shuttle bombing," told me he had asked Soviet fliers about this and was informed that by omitting de-icing equipment, Soviet air industry could produce about eight per cent more planes. Losses due to its absence were only about four per cent on the average, the Russians added, and this meant a net gain in planes of four per cent. Our man thought it was a little hard on the pilots of the other four per cent.

However, if the Soviet Union does not at this time have what we call air power—the ability to carry on a strategic air war—she certainly has the resources to create this power, and undoubtedly is straining every nerve to do so.

The total effort in all fields which contribute to military strength obviously is much greater than should be expected of a nation which for the first time in history is without any strong neighbor on the entire Eurasian land mass. Intrinsically, Soviet military, economic and scientific strengths outweigh corresponding weaknesses, and Soviet power bulks overwhelmingly larger than that of any other European or Asiatic state.

The continued strenuous efforts which the Kremlin is making to increase this power, the irreconcilable hostility of communism toward the capitalist world, and the increasing violence of the Soviet propaganda line toward the West would justify the most gloomy conclusions, were it not for these three considerations.

The United States is still stronger than the Soviet Union. If Stalin lives, and carries out his objectives, it is probable that during the next five to ten years the economic position of the Soviet Union will advance relatively more rapidly than that of the United States. But the Soviet Union will not, in my opinion, overtake the United States during this period.

The Soviet Government, by a series of well-timed moves, has been able to seize control of vast new areas of Europe and Asia, some of them areas to which Russian power has never before extended. Since the war, Soviet control has been extended over

Poland, Czechoslovakia, Hungary, Rumania, Bulgaria, Albania, a large part of China, Northern Korea and, until recently, Yugoslavia. These conquered provinces must now be held in submission, and millions of their peoples are impatient and resentful of Soviet rule. Successful revolts against Moscow's authority might shake the entire structure of Soviet power. Tito's defection is evidence that the Soviet "orbit" is still far from consolidated. The Politburo is well aware that Russia in the past swallowed more than she could digest, and, as the strain of retaining power became too great, had to disgorge in a convulsion of violence and confusion. It is conscious also of the fact that the Russian machine in Eastern and Central Europe is not without serious weaknesses.

It carries the inevitable handicap of foreign rule over people who are familiar with the devices of puppet government. After their experiences with the Germans, it is not easy to mislead them in this respect. Europe has not spent five years smelling out quislings and collaborationists for nothing, and it is very difficult for any man in this area to conceal or disguise his efforts in the service of a foreign state.

Added to this handicap is the wave of chauvinism and arrogance which has swept over the Soviet Army and bureaucracy as a result of Russian victories. Many of the heavy-handed generals and political commissars who now rule in the capitals of Central Europe have given to Soviet imperialism a naked bluntness, little calculated to inspire confidence and sympathy in foreign minds.

To all this must be added the fact that Soviet policy in the conquered territories, though superior in discipline, drive and ruthlessness, has behind it no great idea which could inspire the various peoples of these areas and bind them together into a single political entity with a single purpose. Pure Marxism is dated; and if its flame still animates to any appreciable degree the power of the Kremlin—which to me seems highly questionable—the Soviet rulers have never dared to put it to a test as a straight political program for Eastern Europe. Lacking this, they have themselves no magnetic doctrine to advance and their appeals, so far, have not been impressive.

On the other hand, by Soviet calculations, the capitalist system, including the United States, should be rapidly approaching

a disastrous economic crisis, which will lead to large-scale unemployment, reduce standards of living and intensify the battle
for world markets between the capitalist states. Although the
Marshall Plan has been a severe shock, as it raised the possibility that this crisis in the capitalist world might be deferred
for the immediate future (the Soviet economist, Varga, suggested a deferment of ten years, but has since recanted), the
prospects are so attractive that the Soviet Union can afford to
wait in the confident expectation that there will develop a true
revolutionary situation, during which proletariats may seize
power and carry the world revolution a huge stride forward.

What, then, is the general outlook? The vast empire of the
Soviet Union has nearly all the raw materials necessary for a
war economy, and an industry capable of supporting in the field
armies substantially larger than those of any other country in
Europe or Asia. Its population is young and expanding rapidly;
it is bringing its young people up in a spirit of patriotism,
physical fitness and preparedness for war. It believes in the
hostility of the outside world. It is increasing its war potential.
Its ideology advocates encroachment on the outside world,
which will become ever easier as the population of the Soviet
Union increases and its war potential is built up. Thanks to
its totalitarian regime, it is able to maintain a strictness of
internal discipline and a consistency of political strategy unthinkable in democratic countries. It believes that its star is
rising and that the star of the capitalist world is setting.

The post-war disposition of world forces, as seen by Moscow,
was clearly stated at the Cominform meeting of September,
1947, by Zhdanov, who took precisely the same starting point
that Stalin did in 1925:

"The world has been divided into two camps, the imperialist
camp and the anti-imperialist camp . . . The two most important capitalist countries, Britain and the United States, present
themselves as an Anglo-American alliance leading the other
capitalist countries. On the other hand, at the head of the various countries which are dissatisfied with imperialism and carry
on a life and death struggle with it is our country, the Soviet
Union."

The relative strength of the two camps, Zhdanov pointed out,
had, however, radically altered. The imperialist camp had lost

three of its six major powers—Germany, Japan and Italy—as a result of the war; the new democracies of Eastern Europe had transferred to the rival grouping; France had ceased to be a great power and Britain was greatly weakened; only the United States remained unimpaired and indeed strengthened. In addition, the peoples of the colonial and dependent countries were clamoring for liberation, the aspirations of the proletariats of the capitalist countries were being ruthlessly suppressed, and serious antagonism could be seen in the relations between the capitalist states themselves. The "anti-imperialist camp" on the other hand had enjoyed a great accession of strength. It had recruited the "new democracies," the strength of local Communist parties had grown enormously, and the prestige of the Soviet Union had made it more than ever a rallying point and beacon of hope for all oppressed peoples.

Malenkov, also at the Cominform foundation meeting, summarized the Soviet appreciation of the post-war position when he said that "the center of class struggle has shifted to the international arena." He then went on to describe the methods which the All-Union Communist Party was adopting to meet the situation. Soviet policy, he asserted, was directed toward "undermining imperialism"; it would continue to unmask all the enemies of peace and resist attempts to "ignore the democratic camp or minimize its significance, to sow intrigues against it or form hostile blocs and groups." Soviet diplomacy was to be entrusted only to selected cadres capable of ensuring that the party line was followed in foreign policy, and it would be assisted in its work by the "moral-political, ideological and cultural links between the U.S.S.R. and working class and progressive circles abroad" which had been forged during or as a result of the war. This amounted to an assertion that the Soviet Union would utilize for its own purposes organizations into which Communists had infiltrated and gained power, such as the trade unions, the youth and women's movements, and the various Soviet Friendship Societies abroad. Proof of the success of this line was afforded in the recent coup in Czechoslovakia where the Communist-dominated trade union organization played as important a role as the Communist-controlled police force in ensuring the Communist victory. Such successes naturally confirm to the Politburo the correctness of their policy of attempting to infiltrate national and international trade union organizations.

In practice, the Cominform Declaration, despite its presentation of capitalism in the guise of aggressor, was an announcement that the Soviet camp was taking the offensive, that the national Communist parties represented in the new organization were to be controlled by Moscow on a tighter rein, and that the strategy and tactics of Leninism were to be followed more strictly than previously.

The strike action organized by the French Communist Party in the autumn of 1947 was an example of the new line in action. It was almost certainly dictated from Moscow and contrary to the judgment of the local Communist Party. It was designed to nullify Marshall Plan aid to France in advance by creating economic chaos and, by discrediting the "Third Force" in France, to lead to a situation in which Frenchmen would have to choose between De Gaulle, painted as black reaction on the one hand, and the Communists, depicted as the defenders of democracy and progress, on the other. In the second respect, at any rate, the plan failed in its object, thus suggesting that the Stalin technique is most likely to blunder when provoked into hasty counter-action. The Rome strike in December, 1947, also was an abortive move. The recent developments in Czechoslovakia, on the other hand, were an example of Stalinist tactics perfectly executed and calculated to establish the initiative once more on the Soviet side.

The long-term policy of the Soviet Union has always been based on the fundamental theory that capitalism is doomed and has entered its final stage before dissolution. The Soviet Union, as the base of expanding communism, has accepted the obligation to work by all possible means for the overthrow of capitalism everywhere and its replacement by the dictatorship of the proletariat as the preparatory phase preceding the advent of a world Socialist society. However, the Soviet Government has never in the past been prepared to expose the Soviet state to the risk of disaster. Although, since the last war, it is genuinely believed in the Soviet Union that there has been a vast swing of power in favor of the rising forces of communism and that the capitalist system is greatly enfeebled, it seems to me a reasonable assumption that the Soviet state still will be guided by that principle. In pursuit of the final Communist goal, the Soviet leaders will limit themselves to "all means short of war," so long as they believe that the outcome of a war would be uncertain, i.e., until they are confident that the strength controlled by the Soviet Union has far surpassed that of the United States.

The several assertions of Stalin, Zhdanov, Molotov and other Soviet spokesmen that Soviet foreign policy envisages the coexistence "for a long time" of the capitalist and Socialist systems and that "cooperation is therefore possible between them on terms of reciprocity and the fulfillment of obligations undertaken," cannot, however, be taken at their face value. To be properly understood, such statements must be considered in conjunction with Lenin's statements and his more candid dictum, reaffirmed by Stalin at the fourteenth party congress, that "we are living not merely in one state but in a system of states, and it is inconceivable that the Soviet Republic should continue to exist interminably side by side with imperialist states. Ultimately, one or the other must conquer."

This latter doctrine means in theory that war is ultimately inevitable between the capitalist world and the Communist world, unless the former allows itself to be swallowed up by the latter without opposition. Since that alternative obviously cannot be prudently assumed, Soviet policy must be to prepare by all possible means for inevitable conflict.

The professions of belief in the mutual compatibility of the two systems, which always contain loopholes in the form of conditions, are part of the preparation for the harsher probability. They are calculated to lull suspicion and to throw the blame for failure to cooperate on other shoulders; and they cost nothing. In another passage, also quoted with approval by Stalin, Lenin showed plainly what the Soviet Communist regards as the only basis of international cooperation.

"In no circumstances," he wrote, "under no possible conditions can it [international imperialism] live at peace with the Soviet Republic. . . . Here is the greatest difficulty of the Russian Revolution, its supreme historical problem—the need to solve international problems, the need to promote the world revolution."

We must expect an increase of pressure with the advance of

the series of five-year plans, and particularly if ever the Russians should achieve their declared aim of equalling American levels of production.

The difficulty of preventing our relations from deteriorating will be increased by the fact that the Soviet Government, convinced as it is of the hostility of the outside world, receives all advances with mistrust and suspicion. Our every act is distorted and misinterpreted by Soviet propaganda. Any concessions we may make will be regarded as gains to be taken without reciprocity, and to be immediately consolidated and exploited. Resistance to or dissatisfaction with Soviet policy on our part will be interpreted by them as further proof of our active malevolence. The possibility of preventing deterioration is complicated further by the declared intention of the Soviet Union actively to continue to attempt to undermine the capitalist system and Western democracy.

Given this ideological background, it would seem quite unjustifiable to hope for a change of heart. Although the members of the United Nations are pledged to the settlement of disputes by pacific means, and although through the conscientious efforts of most of its members the effectiveness of the United Nations as an instrument for preserving peace is increasing, there is little indication that our relations with the Soviet Union will really become much better in the foreseeable future. The general outlook is one of friction, disputes, recrimination and tension.

It would be foolish to disregard the danger of war that is inherent in such a situation. This danger exists, and will continue. The Kremlin has embarked on an aggressive line of action which carries with it the possibility of war. That danger is enhanced by the Communist belief in the inevitability of such a conflict. However, the Kremlin's test of the desirability of any policy presumably is whether it will yield a substantial gain in achieving the ultimate objective of world communism under Bolshevik dictatorship without great risk. Being very practical men, the Politburo might conceivably ask themselves the question:

"Since the Western states, contrary to our expectations, have apparently drawn closer together, since the Marshall Plan seems for the time to be improving the economic situation, and since we know that ultimately a clash is inevitable, why should it not come now, rather than later?"

The fact is that such a decision, involving as it does some very fundamental questions of Communist doctrine, would probably be made not on the basis of any short-term evaluation, but within the framework of long-range Communist theories. One of the most fundamental of these theories is that capitalism is in its final period of decay, moving from crisis to crisis in its path toward chaos, whereas the Soviet Union as it advances triumphantly through socialism to communism, will prove to all the world that it is as healthy and vigorous as capitalism is sick and failing. Accordingly, Bolsheviks will feel that they have no more than a temporary stabilization to fear from the success of the Marshall Plan, and however favorably they might rate their prospects today, they must rate them even better as time goes on and the contradictions of capitalism have produced their next major spasm. So why take a chance? The thieves will fall out, as Lenin said, and then honest men will come into their own.

This conclusion would be supported by Soviet estimates of the actual state of fighting morale on both sides of the Iron Curtain. War weariness and a desire for the fruits of peace may appear roughly the same in Western and Eastern Europe, but the United States has been singled out by Stalin as the one country that emerged from the last conflict stronger and more vigorous than before. Accordingly, in his view, the relative position of the Soviet Union would be better after a decade of peace has refreshed its population, and more five-year plans are completed.

A short time ago, one would have added another condition —"and when the Soviet Union is adequately supplied with atomic weapons."

In 1947, I was present at the annual celebration of the October Revolution, when Mr. Molotov, during the course of his address, made the statement: "The atomic bomb is no longer a secret." This was reported by the world press, so President Truman's announcement that an atomic explosion had occurred in the Soviet Union should not have come as a great surprise to anyone. At the time, I interpreted Mr. Molotov's statement to mean that Soviet scientists had reached a laboratory solution, and that the next step would be some sort of test, which might well come in the near future.

Nearly four years ago, the President pointed out very clearly that "scientific opinion appears to be practically unanimous that the essential theoretical knowledge upon which the discovery is based is already widely known," and that there "is also substantial agreement that foreign research can come abreast of our present theoretical knowledge in time."

The Soviet Union has made no secret of the fact that it was concentrating its efforts in this direction, and that a substantial slice of the annual budget was allotted to atomic research. We have naturally been concerned that, before any effective international system of atomic control has been established, atomic weapons might come into the hands of a nation whose policies have in so many respects retarded world stability.

However, we do not think of war as inevitable, nor that Soviet possession of the atomic bomb necessarily makes war more probable.

The atomic weapon is only one of the complex pattern of political and military factors, and, in itself, neither confers on its possessor any guarantees of achieving victory in war nor provides protection against retaliation in kind. Nor does the mere fact that a country might have the ability to make an atomic bomb constitute any assurance to that country of superiority, either in that special field or in the general field of military effort.

During the last war, the Germans, although they had a gas which was considerably more effective than our own, never used it. We captured quantities of it, but the German General Staff was well aware that we had greater quantities of mustard and lewisite and that we had a mighty air armada which could deliver twenty or thirty times as much gas to targets in Germany as the Germans could send over to us.

So far as the atomic bomb is concerned, it is to be hoped, however, that the consciousness of possessing such a terrible and destructive weapon will bring to the Soviet leaders the same sense of responsibility to the peoples of the world which impelled the governments of the United States, Britain and Canada to announce on November 15, 1945, their intention to seek an effective system of international control of atomic energy. Our awareness of what the A-bomb had done and could do had made us, and the nations associated with us, willing to make a substantial deposit of sovereignty in the United Nations in order to secure really effective control.

If the Russians now react as we did, the road to world peace and world stability will have been opened. If not, then distance, necessity, patience, firmness and the united strength of the West, now being organized under the Atlantic Pact, may enable us to continue for a protracted period that precarious and uncertain but relatively peaceful co-existence which we have managed to lead with the Russians up to this time. Of these factors, the one most appreciated and best understood by the collective mind of the Kremlin, is the factor of strength.

No matter from which direction we approach the problem, it is impossible to escape the conclusion that the best assurance of peace is the strength and determination to support our convictions, and our strength must exist and be apparent, since by its very existence it serves its highest purpose—the prevention of war and the assurance of peace.

It is not military and economic strength alone which is required, important though these are. The total strength of the nation encompasses such factors as education and national health, family life and opportunity, and the incentive for individual achievement. Basic to that strength is the passionate devotion of our people to the free way of life. We can maintain the material, moral and spiritual strength of America if our democratic faith remains strong, and we can draw from this deep wellspring of faith the firmness and fortitude necessary to carry out the tremendous responsibilities of world leadership that have devolved upon us.

XV

POSTSCRIPT TO MOSCOW

This is the best school in which to Americanize our countrymen, perhaps that can be found. They are enabled to view their own Government by the law of contrast, and inspect it from new points of observation; and I envy not him who can do so, and return without an increased attachment to our institutions.

—Excerpt from a dispatch of the American Minister to Russia, Neill S. Brown, dated St. Petersburg, January 27, 1853

I T IS disturbing to remember that only a few years ago communism was dismissed by the world in general with the same contemptuous indifference that inspired the Corn-Law Rhymer when he wrote:

> What is a Communist? One who has yearnings
> For equal division of unequal earnings;
> Idler or bungler, or both, he is willing
> To fork out his penny and pocket your shilling.

This total failure to appreciate the importance of a vital movement based initially on the deepest moral motives and impelled by strong historical and economic forces is pitiful, but typical. Even now, there are many who are fatuous enough to minimize the threat of this political ideology which is unique in the profound belief that the termination of class conflict by transfer of the means of production to national ownership is attainable only by force and revolution, and that subsequent to this necessary revolution an apparently unlimited period of dictatorship based on open terror is inevitable.

The events which have taken place in Eastern Europe during the past four years form a clear pattern of Soviet consolidation through Communist political control. This control has accomplished the integration throughout a vast European area of the

military, police, communications and economic systems under
Soviet direction. The methods which have been used are now
plain to all observers. They follow the all too familiar pattern
of infiltration, vilification and intimidation by every possible
means including physical violence extending even to legalized
murder. These tactics are supported by the power—sometimes
hidden, sometimes nakedly exposed to view—of great military
strength directed by forces undeterred by any scruples and
determined to attain their aim regardless of the methods used.
Such a pattern has been seen in Europe before. The one thing
new about it is the state of perfection which has been attained
as the result of Soviet experience, and the power which it de-
rives from a firm and undeviating policy with but one objective
—the extension of Soviet power. The sequence of events since
the Communist coup in Czechoslovakia has highlighted, as
never before, the danger of the situation.

When the leaders of the Soviet Union decided to turn away
from the cooperation which we hoped would prevail after the
war, and instead to seek to impose communism upon their
neighbors and ultimately upon the rest of the world, it was
inevitable that the Western European nations would draw
closer together in mutual self-defense. Most of them emerged
from the war practically defenseless, and they were acutely conscious of their individual helplessness. The Brussels Pact put
new heart into the democratic states, and gave the Soviet Union
cause for reflection.

Since then, impressive progress has been made. The repudia-
tion of communism by the Italian people has had a powerful
effect in those exposed nations who have anxiously awaited
some sign that Communist plans can be countered successfully.
Then came the European Recovery Program, an essential and
effective means of assuring peace.

The change that has taken place since the Marshall Plan has
been in operation is profoundly impressive. A short time ago,
Western Europe was disorganized economically, depleted physically and depressed spiritually. The position of its free nations
was precarious. The situation approached a crisis in which anything might happen.

The contrast today is remarkable. The free nations of Western Europe have literally taken a new lease on life. Their

people have been given more than new hope, important though
that is: they have been given something to work with and
their production record proves that they are eager to work and
that they have the skill and the determination to re-establish
themselves in the world. Of course, the Marshall Plan has not
been the only factor in effecting this transformation, but it has
been the major force in the stabilization of Europe—it marked
the turning point.

In the great increase of production achieved in Europe during the past year, the contributions of farm and labor groups,
both in this country and in Europe, have been outstanding.
The organized labor movement in this country and the non-
Communist labor movements in the participating countries of
Europe have strongly supported the Marshall Plan, and these
movements on both sides of the Atlantic joined in establishing
a trade union advisory committee to assist in carrying out the
recovery program. The support of labor is vital to success. It
is the workers who hold the key to industrial production. Similarly, the representatives of farm organizations in this country
have accepted the Marshall Plan and have likewise been active
in an advisory committee to assist the European Recovery Program. The farmers of Europe, on their part, have substantially
increased the production of food crops. Here is evidence, if
such were needed, that the Marshall Plan is not merely an
arrangement among governments but actually a cooperative
effort among peoples.

While the recovery of Europe is a primary requisite for maintaining the free way of life and preserving peace, it actually is
only part of a larger design. Economic revival of Western
Europe is essential to give its people the strength to assure their
own security. They do not have that strength at present. Rebuilding defenses is a slow, laborious process, particularly since
economic recovery has priority. Realization of their helpless
condition, in the face of the aggressive and expansive tendencies of the Soviet Union, has caused a pervading sense of insecurity that weighs heavily on Western Europe. Its people have
been haunted by the fear that they might be rebuilding only to
have the fruits of their labor again destroyed, and the Kremlin
has used this fear of war as a potent weapon against economic
recovery. Thus, if we are to achieve our objectives in Europe, it

devolves upon the United States to use its own strength to shield the free nations of Europe from aggression while they rebuild their own defenses, just as we are using our material resources to help them revive their economies. The two go hand in hand. This is the purpose of the North Atlantic Treaty and of recent legislation for military assistance.

The great, the priceless benefit to be derived from this treaty is peace, and its makers have sought that benefit by clearly stating in advance their determination resolutely to resist armed attack with all the strength available to us all. Determination is not enough; it must be backed by strength.

The greatest single achievement toward the creation of conditions that would assure lasting peace in the world would be the re-establishment in Europe of a group of strong, free, virile and progressive states, living together in harmony and cooperating politically, economically and militarily. Such a group, no longer dependent on the United States or fearful of attack from the East, would be a stabilizing force of the most vital significance.

It would contain a population greater than that of the Soviet Union, much further advanced in science and technology, with resources much better developed, and an industrial organization much more efficient and productive. Such a Europe would be able effectively to resist the encroachments of communism and provide a living, dynamic demonstration of the superior values of the free way of life; it would exert a profound attraction for the repressed and impoverished peoples now under the Communist yoke.

Above all, this Europe would be a great constructive force for peace. It shares our aversion for war and that aversion has been intensified by the tragic and bitter experiences of the recent conflict. Strength in the hands of its free peoples will be strength dedicated to the defense of peace. We can make no better investment than the restoration of this strength. This is the object of our nation's foreign policy.

The turn of events since the end of the war has placed upon the United States, as the citadel of freedom and the strongest of the free nations, the major responsibility for world recovery, peace and progress—and at the same time has confronted this nation with the gravest challenge ever offered to our principles and our way of life.

We have ample strength to meet both the responsibility and the challenge. We can, if we so resolve, call into being a sufficiently coherent and self-confident system in Western Europe to discourage any adventurous attempts in that direction.

There are still two danger spots in Western Europe—Berlin and Vienna—where, as Mr. Bevin once said, "We are face to face with Soviet aggression and can expect them to be up to every sort of devilment." Here, as in such other sensitive spots as Trieste, Turkey, the Adriatic Area and the Middle East, we may at any moment be faced with a serious incident which will require the most careful handling, and where a vast amount of moderation and firm patience will be required, combined with the determination not to be provoked into any ill-considered action.

It is extremely important, therefore, never to lose sight of the fundamental fact that we are forced to a continuing struggle for a free way of life that may extend over a period of many years. We dare not allow ourselves any false sense of security. We must anticipate that the Soviet tactic will be to attempt to wear us down, to exasperate us, to keep probing for weak spots, and we must cultivate firmness and patience to a degree we have never before required.

We must continually remind ourselves to take the long view, particularly at the conclusion of some dramatic or frustrating experience, whether it be the end of a blockade or the termination of a conference of Foreign Ministers. We cannot deviate from our ultimate purpose because of the elations or the disappointments of the moment.

The time has passed when foreign affairs and domestic affairs could be regarded as separate and distinct. The borderline between the two has practically ceased to exist. Mr. Stimson, one of our greatest living statesmen, has summed it up this way:

"No private program and no public policy, in any sector of our national life, can now escape from the compelling fact that if it is not framed with reference to the world, it is framed with perfect futility."

Accordingly, having adopted a policy which has already attained a considerable measure of success, we must follow it through to its logical conclusion if it is to accomplish its purpose. If we turn back, or slacken our efforts, we not only risk losing the momentum thus far achieved, we may waste what we have already invested; and aside from these material factors, any sign of vacillation or indecision on our part will profoundly discourage our friends and strengthen the belief of the Communists that they have only to keep up the pressure until we grow tired and give up the struggle. We must face the fact that we are engaged in a contest of indefinite duration; that we must decide our course and stick to it.

If we do stick to it calmly, determinedly and courageously, we can go forward, step by step, to the peace and security which we and all the free world so ardently desire. The stakes are too high, and the alternatives are too terrible, to permit even a suspicion of irresolution.

INDEX

Aggression, Soviet, 330-331
Agriculture, Soviet, 134-135
  collectivization in annexed territory, 150-151
  excessive taxation to eliminate independent farmers, 150-153
  exports of grains, 154
Aims and policies of Soviet leaders, 316
Air force, Soviet, strength and development of, 319-320
Alexandrov, M., 61, 103, 104
Alexii, Patriarch, 269
Allard, Brigadier, 107
Allen, Ronald, 87
Allied Control Council in Germany, 225, 235
All Russian Extraordinary Commission (Cheka), 115
All-Union Central Committee of the Communist Party, 65
  methods of, 323-324
All-Union Society for the Dissemination of Political and Scientific Knowledge, The, 294-295
Amerika, Russian-language magazine, 177
Andreyev, A. A., 66
Anti-Semitism in the Soviet Union, 266, 273-276
Apostolic Church of Armenia, tolerance for, 265, 272
Army, Soviet, strength and development of, 317-318
Ashraf, Princess, 107-108
Atomic bomb, 327-329
Attlee, Clement, at Potsdam Conference, 24

Benidiktov, Minister of Agriculture, 150
Berg, Ambassador, 108
Beria, L. P., 66, 71, 75-80, 83, 126
Berlin, access to Allies assured by Stalin, 234

city elections (Dec., 1948), 257
conference on blockade and currency, 251-252
international agreements for control of, 234
right of Western powers to occupy, denied by Stalin, 244
Berlin blockade, imposed by Soviet authorities, 237
  lifted, 231, 257
  Melnikov's article as Soviet propaganda, 253-257
  protests to Soviet Government, 237-253
    Ambassador's first meeting with Stalin, 242-245
    Ambassador's second meeting with Stalin, 248-250
    through Molotov, 241, 246-248, 251-252
    through Zorin, 240
  underestimation of effectiveness of airlift by Soviets, 253
Bevin, Ernest, 198
  at Moscow Conference, 215, 217, 218, 220, 225, 228
Bidault, Georges, 215, 217-220, 225, 228
Bierut, Boleslaw, 193
Bitossi, 168
Bizonia, establishment of, 236
Blazejczek, Mirion, 33, 87
Bogomolets, Professor, 290, 291
Bohlen, Charles, 27, 220, 221, 228
Bolshevik Party, 310
Boswell, Minister, 108
Braun, Leopold, 276-277
Brosio, Ambassador, 106
Briggs, Ruth, 33, 86, 87, 263
Brussels pact, 331
Bucar, Annabelle, *The Truth About American Diplomats*, used by Soviet propagandists, 186-187
Bulganin, N. A., 66, 79-80, 83

337